25 Reasons
why christians are not healed

by:

Revivalist Dan Nolan

© 2017 Dan Nolan. All Rights Reserved. Unauthorized Duplication is Prohibited.

Copyright © 2017 Dan Nolan. United States of America. All Rights Reserved under international copyright laws. Contents and/or cover may not be reproduced in whole or in part without prior written consent of Dan Nolan.

Printed in the United States of America

Published by Aion Multimedia
20118 N 67th Ave
Suite 300-446
Glendale AZ 85308
www.aionmultimedia.com

ISBN-13: 978-0-9976046-7-2

Scripture quotations marked (NASB) are taken from the NEW AMERICAN STANDARD BIBLE®, Copyright © 1960, 1962, 1963, 1968, 1971, 1972, 1973, 1975,1977,1995 by The Lockman Foundation. Used by permission.

Scripture quotations marked (KJV) are taken from the King James Bible, New York: American Bible Society: 1999.

Scripture quotations marked (AMP) are taken from the Amplified Bible, Copyright © 1954, 1958, 1962, 1964, 1965, 1987 by The Lockman Foundation. Used by permission.

Scripture quotations marked (NKJV) are taken from the New King James Bible, Copyright © 1979, 1980, 1982 HarperCollins Publishers. Used by permission.

Scripture quotations marked (WEB) are taken from the World English Bible: Rainbow Missions: 2000.

Scripture quotations marked (MEV) are taken from the Modern English Version. Copyright © 2014 by Military Bible Association. Used by permission.

Scripture quotations marked (NLT) are taken from the Holy Bible, New Living Translation, Copyright © 1996, 2004, 2007 by Tyndale House Foundation. Used by permission of Tyndale House Publishers, Inc., Carol Stream, Illinois 60188. All rights reserved.

Scripture quotations marked (YLT) are taken from the Young's Literal Translation Bible (Public Domain).

Scripture quotations marked (NIV) are taken from The Holy Bible, New International Version, Copyright © 1973, 1978, 1984, 2011 by Biblica, Inc. Used by permission. All rights reserved.

Scripture quotations marked (ESV) are taken from the English Standard Bible, Copyright © 2001 by Good News Publishers. Used by permission. All rights reserved.

Scripture quotations marked (KJ21) are taken from the King James 2000 Bible, Copyright © 2000, 2003 by Doctor of Theology Robert A. Couric. Used by permission. All rights reserved.

Scripture quotations marked (NIRV) are taken from the Holy Bible, New International Reader's Version, Copyright © 1996, 1998 Biblica. Used by permission. All rights reserved.

Scripture quotations marked (BSB) are taken from the Berean Study Bible, Copyright © 2016 by Bible Hub and Berean.Bible. Used by permission. All rights reserved.

Scripture quotations marked (HCSB) are taken from the Holman Christian Standard Bible, Copyright © 1999, 2000, 2002, 2003, 2009 by Holman Bible Publishers. Used with permission by Holman Bible Publishers, Nashville, Tennessee. All rights reserved.

Scripture quotations marked (ISV) are taken from the Holy Bible: International Standard Version, Copyright © 1995-2014 by ISV Foundation. Used by permission of Davidson Press, LLC. All rights reserved.

Scripture quotations marked (TLV) are taken from the Tree of Life translation of the Bible. Copyright © 2015 by The Messianic Jewish Family Bible Society. Used by permission. All rights reserved.

Scripture quotations marked (CSB) are taken from the Christian Standard Bible. Copyright © 2017 by Holman Bible Publishers. Used by permission. All rights reserved.

Scripture quotations marked (BLB) are taken from the Berean Literal Bible, Copyright © 2016 by Bible Hub and Berean.Bible. Used by permission. All rights reserved.

Scripture quotations marked (GW) are taken from God's Word®, Copyright © 1995 God's Word to the Nations. Used by permission of Baker Publishing Group. All rights reserved.

Scripture quotations marked (TLB) are taken from the Living Bible, Copyright © 1971 by Tyndale House Foundation. Used by permission. All rights reserved.

Table of Contents

Preface	1
Introduction	21
The Law of the Spirit of Life	27
1 to 25 Reasons Why Christians Are Not Being Healed	65
100 Healing Scriptures	267
About The Author	275
Conclusion	279

Preface

The first thing you need to know is this: None of the principles and truths (for healing) of the Word of God apply to the nonbeliever. Jesus and His disciples—and later the apostle Paul—all healed the multitudes that weren't saved so they would believe that Jesus is the only way to salvation.

That's how I became a Christian. My brother took me to a church. They prayed for me, and I was miraculously healed by God's awesome power of a serious spinal injury. The doctors wanted to do major surgery on me by sticking two rods up my back. I then gave my life to Jesus Christ as Lord and Savior. Before I became a Christian, I was a very filthy sinner, and none of these principles in this book applied to me. **But now that I am a Christian, they do apply to my everyday life, and yours too!**

> *"My son, give attention to my words, incline your ear to my sayings. Do not let them depart from your eyes, keep them in the midst of your heart. For they are life to those that find them, and health to all their flesh."*
>
> **—Proverbs 4:20-22, NKJV**

> *"You shall also decree a thing and it shall be established to you."*
>
> **—Job 22:28, WEB**

> *"Now to Him who is able to do exceedingly abundantly beyond all that we ask or imagine, according to the power that works in us..."*
>
> **—Ephesians 3:20, MEV**

> *"For assuredly I say unto you, whoever says to this mountain, 'Be removed and be cast into the sea,' and does not doubt in his heart, but believes that those things he says will be done, he will have whatever he says."*
>
> **—Mark 11:23, NKJV**

> *"Believe me that I am in the Father and the Father in Me, or else believe Me for the sake of the works themselves."*
>
> **—John 14:11, NKJV**

> *"That I should be the minister of Jesus Christ to the Gentiles, ministering the gospel of God, that the offering up of the Gentiles might be acceptable, being sanctified by the Holy Ghost. I have therefore whereof I may glory through Jesus Christ in those things which pertain to God. For I will not dare to speak of any of those things which Christ hath not wrought by me, to make the Gentiles obedient, by word and deed. Through mighty signs and wonders, by the power of the Spirit of God; so that from Jerusalem, and round about unto Illyricum, I have fully preached the gospel of Christ."*
>
> **—Romans 15:16-19, KJV**

Therefore, this book is written to Christians only, and is all about the truth as Jesus came with grace and truth (see John 1:17) that our loving God and Creator (Jesus Christ) not only died on the cross to give us free salvation, but to also give us soundness of mind and total physical healing to our bodies as well if we'll believe Him. Salvation is free, and so is our healing. There's nothing we can do to merit our salvation or healing or soundness of mind. The blood of Jesus Christ paid for it all on the cross. Thank You, Jesus, for Your love and grace to us. Thank You for Your free gift. When Jesus died, He said, "It is finished" (John 19:30) and it was—and still is.

We all know that salvation is the greatest gift of all, unquestionably so. But for the purpose of this book, we are talking about the lesser gift of healing.

Although our healing is free, and there's nothing we can do to earn it, there are many blockers, obstacles, barriers, and hindrances that we can inadvertently place in-between us and our receiving from the Holy Spirit this free gift of healing. This book is about uncovering and disclosing those hindrances, so we can become enlightened with the truth, whereby we can receive our free gift of healing that's available to all Christians through the blood of the cross.

> *"And ye shall know the truth, and the truth shall make you free."*
>
> **—John 8:32, KJV**

> *"All scripture is given by inspiration of God, and is profitable for doctrine, for reproof, for correction, for instruction in righteousness: That the man of God may be perfect, thoroughly furnished unto all good works."*
>
> **—2 Timothy 3:16-17, KJV**

> *"In the same way, you husbands must give honor to your wives. Treat your wife with understanding as you live together. She may be weaker than you are, but she is your equal partner in God's gift of new life. Treat her as you should so your prayers will not be hindered."*
>
> **—1 Peter 3:7, NLT**

When I first started out in the healing ministry 39 years ago, I'd preach about faith and would put a lot of emphasis on just believing God's Word to be healed. Some people were healed; most weren't. As I'll mention several times in this book, this was a long and tedious journey for me discovering that yes, God is our healer, but there are many other factors to take into consideration when looking at all the whole Word of God. I'd call out to the crowd, "Just come down to the front and believe God." They would come, but still most didn't get healed. I've now learned the hard way that we need to apply the whole of the teachings of the Word of God, and not just faith, to uncover the overall truths in God's Word concerning healing. People would come to me and say, "I believed and my family believed, and my sick mother believed for her healing, yet she wasn't healed and she died. Why?" My heart goes out to people such as those. Thus, this and other factors are the motivating force behind writing this book.

> *"Who his own self bare our sins in his own body on the tree, that we, being dead to sins, should live unto righteousness: by whose stripes ye were healed."*
>
> **—1 Peter 2:24, KJV**

> *"Now may the God of peace Himself sanctify you entirely; and may your spirit and soul and body be preserved complete, without blame at the coming of our Lord Jesus Christ."*
>
> **—1 Thessalonians 5:23, NASB**

> *"For God did not give us a spirit of fear, but of power and love and of a sound mind."*
>
> **—2 Timothy 1:7, YLT**

Some Hindrances to Prayer Scriptures

1) **Sin in the life. Not walking in fellowship** (John 4:22-23; Jude 20; Ephesians 6:18; Psalm 66:18; Ephesians 4:30; 1 John 1:9).

2) **Failure to spend time in the Word of God** (Proverbs 28:9; John 15:7; Psalm 119).

3) **Failure to pray in faith** (Matt. 21:22; 1 John 5:14-15; James 1:5-7; Hebrews 11:6).

4) **Failure to ask because of a spirit of self-dependence** (James 4:2).

5) **Failure to ask from the right motives, without concern for God's will** (James 4:3, 15; 1 Corinthians 4:19; Matthew 6:10; 26:42).

6) **Failure to endure, fainting under pressure** (Luke 18:1; cf. 1 Samuel 27:1-3 with Isaiah 40:31).

7) **Wrong relations with people, an unforgiving spirit** (Mark 11:25-26).

8) **Pretentious praying, praying to impress people** (Matthew 6:5-8).

9) **Religious zeal in the form of vain repetitions and cultic ritual** (Matthew 6:7; 1 Kings 18:26-29; Romans 10:2-3).

10) **Iniquity in my heart.** *"Had I cherished iniquity in my heart, the LORD would not have listened"* (Psalm 66:18).

11) **Not being persistent in prayer. Jesus said, "I tell you, though he will not get up and give him the bread because he is his friend, yet because of the man's persistence he will get up and give him as much as he needs" (Luke 11:8). The ultimate in prayer power seems to be in persistence, according to Isaiah 1:15 and Luke 18:1. Healing is a free gift from God, but sometimes we have to press in like bulldogs, and fight the good fight of faith. (See 1 Timothy 6:12.)**

12) **Domestic breakdown in the home; husbands not loving your wives, or wives not loving your husbands. This will bring a hindrance to prayer big-time** (1 Peter 3:7). **"What's good for the goose is good for the gander**[1]**."**

My many personal testimonies of healing as a Christian (and I give all the glory to God).

I was raised in Adelaide, South Australia, in a very poor, dysfunctional and abusive family. After dropping out of school, I became a street kid at age 15. By 19, I was a biker gang-leader, involved in drugs, rock 'n roll, and the occult. When I was 20, a work accident took me off the job and in need of a major back operation. It was so severe that the doctors wanted to stick two rods up my back. They said if I didn't, that by my 30s I would be confined to a wheelchair for the rest of my life. I was angry, broken, and had no hope. I was not a born-again Christian, and all I did was get drunk.

---

[1] "What's Good for the Goose Is Good for the Gander." *Merriam-Webster.com*. Merriam-Webster, n.d. Web. 19 June 2017.

Miracle #1

My brother eventually took me to a church that prayed for the sick. The preacher called me out by a word of knowledge, and as he prayed over me, I fell out under the power. A ball of fire shot into my right side of my body, then moved up and down inside my body and God did an instant, creative miracle in my back. I was completely healed. Being overwhelmed with God's love, I accepted Christ into my heart. I also was filled with the Holy Spirit, with praying in tongues and I have loved God and served Him ever since. Not long after that the Lord healed me of a major learning disability, and I was able to go back to school and get my G.E.D. I went on to Building College and then onto Business College. Later I got my bachelors and masters in theology. God is a healer, and a restorer, big-time. I was born again on July 6, 1975, about 8 p.m. I've never looked back, not once.

Miracle #2

Easter 1977, I was a cook at a large church camp in the hills country, about 40 miles south of the city of Adelaide, South Australia. About 650 people were in attendance. In-between cooking sessions we would go out on the football field and play ball. I was running to catch the ball when my right foot went down a hole in the ground, snapped, and bent around the other way. They took me down the mountain to the ER to the Flinders Medical Center in Adelaide. After x-rays, the doctors said that I would have to have several pins and plates put into my leg and foot to hold it all together, and I would be in a cast for three months. After my cast was taken off they would have to operate on my foot the second time and maybe even a third time before I could walk on it again. They gave me a 75 percent chance I'd never walk without a limp. As I lay in the bed, with no one else in the room and my feet up on a bed rest, I prayed and told God if He would heal my ankle, I would tell people all over the world and everyone I could what He had done. Suddenly, a pillar of fire came down from the ceiling, stood at the end of my bed, and out of it came the words, "I have called you to carry My healing power and anointing around the world." I was then healed instantly. I was shocked at what I saw and experienced. My crushed, twisted, and very swollen ankle just shrank, turned the other way around, and was instantly made whole, just like the other one. I was absolutely taken aback, surprised, and flabbergasted at this whole ordeal of God's mercy, love, and His absolute awesome power. I'm still to this day undone by what I heard Him say I was called to do. I had no pain or broken and smashed bones. This was my introduction to the healing ministry. The doctors came back and they also were amazed at what had taken place and they let me go back to the church camp. My brother, Ray, picked me up in his car, and when I walked totally normal into the building where the whole camp was eating, they honestly couldn't believe what they saw. See, Jesus is the God of miracles.

Miracle #3

In the year of 1978 I was diagnosed with a cancerous growth in my chest. The doctors said I needed to have immediate surgery the next day. I told them they were not going to operate on me. They said it was imperative that they do otherwise it would spread. They were very concerned for my life. I went home and called my brother, Ray (who had a healing ministry), and he anointed me with oil and prayed the prayer of faith over me (James 5:14-15), and I was healed completely over the next few weeks. I went back to the doctors and they were amazed and kept saying over and over, "How could this possibly be?" "Only because of Jesus," I said to the doctors, "is this possible."

Miracle #4

In the year of 1979 I was diagnosed with a very large peptic stomach ulcer, and the doctors again said I needed immediate surgery. I refused, but they said "Look, young man, the lining of your stomach is about to burst open on the inside. If we don't operate now, your stomach fluids will seep through the hole into and around your organs on the inside of your body and eventually you will die from toxic sepsis poisoning." I walked out, and drove home and got my brother, Ray, to come over and pray the prayer of faith that shall save the sick one and God raise them up. God healed me over the next few weeks. Then I went back to the doctors. Of course they were dumbfounded and said, "We have never seen anything like this ever." To God be the glory...AMEN!

Miracle #5

Early In the year of 1981, I was rushed to the hospital with excruciatingly unbearable pain, and my urine was red with blood. After x-rays the diagnosis was a huge kidney stone nearly an inch long and half an inch wide cutting its way through my right kidney. The doctors said that I needed to have surgery first thing in the morning. As I lay in the hospital bed, my brother came in to see what was the problem, and how could the church pray for my condition. I said to him, "Get the prayer team together and pray in the Holy Ghost for several hours. When you all get the anointing, lay hands on a handkerchief and anoint it with oil. Then bring that cloth to the hospital and lay it on my body and God's power will move over me and the huge kidney stone will dissolve." So they did just that, and I was completely healed. The stone dissolved and the doctors couldn't ever find the particles in sifting the urine. They said to me, "This is a miracle indeed. We have never seen anything like this before. You must have someone up there [meaning God] looking after you big-time." To me this is normal Christianity. To God be the glory in Jesus' name.

Miracle #6

In the year 1982 I was seriously injured in a work accident in which my right shoulder was torn out of the socket. The company I worked for rushed me to the hospital and by that time my right shoulder had swelled up big-time. They x-rayed me and said I would have to have major surgery and I'd be in plaster for about six weeks. My brother, Ray, came over to see me, and he anointed me with oil and prayed the prayer of faith. A powerful fire came on my right shoulder, and I was healed instantly by God's power. The doctors found it hard to believe, as they had never seen such a miracle as that. To God be the glory. Jesus said you shall lay hands on the sick and they will be healed. Just believe, okay?

Do I believe in doctors and the medical profession?

Yes, I do believe in physicians and the medical profession. And yes, they do our society a great service and definitely help a lot of people on this earth.

Although doctors do a tremendous job helping people, do they actually heal people?

A woman said to me once that she went to her doctor to get healed. I said to her,
"How did the doctor heal you?" She said, "I had cancer, and the doctors cut out a small part of my bowels." I said to the woman, "It's a good thing

that you are free from that cancer, but the doctor didn't heal you. Rather, he cut it out of your body; therefore, that's not healing." Then I said to her, "Doctors do a tremendous job in helping people by prescribing all sorts of medicines and teaching us how to live right, but if the medicines don't work, and the sickness gets worse, they then proceed with an operation and cut out the body part that is sick."

Yes, it's better to have a body part removed through surgery than to be in great pain and maybe even die from the sickness. No one can dispute this, but again, that's not healing, even though it's a tremendous blessing. God's healing is from the Holy Spirit, and His Word, as I have shared in the six miracles above I've received from the Holy Ghost and fire.

How Modern Medicine Saves Lives

Because of vaccinations, we no longer see smallpox or polio[2], and many other diseases have been virtually eliminated including whooping cough, diphtheria, and meningitis C.

No wonder vaccination is considered a modern miracle. It is one of the greatest breakthroughs in modern medicine. No other medical intervention has done more to save lives and improve quality of life. So, we need to thank God for His giving of such wisdom and knowledge to men on the earth.

How Much Good Does Medicine Do?

Life expectancy in the U.S.A. was around 47 years in 1900; it is now about 80[3]. To what degree can medicine take credit for this vast improvement?

---

[2] "Post-polio syndrome." *NHS Choices*. NHS, 26 Aug. 2015 Web. 25 Jun, 2017.

[3] "World Development Indicators." *World Development Indicators-Google Public Data Explorer*. World Bank, 27 Apr. 2017. Web. 25 Jun, 2017.

During the last century the population in the developed world became better fed, wealthier, better educated, and living in safer and more hygienic environments. Our longer lives are due to all of the above, including our marvelous breakthroughs in modern medicine. Surgeons, doctors, and nurses save tens of millions of people's lives every year around the world. **Now thank God, because that's a very good thing!**

In November 1974, before I was a Christian, I had a serious ruptured appendix and was rushed to the hospital for an emergency appendectomy. I spent the next 10 days in the hospital whereby the doctors worked hard to save my life using the most potent penicillin available because of sepsis poisoning. See, God used those doctors.

But now that I'm a Christian, I put all my hope and trust in the finished work of the cross. (See Isaiah 53:4-5; Matthew 8:17; 1 Peter. 2:24; James 5:13-15.)

The following is an excerpt from the article *Do Doctors Really Heal?* by Brian Shilhavy[4]

Who Were "Doctors" in the Ancient World?

So who were these "doctors?" How was this title used in biblical times?

When we use this word today in English, we automatically imagine someone in a white coat at a clinic or hospital who examines people and prescribes medicine or other medical procedures designed to deal with physical sicknesses. We

---

[4] Shilhavy, Brian. "Do Doctors Really Heal?" *Created4Health, 4 Apr. 2015.* Web. 26 Jun 2017.

would not think of a doctor as someone who looks at spiritual issues in addition to physical issues, and tries to find remedies through invoking certain spirits through incantations, spells, or magic. We would not imagine someone working in a temple offering up sacrifices to gods bearing the title "doctor." No, we would not imagine doctors like this today in the modern world. Since the days of enlightenment and since the time when science came into vogue, such practices have for the most part ceased to be a part of popular western culture.

When you see the English word "doctor" or "physician" in the biblical literature, however, this is just how the word was understood in those days. They were usually temple priests, seen as having experience with the spiritual world, in addition to experience with physical medical remedies. They bore some resemblance to the doctors people pay to see today in that they accepted money in exchange for health services or products. But the types of services and products were vastly different in the ancient world. Today's doctors deal only with the physical and mental realm of health, and not spiritual, which is a recent development in human history.

In the ancient world, if you went to see a doctor you would most likely be going to some temple where sacrifices were made to appease the spirits or gods that were causing the illness, and trying to get on the good side of the spirits or gods that supposedly had the power to heal you. There were also remedies from plants and herbs that were used in the physical realm. The Greeks, for example, were strong in empiricism and rationalism and used empirical examinations to find causes and effects to problems. But they combined this with their belief system in their gods, especially Apollo who for a period of Greek history was considered the mediator of healing between men and Zeus, one of the highest Greek gods.

Consider What the Apostles Paul and Barnabas Went Up Against

"In Lystra a man sat who was lame from birth and had never walked. He listened to Paul as he was speaking. Paul looked directly at him, saw that he had faith to be healed, and called out, 'Stand up on your feet!' At that, the man jumped up and began to walk. When the crowd saw what Paul had done, they shouted in the Lycaonian language, "The gods have come down to us in human form!" They called Barnabas Zeus, and Paul they called Hermes because he was the chief speaker. The priest of Zeus, whose temple was just outside the city, brought bulls and wreaths to the city gates because he and the crowd wanted to offer sacrifices to them" **(Acts 14:8-13).**

The Jewish people did not seek out these doctors, but instead went to the Jewish priests (doctors) in their own temple or synagogue, as this is what was prescribed in the Law of Moses.

Many have said to me, "What about Luke, the beloved physician?" (See Colossians 4:14.) He was part of the Jewish priesthood and worked in the synagogue as a doctor or physician. There they helped the people with remedies from plants, spices, and herbs that were used only for physical health and healing. They also set people's bones, and washed and dressed their wounds.

What About In The Old Testament Times?

"And the Lord will take away from thee all sickness, and will put none of the evil diseases of Egypt, which thou knowest, upon thee; but will lay them upon all them that hate thee."

—Deuteronomy 7:15, KJV

"Because thou hast made the Lord, which is my refuge, even the most High, thy habitation; There shall no evil befall thee, neither shall any plague come nigh thy dwelling."

—Psalm 91:9-10, KJV

"Bless the Lord, O my soul: and all that is within me, bless his holy name. Bless the Lord, O my soul, and forget not all his benefits: Who forgiveth all thine iniquities; who healeth all thy diseases; Who redeemeth thy life from destruction; who crowneth thee with lovingkindness and tender mercies; Who satisfieth thy mouth with good things; so that thy youth is renewed like the eagle's."

—Psalm 103:1-5, KJV

"Then they cry unto the Lord in their trouble, and he saveth them out of their distresses. He sent his word, and healed them, and delivered them from their destructions."

—Psalm 107:19-20, KJV

> *"My son, attend to my words; incline thine ear unto my sayings. Let them not depart from thine eyes; keep them in the midst of thine heart. For they are life unto those that find them, and health to all their flesh. Keep thy heart with all diligence; for out of it are the issues of life."*
>
> **—Proverbs 4:20-23, KJV**

So, when we read about what King Asa did when he was crippled in his feet and how he went to the physicians instead of to the Lord, we may be tempted to think, "What was so bad about that?", given modern-day Christians' acceptance and high regard of the current medical-pharmaceutical system. But what was more than likely happening was that the king of Israel was running away from God and seeking a pagan priest with his magic, spells, and potions instead of seeking the one true God of Israel through the Levitical priests:

> *"And Asa in the thirty and ninth year of his reign was diseased in his feet, until his disease was exceeding great: yet in his disease he sought not to the Lord, but to the physicians. And Asa slept with his fathers, and died in the one and fortieth year of his reign."*
>
> **—2 Chronicles 16:12-13, KJV**

The Ministry of JESUS

> *"And all the people were trying to touch Him, for power was coming from Him and healing them all."*
>
> **—Luke 6:19, NASB**

Preface

"A large crowd followed and pressed around him. And a woman was there who had been subject to bleeding for twelve years. She had suffered a great deal under the care of many doctors and had spent all she had, yet instead of getting better she grew worse. When she heard about Jesus, she came up behind him in the crowd and touched his cloak, because she thought, 'If I just touch his clothes, I will be healed.' Immediately her bleeding stopped and she felt in her body that she was freed from her suffering. At once Jesus realized that power had gone out from him. He turned around in the crowd and asked, 'Who touched my clothes?' 'You see the people crowding against you,' his disciples answered, 'and yet you can ask, "Who touched me?"' But Jesus kept looking around to see who had done it. Then the woman, knowing what had happened to her, came and fell at his feet and, trembling with fear, told him the whole truth. He said to her, 'Daughter, your faith has healed you. Go in peace and be freed from your suffering.'"

—**Mark 5:24-34, NIV**

What the doctors could not do for 12 years while taking all of her money for their services and products, Jesus accomplished in a moment through the faith of the woman – free of charge.

"Is any one of you sick? He should call the elders of the church to pray over him and anoint him with oil in the name of the Lord. And the prayer offered in faith will make the sick person well; the Lord will raise him up. If he has sinned, he will be forgiven. Therefore confess your sins to each other and pray for each other so that you may be healed. The prayer of a righteous man is powerful and effective."

—**James 5:14-16, NIV**

"And He Himself bore our sins in His body on the cross, so that we might die to sin and live to righteousness; for by His wounds you were healed"

—1 Peter 2:24, NASB

"But he was pierced for our transgressions, he was crushed for our iniquities; the punishment that brought us peace was upon him, and by his wounds we are healed."

—Isaiah 53:5, WEB

"And all the people were trying to touch Him, for power was coming from Him and healing them all."

—Luke 6:19, NASB

What Are God's Instructions To The Sick In His Church Today?

"Is anyone among you suffering...Let him sing praises. Is anyone among you sick? Let him call for the elders of the church, and let them pray over him, anointing him with oil in the name of the Lord; and the prayer offered in faith will restore such a one who is sick, and the Lord will raise him up, and if he has committed sins, they will be forgiven him. Therefore, confess your sins to one another, and pray for one another, that you may be healed. The effective prayer of a righteous man can accomplish much."

—James 5:13-16, ESV

This phrase, "Is anyone among you sick?" means all the sick people in the body of Christ.

I can confidently say with faith, *"Lord, I believe that you are Jehovah-Rapha, the **Healer of all my sickness** or diseases,"* because we find in the Bible God's promises of divine healing.[5] (See **1 Peter 2:24.**)

In 2 Corinthians 4:13 it is written, *"I believed; therefore I have spoken."* With that **same spirit** of faith **we also believe and therefore speak**[6].

> *"My son, give attention to my words, incline your ear to my sayings. Do not let them depart from your eyes, keep them in the midst of your heart. For they are life to those that find them, and health to all their flesh."*
>
> **—Proverbs 4:20-22, NASB**

---

[5] Feeney, James H. "God Heals Today | Faith-Building Articles Full of Healing Scriptures." *God Heals Today | Faith-Building Sermons on Divine Healing.* Web.<http://www.jimfeeney.org/divine-healing-today.html>.

[6] Feeney, James H. "You Have the Same Spirit." *You Have the Same Spirit.* Web. <http://www.jimfeeney.org/thesamespirit.html>

Introduction

"Examine yourselves, to see whether you are in the faith. Test yourselves. Or do you not realize this about yourselves, that Jesus Christ is in you? —Unless indeed you fail to meet the test!"

—2 Corinthians 13:5, ESV

Back in 1988, I read an article in a major popular Christian magazine stating that most Christians were sick and dying of disease at almost the same rate as nonbelievers. The numbers were shocking and I asked the Lord, "If Jesus redeemed us from the curse of the law of sin and death, why do so many Christians fail to receive or maintain healing?" What is the problem? What is the answer? If its God's will to heal all, then why aren't all healed? Why was I supernaturally and miraculously healed before I got saved and had no faith to believe or receive that touch from heaven while many Christians struggle to receive?

How I Was Called To The Ministry

On Easter Sunday 1977, I was a cook at a large church camp in the hills country, about 40 miles south of the city of Adelaide; South Australia. About 650 people were in attendance. In-between cooking sessions we would go out on the football field and play ball. I was running to catch the ball when my right foot went down a hole in the ground, snapped, and bent around the other way. They took me down the mountain to the ER to the Flinders Medical Center in Adelaide. After x-rays, the doctors said that I would have to have several pins and plates put into my leg and foot to hold it all together, and I would be in cast for three months. After my cast was taken off, they would have to operate on my foot the second time and maybe even a third time before I could walk on it again. They gave me a 75 percent chance I'd never walk without a limp. As I lay in the bed, with no one else in the room and my feet up on a bed rest, I prayed and told God if He would heal my ankle, **I would tell people all over the world and everyone I could what He had done.** Suddenly, a pillar of fire came down from the ceiling and stood at the end of my bed. Out of it came the words, **"I have called you to carry My healing power and anointing around the world."** I was then healed instantly. I was shocked at what I saw and experienced. My crushed, twisted, and very swollen ankle just shrank, turned the other way around, and was instantly made whole, just like the other one. I was absolutely taken aback, surprised, and flabbergasted at this whole ordeal of God's mercy, love, and His absolute awesome power.

I'm still to this day undone by what I heard Him say I was called to do. I had no pain or broken and smashed bones. **This was my call and introduction to the healing ministry.**

Up to that time, a few pastors from different churches had invited me to minister at their churches. After the healing, I felt strongly led to become a full-time evangelist so I quit my executive job, bought a motor home, and hit the road. I would have a revival meeting and about 100 to 300 people would be saved because of the healing power of the Holy Ghost with signs, wonders and miracles. My own salvation experience (July 6, 1975) in church had been with a demonstration of power and a miraculous healing. I believed and had the same expectation when I preached and ministered. Every time, the Lord showed up powerfully. People were delivered and healed, some miraculously.

I later moved to Brisbane, Queensland Australia, where I pioneered four churches through outreach revival crusades. I would hand the churches over to the organization that I was under, and they would place pastors in

Introduction

those churches. Eventually I took a pastoring job where I was happy and comfortable. Things were great. I had a good salary, a nice home provided by the church, a good car, and blessings on top of blessings.

One Monday morning I sat at my desk going over church finances when the Lord dropped a bomb on me.

"It is time for you to leave Australia and evangelize and help towards bringing a revival to America," the Holy Spirit spoke clearly into my spirit. This was a rekindling and a reminder of a powerful word I'd received from the Lord about 11 years earlier.

I felt like I was nearly knocked out of my chair the moment He spoke. "But Lord," I reasoned, "I like pastoring this church. I am enjoying my life, things are good." Plus, the Assemblies of God churches in Perth, Western Australia, wanted me to do a citywide revival there in a few months. The truth was, I really, really, adamantly did not want to go to America to live. Period. "Lord, I said again, "things are good here."

So He gave me a choice: I could stay to pastor the church, but the powerful anointing to minister in healings and miracles would be lifted, and He'd give it to another. I hesitated. I could continue to pastor the church with all the perks and benefits or leave everything behind to go to America. His anointing and blessings went with the calling to evangelize and bring revival. The choice was mine.

After moments of wrestling with my flesh, which was quite happy and content doing what it was doing, I decided that I couldn't fathom a halfhearted existence of attempting to minister out of my flesh (with a gift-only approach) without His anointing power. I imagined standing behind the pulpit preaching nice little sermons and having men's breakfasts, church workdays, and potlucks with the anointing upon me to minister in power **gone forever.** I could go through the motions of pastoring that church in God's permissive will, or follow Him, in His perfect will with purpose, anointing and covering, and blessing. His anointing was my life. It was greater than the comforts of a good job with full benefits. It was my covering and protection beyond ministering to others. I made my decision. I said yes to the good Lord's call. It's not always easy, but we must do it.

I came to America on the March 5, 1990, and lived in Chicago for one year, and then to Tulsa, Oklahoma, from 1991 to 1994. I pastored a church for three years and traveled around the country preaching healing and revival meetings in hundreds of churches.

Although I was seeing a considerable amount of people healed in these meetings, including some very powerful miracles, like people getting out of wheelchairs, I was becoming increasingly despondent of the healing ministry. Why? Because, the majority of people were not getting healed by the power of God through the laying on of hands. I also noticed this was the case with all the other healing evangelists I spoke to, including some very prominent well-known ministers with large public ministries.

In 1993, a notable healing evangelist came to Tulsa to do a revival. I went to the meeting yearning to experience Christ at work, expecting to see a powerful move of God with miracles and people receiving healing and deliverance. I wanted to leave the meeting feeling encouraged and filled with hope in my own ministry.

Choosing a high vantage point with a view of the whole church, I counted about 150 people in wheelchairs, 25 people on beds, and about 35-40 people with oxygen bottles. About 150 other people had canes, crutches, and walkers, besides hundreds of other very sick people who were all seated together on the front floor of this large church. They had designated the front floor area for the sick only.

I saw one woman with a very bad back in a wheelchair. She wasn't a cripple, but she could barely walk and was in need of surgery. She was instantly healed, and got up and walked around normal. Praise the Lord!

Introduction

A handful of people were healed of arthritis, and about a dozen others were healed of various conditions, some serious. However, I saw none of those on the main floor with grave illnesses touched or healed. I felt devastated. Overwhelmed with grief, I got up and left. I thanked the Lord for the few who were healed in Jesus' name, but drove home in tears, feeling crushed and broken.

I shut myself into my office and collapsed to the floor. Trembling and sobbing in utter brokenness, I cried to God, "That's it for me! No more! Look at all those hurting, broken and emotionally devastated people who didn't get healed tonight. How do they feel? I bet most of them will never go near another healing evangelist again. If that powerful evangelist can't get them healed, what hope do I have? That's it, I'm done."

As I lay on the floor crying, the Lord spoke to me in an audible voice, and said, "For the world, the nonbelievers, are under total grace and mercy to receive and I heal many so they can get saved. **See, son, that's the way you came to know Me.** I healed you of a major spinal injury and then you got saved. After they are healed and become children of God, then they must learn to walk in the grace and the covenant of God, the Word of God. My people have been redeemed from the curse of the law through Jesus Christ dying on the cross and shedding His blood for all their sin, but they are mostly walking in the flesh and not the Spirit. That's why they are sick and weak and many are dying before their time."

He then instructed me not to give up the healing ministry, but to pray for the sick under the anointing and to teach the spiritual laws of the word of the covenant—the law of the Spirit of life in Christ—and I would see greater results. I spent many years studying and prayerfully meditating on the subject of **why Christians are not receiving their healing.** The Holy Spirit revealed many things in the carnal or fleshly nature in Christians that can manifest sickness in the body, mind, and soul from the law of sin and death.

The purpose of this book is to set the captives free by revealing the Truth in the Word, which has the power to break the yokes of bondage and to bring abundant life and healing according to the promises in God's Word. 1 Peter 2:24 says, *"By his stripes ye are healed."*

The blessings of health, healing and abundant life are found in the simplicity and power of the gospel, and walking according to the law of the Spirit of life in Christ. Just as a seed contains the locked potential to explode with life and growth, the Word contains life to the hearers whose ears are like fertile soil and their hearts a prepared field.

Perhaps you are sick, or know someone who is, and are in need of a miracle but don't understand the keys to unlock the answers that have been spelled out in the Word of God. As you read this book, it is my prayer that the Lord will give you revelation of the law of the Spirit of life, specifically in the realm of divine health; mentally, emotionally, spiritually and physically. Although these 25 reasons why Christians are not receiving their healing is not an exhaustive list, it offers an explanation of the most prevalent road blocks and hindrances which the Lord has revealed to me during the decades of ministering in the gifts of healing and miracles.

The Law of the Spirit of Life

"This is the covenant that I will make with them after those days, says the Lord, I will put My laws into their hearts, and in their minds will I write them."

—**Hebrews 10:16; 8:10, KJ21**

"If you love me, keep my commandments."

—**John 14:15, 21, WEB**

"By this we know that we love the children (brethren) of God, when we love God and keep His commandments."

—**I John 5:2, KJV**

"For this is the love of God, that we keep His commandments: and His commandments are not grievous."

—**1 John 5:3, KJV**

"And this is love, that we walk after His commandments..."

—**2 John 6a, KJV**

"If we love one another, God dwells in us, and His love is perfected in us,"

—**1 John 4:12, AKJV**

25 Reasons Why Christians Are Not Healed

> *"God is love, and he that dwells in love dwells in God, and God in him. Herein is our love made perfect, that we may have boldness in the day of judgment: because as He is, so are we in this world."*
>
> —**1 John 4:16b-17, AKJV**

> *"He that keeps His commandments dwells in Him and He in him. And hereby we know that He abides in us by the Spirit which He has given us."*
>
> —**1 John 3:24, AKJV**

The sun hung low and the air was beginning to cool slightly in the evening June sky over Hillsboro, Oregon, as I drove past the municipal airport toward the Washington County fairgrounds. I talked out loud to the good Lord. "This thing is Yours, Jesus."

Just a few weeks earlier a five-day revival—hosted by an awesome Pentecostal church in Cornelius, Oregon situated on the outskirts of the Portland Metroplex—had exploded. Within days of preaching, the church was packed with standing room only, as word got out that people were being healed every night, some who'd been given only months to live. Others were throwing away their crutches and walkers after being healed. The crowds started coming to see the miracles and the fire of God at work.

We decided to erect a 600-man tent on the property next to the church to accommodate the growing crowd. By the end of the week that tent went up, the local fire chief was on hand to shut it down because the revival meeting was gathering too many people. They explained it was a safety hazard to attempt to pack all these people into a 600-man tent. Not only was the tent full, but also there was an additional 3 to 400 people on the outside and all the way up the street, trying to get into the healing revival service.

We announced that the meetings would resume in a week. We didn't know how, when, or where. But we'd let everyone know soon through advertising.

Pastor Eddie was a ball of fire to push the revival to the next level. He found a 2,000-man revival tent and talked to the county who allowed him to use the fairgrounds at no cost. He put out advertising and word spread quickly. People were hungering to hear the gospel, to experience a real move of the Holy Spirit, and to soak in the Lord's presence and corporate anointing.

I turned onto the gravel fairground entrance and looked over to the large white tent and the many hundreds of cars parked neatly in the grassy field next to it. My revival schedule meant that I prayed all night in the Holy Ghost, spent time studying the Word and waiting on the Lord, and slept by day. It is critical to not have distractions that stop the anointing, especially just before preaching and ministering, so I'd arrive during the praise and worship segment of services. The other thing was that I didn't want to distract people from their time of worship.

For a revival, their worship was excellent, passionate, anointed, on fire big-time, and their musicians were dedicated. The pastor's wife led the worship band singing and playing keyboard along with the guitarists, a drummer, and the handful of other singers. I parked my car and stood for a few minutes with eyes closed, listening to the worship band and the muffled sound of the people singing inside the canvas walls. Although I felt a heavy anointing on me, I also experienced intense warfare from a dark insidious power that attempted to push against this revival and me. But through intercessory prayer in the Spirit, this was broken down early into the tent meetings. I sought the Lord regarding the heavy oppression and His answer was to pray more in the Holy Spirit… and I did.

The music seemed to ebb and flow and ride the breeze as I walked across the uneven dirt and grass toward the tent opening. The night before, several people sat in the front in wheelchairs. People from all walks of life and every denomination came to the meetings.

In the New Testament, many times the Bible references Jesus "knowing their thoughts".[7] As I preached, I sensed people's thoughts. "How come you don't just pull people out of their wheelchairs to walk if you are ministering under His anointing and operating in the gift of miracles? Why is one person healed and another person is not, if God is not a respecter of persons?"

I opened the flap and stepped in. Almost all the chairs were full. The one person looking for me was the pastor's wife, and my presence meant that she could begin to bring worship to a close. One thing for sure is no matter how much I pray and study and wait on the Lord, He makes sure I realize that I never rely on my own strength or power or understanding. The more I grow as a believer and a minister of the gospel, the more I become dependent on His grace, His power, His leading, and His anointing.

I put the microphone headpiece in place and clipped the battery pack onto the side of my belt. I walked down to the front and sat in a foldout chair where a hot pink sheet of paper lay with "RESERVED" hand scrawled in permanent marker. Pastor Eddie came forward and welcomed everyone as the musicians stepped off the plywood stage.

"We just praise the Lord for God sending us Australian evangelist, Dan Nolan. Brother…."

---

[7] Matthew 9:4; Matthew 12:25; Matthew 22:18

As Pastor Eddie took a seat in the front, I stepped up and looked over the group with a smile.

"Praise the Lord. G'day, mates! That's what we say in Australia. We're going to have a very powerful night with the Holy Ghost! The Holy Ghost and fire are here now, amen. What's going to happen is that I'm going to preach, then the power and fire of God are going to show up and then I'm going to call people out with words of knowledge. People are going to receive miracles, others will be healed, and many will be saved tonight. Halleluiah!"

I took in a deep breath and looked at the crowd of people. "So let's just pray. Thank You, Jesus. Praise You, Jesus. Lord, we give You thanks for Your Word and for touching people's hearts and lives. We give You all the glory. We give You thanks for the people who are to be saved, and those who are going to come back to You. We thank You for all the broken hearts You're going to mend and for those who are to be healed and set free. In Jesus' name, amen."

"HA!" I laughed a big belly laugh and lifted up my large worn black Bible. "I'm going to be reading Scriptures tonight from the New King Jimmy. I feel like the good Lord wants me to preach on a subject that will shed some light on why some people are not healed. Tonight He wants you to have an understanding of some spiritual laws. Sometimes people are sick or are sitting in wheelchairs, for example. People may wonder, 'Brother Dan, why did you ignore all those poor people sitting in wheelchairs? Why did you command those two persons to stand up out of their wheelchairs in Jesus' name, and they stood and walked, while you didn't even look at the others? Why did one Christian receive healing and another did not? Why did the Lord supernaturally heal one person who was not even saved and had no faith?'

When I minister, I can't just walk around and say, "The Lord has given me the gift of healings and miracles and I go do my own thing." The Spirit leads me. You can't just walk around trying to yank people out of wheelchairs. That's in the flesh and it will not work. The Word of God says in **Ephesians 6:18 that we are to pray always with all prayer and supplication in the Spirit.** There are different kinds of prayer, but it all needs to be in the Spirit. If we don't pray from the Spirit, we are praying in the flesh. We will not see results when we operate out of the flesh. But in the Spirit, and through the Spirit, it always works. In James 5:14-15, that's called the prayer of faith.

We've seen thousands of people healed and lots and lots of creative miracles over the years by the power of the Holy Ghost in Jesus' name. I've seen blind eyes open, deaf ears open, broken bones healed, and people have been healed of cancer and all types of diseases. Others, who have been told they would never walk again leave the meeting pushing their own wheelchair out the door. I'm not the healer; He is. Jesus is. I do the praying, and He does the healing or miracle. Amen!

Years ago, I sought the Lord as to why so many Christians are sick and many die before their time. If we have been redeemed from the curse of the law of sin and death through Jesus (see Galatians 3:13), who took sickness and the wages of sin and death on Himself when He was crucified, then what's the problem? I've cried out to the Lord, and He spoke to me as to why this is so. And over the years He's borne witness through His Word, and confirmed what I've seen in the ministry—that healing is for everyone.

Here's what you need to understand about the law of the Spirit of life versus the law of sin and death. When you get revelation of what the Word says, you can begin to understand the reason why many people do not walk in divine health or receive healing. If you are in need of an answer, I pray you will find your answer and the key to unlock the door for healing to flow.

For some of you reading this, this is the first time you've heard someone preach that it's God's will to bless and that it's God's will to heal, or that He's still in the miracle-working business. Some of you might think that the gifts of the Spirit and healing passed away with the 12 apostles. He didn't do away with preachers and evangelists and He didn't do away with the gift of hospitality or the gift of giving, and He didn't do away with the gifts of healings and miracles.

We need to get out of thinking that it is His will for us to walk on a barely getting along street, and stumbling down grumble alley, holding onto an insecurity post, beat down, broken and bruised, busted and disgusted in this life. His Word says that we are more than conquerors in Christ Jesus. (See Romans 8:31-39.)

His blessings are for all. His Word says in **Jeremiah 29:11:** *"For I know the thoughts that I think toward you, says the Lord, thoughts of peace and not of evil, to give you a future and a hope."* That's good news. Some of you need to know that deep in your spirit.

Jesus said in **John 10 verse 10:** *"The thief does not come except to steal, and to kill, and to destroy. I have come that they may have life, and that they may have it more abundantly."*

We serve a good God. The devil is behind sickness and disease. He's the bad one. He wants to put sickness on people and have them blame God for it.

> *"[Only good things come] down from the father of lights, with whom there is no variableness, neither shadow of turning."*
>
> **—James 1:17, KJV**

In the book of Romans, Paul talks about the law of the Spirit of life in Christ. The other law is the law of sin and death. We read from Romans 8:1-6 NKJV:

> *"There is therefore now no condemnation to those who are in Christ Jesus, who do not walk according to the flesh, but according to the Spirit. For the law of the Spirit of life in Christ Jesus has made me free from the law of sin and death. For what the law could not do in that it was weak through the flesh, God did by sending His own Son in the likeness of sinful flesh, on account of sin: He condemned sin in the flesh, that the righteous requirement of the law might be fulfilled in us who do not walk according to the flesh but according to the Spirit. For those who live according to the flesh set their minds on the things of the flesh, but those who live according to the Spirit, the things of the Spirit. For to be carnally minded is death, but to be spiritually minded is life and peace."*

Many Christians know and can quote the first half of that verse: *"There is therefore now no condemnation for those who are in Christ Jesus..."* Then they stop and do not quote the second half of that verse: *"...who do not walk according to the flesh, but according to the Spirit."* This second half happens to be the condition that must be met to receive the promise. As believers, we have a choice to walk after the flesh or after the Spirit. One cannot give himself to the dictates of their flesh and expect to reap the benefits of a life that's submitted to the Spirit.

Some scholars say that Romans 8:1 was altered about 1500 years ago by some priest, by adding to the text, "who walk not after the flesh, but after the spirit."

Well, consider this. Romans 8:4 says the same thing. Romans 7:6 spells out the same principle. Romans 8:12-13 is spelling out the same principle. Galatians 5:16-21 spells out and makes this principle of walking in the spirit vs. walking in the flesh very clear indeed. Maybe those who oppose this principle of "walking in the flesh vs. walking in the spirit" really want to have a flesh walk and to be able to justify it so. Romans 6:1-2 says, *"What shall we say then, shall we continue in sin, that grace may abound? God forbid. How shall we, that are dead to sin, live any longer in it?"* Also, in **Romans 6:14-15:** *"For sin shall not have dominion over you: for ye are not under the law, but under grace. What then? shall we sin, because we are not under the law, but under grace? God forbid."*

Titus 2:11-12 tells us, *"For the grace of God has appeared, bringing salvation for all people, training us to renounce ungodliness and worldly passions, and to live self-controlled, upright, and godly lives in the present age."* **That means this grace that we have received will train us in holiness and a godly walk in this present age.**

The following is an excerpt from *Walking According to the Spirit* by Jon W. Quinn[8]:

Two Kinds of Walk: Flesh and Spirit

"For what the Law could not do, weak as it was through the flesh, God did, sending His own Son in the likeness of sinful flesh and as an offering for sin, He condemned sin in the flesh in order that the requirement of the Law might be fulfilled in us, who do not walk according to the flesh, but according to the Spirit" (Romans 8:3-4 NASB).

---

[8] Full article found online at http://www.bible.ca/ef/expository-romans-8-1-17.htm

The Law of Moses could not save sinners. It was not designed to forgive, but to demonstrate how far everyone fell short of righteousness. "Weak as it was through the flesh" refers to our flesh, or carnality. The Law could not take away our sins. Jesus came and died the death that the Law required of us, taking our sins with Him to the cross so we who walk according to the Spirit and are in Christ Jesus will not suffer condemnation (vs. 1).

There are two words which Paul contrasts with one another throughout Romans 8:1-17. They are "flesh" (sarx) and "Spirit" (pneuma). The Greek word "sarx" (flesh) is used several different ways. Sometimes, it literally means our skin and muscle (Luke 24:39). Other times, it simply means from a human point of view. For example, Jesus is the son of David on his human or "fleshly" side (Romans 1:3). Neither of these uses is negative at all.

But Paul also uses the word in a very negative way, as he does in Romans 8. In this chapter he talks of "sinful flesh" and "sin in the flesh" (v. 3); that the mind "set on the flesh is death" (v. 6) and is "hostile toward God" (v. 7); that those "in the flesh cannot please God" (v. 8). Living "by the flesh" means that we allow our desires and whims to override righteousness and moral good in our conduct.

Allowing ourselves to be controlled by lusts makes us slaves and ultimately leads to the practice of "...immorality, impurity, sensuality, idolatry, sorcery, enmities, strife, jealousy, outbursts of anger, disputes, dissensions, factions, envyings, drunkenness, carousing, and things like these of which I forewarn you just as I have forewarned you that those who practice such things shall not inherit the kingdom of God" (Galatians 5:19-21).

The other word is "pneuma" (Spirit). We read of the law of the Spirit of life in Christ (v. 2) and that the mind set on the Spirit is life and peace (v. 6). We are told that those in the Spirit have the Spirit of God dwelling in them and if one does not have the Spirit of Christ then he does not belong to Him (vs. 9). Finally, we are told that those who are being led by the Spirit are sons of God (v. 14). The fruit of the Spirit is love, joy, peace, patience, kindness, goodness, faithfulness, gentleness, self-control (Galatians 5:22-23).

Walking According To The Flesh

"So then, brethren, we are under obligation, not to the flesh, to live according to the flesh...for if you are living according to the flesh, you must die" (Romans 8:12-13a NASB).

Tragically, we see many extreme examples of utmost depravity in our society today. These include the abduction, exploitation, and even murder of young children; the countless choices being made by mothers to have their yet unborn children slain; uncontrolled greed which results in the highly profitable drug trade and the subsequent human misery; cruelty to the extreme; murder for the thrill of it; bombings and other outrages.

But those are the extremes. Walking "according to the flesh" also includes things many would consider petty: to be hateful of others; to allow one's pride to cause such ungodliness as racial prejudice or other forms of injustice;

to cheat or lie for any reason, perhaps to advance some worldly ambition; to gossip; dress immodestly; divorce for unscriptural reasons; or to delve into impure entertainment. In fact, to simply get so busy with the things of this world that one has little time for God is walking according to the flesh. In short, the vast majority of our neighbors are doing just that. It is the modern American way. Carnality of every sort is increasingly more accepted. The media glorifies it, and I fear our nation is only beginning to pay the consequences of our pursuit of the flesh.

Walking According To The Spirit

"But if by the Spirit you are putting to death the deeds of the body, you will live. For all who are being led by the Spirit of God, these are the sons of God" (Romans 8:14 NASB).

Walking "according to the Spirit" means to be led by Him. It means to live by the moral, doctrinal, and ethical standards of His written revelation, the Bible. It is to love others and to deeply enjoy the blessings of life, both spiritual and physical. Please understand that there is nothing wrong with having and enjoying material things, as long as we are thankful for them and that they do not become our gods (I Timothy 4:4-5). There is peace and contentment in such a life, a life filled with kindness and goodness.

If the Bible is not our standard for the way we live, worship, and serve God, then we are not being led by the Spirit. The apostles' doctrine taught in the first century and made available to us today in the Scripture is the product of the Spirit (Acts 2:4, 42; 1 Corinthians 2:11-13).

Whose Responsibility Is It To Choose The Spirit?

"For those who are of the flesh set their minds on the things of the flesh, but those who are according to the Spirit, the things of the Spirit... you are putting to death the deeds of the body" (Romans 8:5, 13b).

It is up to you to "set" your mind on the things of the Spirit. Do not pray that God do that for you. It is up to you to "put to death the deeds of the body." The Lord died for your sins and arose for your hope. He has revealed how we must live and has invited us to willingly come to Him. He has given us magnificent promises to motivate us, shields us from impossible temptations, and makes His gospel easy to understand and obey. It is up to you to "crucify the old" and "put on the new" and not to let sin reign in your body, but rather righteousness (Romans 6:12-18). "Now those who belong to Christ Jesus have crucified the flesh with its passions and desires. If we live by the Spirit, let us also walk by the Spirit" (Galatians 5:24,25). You see? It is up to you.

We can find more information on walking in the Spirit in Jack Wellman's article *5 Differences Between Walking in the Flesh and Walking in the Spirit*[9]:

---

[9] Full article found online at http://www.whatchristianswanttoknow.com/5-differences-between-walking-in-the-flesh-and-walking-in-the-spirit/

Paul addresses walking in the Spirit with a capital "S" which means that the word Spirit is a proper noun—God the Holy Spirit—as we can tell in Colossians 1:9-10: "And so, from the day we heard, we have not ceased to pray for you, asking that you may be filled with the knowledge of his will in all spiritual wisdom and understanding, so as to walk in a manner worthy of the Lord, fully pleasing to him, bearing fruit in every good work and increasing in the knowledge of God."

If a believer is walking "in a manner worthy of the Lord" and is "fully pleasing to Him," then they will be "bearing fruit in every good work and increasing in the knowledge of God." Thus, someone who is walking in the Spirit of God will be producing good fruit proving that he or she is walking in the Spirit.

It is up to you, not God, to do the walking in the spirit because He's already there.

> "Christ has redeemed us from the curse of the law, having become a curse for us (for it is written, 'Cursed is everyone who hangs on a tree'), that the blessing of Abraham might come upon the Gentiles in Christ Jesus, that we might receive the promise of the Spirit through faith."
>
> **—Galatians 3:13-14, NKJV**

Freedom from curses, which we have been redeemed from, and the blessings that are promised are found in Deuteronomy 28. Verses 1 through 14 list the blessings that were to come upon and overtake a person who kept the whole law. Verse 15 though lists all the curses that come as the penalty of not keeping the law. It's worth looking at to see what the curse entailed so we understand the greatness of our redemption. Let's just read some of them from verse 2 through 6:

> *"And all these blessings shall come upon you and overtake you, because you obey the voice of the LORD your God: Blessed shall you be in the city, and blessed shall you be in the country. Blessed shall be the fruit of your body, the produce of your ground and the increase of your herds, the increase of your cattle and the offspring of your flocks. Blessed shall be your basket and your kneading bowl. Blessed shall you be when you come in, and blessed shall you be when you go out."*

Praise the Lord! We need to read the blessings that God wants to give to those who are in Christ Jesus, **who do not walk after the dictates of the flesh, but after the Spirit of the Law of life.** The flip side of the coin is the law of sin and death…and the curse for those who walk after the flesh.

This was the Old Testament covenant before Jesus. That was God's will for His children then. We can see what God's perfect will looks like and it abounds with His blessings, its abundance, health and prosperity, in business, in work, in agriculture with rain and harvest, in finances and family. The flip side of the coin demonstrates God's sovereignty. He made His will clear and although His will was known, the Lord gave the choice to follow it or not. He spells out in detail the fruit from following Him with all your heart, which is His perfect will. The blessings are pretty easy, short and sweet, you might say in comparison to the ugly list of the curse.

Over 40 curses are listed from Deuteronomy 28:15-68. Since we're talking about those that affect health and healing, I'll highlight those. The fruit of the body would be cursed. That could include miscarriages and inability to have children. The plague that clings is an illness that doesn't go away. Also included are consumption, fever, inflammation, and severe burning fever. The boils of Egypt, tumors, hemorrhoids, the scab and the itch, from which there's no healing…being struck on the legs and knees with severe boils from head to toe which can't be healed. Part of the curse also includes failing eyes.

The curses from the law of sin and death also fall upon descendants. **Those are generational curses that can continue down a family line: "Grandma had cancer, Momma had cancer, all her sisters died of cancer, and they were all Christians."** They are extraordinary, great and prolonged plagues and sicknesses. The illnesses include those they had in Egypt that they feared would cling to them, along with every sickness and plague, which is not written in the Book of the Law. What does that mean? **That's all sickness and disease, even different types of cancer.**

The emotional outcome of being under the curse is trembling heart, anguish of soul, terrifying fear day and night, groping at noonday as a man gropes in darkness, madness, blindness, confusion, and an angry heart.

The apostle Paul wrote that Jesus Christ has redeemed us from the curse of the law (Galatians 3:13). Understand all that we've been redeemed from. What a great redemption Christ paid for us on the cross! Because the law of the Spirit of life has set us free from the law of sin and death—**which is the curse of the law**—we no longer reap the curses listed in Deuteronomy 28:15-68, even though we haven't kept every precept of the Law. Christ redeemed us from these curses of the law. Praise God that we don't have to receive the wages of sin, which is death and sickness in this life.

> *"Christ Jesus has redeemed us from the curse of the law, having become a curse for us (for it is written, 'Cursed is everyone who hangs on a tree.'"*
>
> **—Galatians 3:13, NKJV**

Not only have we been redeemed from the curses, but also through Jesus we have the blessings and righteousness of the law fulfilled in us. So, by walking according to the law of the Spirit of life in Christ, the blessings of Deuteronomy 28:1-14—that we don't deserve—belong to us through Christ, and the curses we deserve, we do *not* receive. Jesus took those upon Himself when He died on the cross and shed His blood for us. That's worth a shout, halleluiah!

God placed the condemnation that was directed toward us upon the flesh of His Son, Jesus. Thank You, Jesus!

Some of you are still scratching your heads, trying to see how the Old Testament teachings pertain to the New Testament church today. Jesus said:

> *"Do not think that I came to destroy the Law or the Prophets. I did not come to destroy but to fulfill. For assuredly, I say to you, till heaven and earth pass away, not one jot or one tittle will by no means pass from the law till all is fulfilled."*
>
> **—Matthew 5:17-18, NKJV**

The Lord placed before Israel life and death, blessing or cursing and told them to choose. And now, even though we have a Savior and Redeemer, Jesus, we still must choose to **walk according to the Spirit and not the flesh** to enjoy the benefits of blessing. God wants to bless, but we will still reap what we sow (Galatians 6:7). Do not be deceived; God cannot be mocked. A man reaps what he sows.

Laws are called laws because they are fixed and unchanging. We are faced with two opposing laws at force. First is the law of the Spirit of life and the other is the law of sin and death. Jesus availed to us the benefits of the Law of the Spirit of life through His death on the cross while giving us freedom from the law of sin and death... but it is our choice to mind the things of the Spirit or mind the things of the flesh. (The word "law" as per Romans 8:2 means "A body of divine commandments, according to the spirit.")

A war is waging, and the frontline of the battle begins in the mind. It's what you decide to put your mind to and what you will to do that will decide the outcome.

> *"For those who live according to the flesh set their minds on the things of the flesh, but those who live according to the Spirit, the things of the Spirit. For to be carnally minded is death, but to be spiritually minded is life and peace."*
>
> **—Romans 8:5-6, WEB**

Our soul embodies our mind, will, and emotions. In that one example, the Word of God says that when we put our mind to things of the Spirit, life and peace follow.

What do you put *your* mind to? Do you put your mind to meditating on the Word? What do you do with thoughts that are contrary to the Word and will of the good Lord? What will you give your thoughts to when the devil tells you his lies? He'll speak through the traditions of men and spiritually dead religious people full of dead man's bones and dogmas who do not have the Holy Ghost. He'll drop thoughts on you. He'll speak through anyone willing to side with him to speak against the Word and will of God. Those thoughts and arguments are from the pit of hell, and they are called strongholds.

We are to pull down the strongholds, and our mighty, spiritual weapon in God is His Word.

> *"For, the weapons of our warfare are not carnal but mighty in God for pulling down strongholds, casting down arguments and every high thing that exalts itself against the knowledge of God, bringing every thought into captivity to the obedience of Christ, and being ready to punish all disobedience when your obedience is fulfilled."*
>
> **—2 Corinthians 10:4-6, NKJV**

Once you are saved, the Lord will not force you to think a certain way. He will not force you to read or meditate on His Word. He will not force you to fellowship with other believers. He will not force you to give up evil companionships that will pull you down the path to destruction. The Holy Spirit guides and leads us and will convict us of those things we need to lay down. He will empower you to walk away from the things of the world that weigh us down and keep us bound. His path brings life. His path brings peace. We choose to walk a life being filled with the Word and the Spirit, because we love and follow Jesus. It's not us trying to change our behavior to comply with a pile of legalistic, dead religious rules and dogma. It's following a Man, and His name is Jesus Christ. We choose to follow Jesus, and obey Him in Word and Spirit because we love Him.

The promise to walk in and abide in life and peace isn't dependent on Jesus. It's on us. He's done all He's going to do. When Jesus sat down at the right hand of the Father and said, "It is finished," it was finished. He sent his precious Holy Spirit, the Comforter, to empower us and guide us into all truth, and much more. According to 2 Timothy 3:16, we have the Word which is given by inspiration of God and is profitable for doctrine, for reproof, for correction, and for instruction in righteousness. From the time of Adam and Eve until the present, the Lord has always given us the choice to follow after Him with all of our hearts, which brings life.

> *"I call heaven and earth as witnesses today against you, that I have set before you life and death, blessing and cursing; therefore choose life, that both you and your descendants may live."*
>
> **—Deuteronomy 30:19, NKJV**

"Aww, Brother Dan, we just want all the blessing. We prayed a prayer of repentance and received Jesus years ago. **What's this 'living according to the Spirit' stuff vs. the law of sin and death?"**

You say, "That's the Old Testament, preacher. We're under grace of the New Testament."

Yes, we are under grace, but the law of sowing and reaping remains. Consequences still exist for being a carnal Christian. In all my decades of ministering, the Lord has revealed to me this reason is why so many Christians are not walking in health, or receive healing from the Lord. See what it says beginning with Romans 6:14-15 (KJV): *"For sin shall not have dominion over you: for ye are not under the law, but under grace. If you say you are under grace, then you have ceased from sin. What then? Shall we sin, because we are not under the law, but under grace? God*

The Law of the Spirit of Life

forbid." This word "forbid" means to prohibit, outlaw, make illegal, disallow, ban.[10]

> *"For what the law could not do in that it was weak through the flesh, God did by sending His own Son in the likeness of sinful flesh, on account of sin: He condemned sin in the flesh, that the righteous requirement of the law might be fulfilled in us who do not walk according to the flesh but according to the Spirit."*
>
> **—Romans 8:3-4, NKJV**

The righteous requirement of the law might be fulfilled in whom? *"In us who do not walk according to the flesh, but according to the Spirit."*

> *"I say then: Walk in the Spirit, and you shall not fulfill the lust of the flesh. For the flesh lusts against the Spirit, and the Spirit against the flesh; and these are contrary to one another, so that you do not do the things that you wish. But if you are led by the Spirit, you are not under the law. (If you are not being led by the spirit, you are now under the law of sin and death. Even though Christ has set you free, you must walk in it.) Now the works of the flesh are evident, which are: adultery, fornication, uncleanness, lewdness, idolatry, sorcery, hatred, contentions, jealousies, outbursts of wrath, selfish ambitions, dissensions, heresies, envy, murders, drunkenness, revelries, and the like; of which I tell you beforehand, just as I also told you in time past, that those who practice such things will not inherit the kingdom of God. But the fruit of the Spirit is love, joy, peace, longsuffering, kindness, goodness, faithfulness, gentleness, self-control. Against such there is no law. And those who are Christ's*

---

[10] "Forbid." *Merriam-Webster.com.* Merriam-Webster, n.d. Web. 24 Jun, 2017.

have crucified the flesh with its passions and desires. If we live in the Spirit, let us also walk in the Spirit."

—**Galatians 5:16-25, NKJV**

So folks, let's walk in the Spirit and not in the flesh, and we will get all the blessings too.

Knowing God's Will

How do we know what God's will is in regard to health and healing? You can't ask with complete certainty for something in particular if you don't know if it's God's will, right? Why do the things of God seem to be an uphill battle so often? Why is so much emphasis placed on the Scriptures? If God has a plan of good, why does it feel like I struggle to receive His good gifts for me?

I believe a good place to start is **in the beginning:**

> *"In the beginning God created the heavens and the earth. The earth was without form, and void; and darkness was on the face of the deep. And the Spirit of God was hovering over the face of the waters. Then God said, 'Let there be light,' and there was light."*

—**Genesis 1:1-3, NKJV**

God said… And it was so.

God's Word held the power of creation, light, life, time, space, and all the elements. We can understand God's will and plan from the beginning of His creation. Everything He made and put into place was good. He planted a beautiful garden filled with herbs and fruit trees, placing Adam and Eve into the Garden of Eden to tend and keep it. One of the trees he planted—the tree of the knowledge of good and evil—had a fatal curse attached if man were to eat of its fruit. The command was given that they were to not eat the fruit of that tree or in that day they would surely die.

> *"Then the LORD God took the man and put him in the Garden of Eden to tend and keep it. And the LORD God commanded the man, saying, 'Of every tree of the garden you may freely eat; but of the tree of the knowledge of good and evil you shall not eat, for in the day that you eat of it you shall surely die.'"*
>
> **—Genesis 2:15-17, NKJV**

God's creation and plan was for man to live, work, be fruitful and multiply, rule, and enjoy perpetual, eternal, fruitful blessing, free from sickness, disease, and death and the knowledge of evil and sin. Even though this was God's will, in His sovereignty, **He gave man freewill to believe, embrace and abide in His Word…. or not.**

The other choice would be to forsake His Word and cast it aside, turning from the blessing, and reaping a curse which ultimately culminated in death. All of God's will for continuous blessing was not contingent upon God, but on man. Perfect alignment in God's will hinged on Adam and Eve not eating of the tree of the knowledge of good and evil. From the very beginning of the creation, God set life or death, blessing or cursing before Adam and Eve, and His will was for them to walk in the commandment, which brought life. Mankind also had the option to choose death by the sin of disobedience.

We have God's Word, which is God-breathed, or inspired, profitable for doctrine, reproof, correction, instruction in righteousness to work wholeness and equipping for every good work (2 Timothy 3:16-17).

When we believe upon the Lord Jesus, the Son of God, He forgives us all our sin and gives us eternal life. He said that He is with us always, even to the end of the age. He has also given us the power to use His name in circumstances, to pray to the Father and against demonic attacks.

> *"For God so loved the world that He gave His only begotten Son, that whoever believes in Him should not perish but have everlasting life."*
>
> **—John 3:16, NKJV**

> *"And these signs shall follow them that believe; in my name shall cast out devils; they shall speak with new tongues. They shall take up serpents; and if they drink [this means accidently] any deadly thing, it shall not hurt them; they shall lay hands on the sick, and they shall recover."*
>
> **—Mark 16:17-18, KJV**

From the beginning of the history of our age, Satan's mission has been to deceive, kill, steal, and destroy. If he can bring deception against God's Word, then he can steal the truth, and corruption, death, and destruction always follow. The old serpent, the tempter, the great dragon, the accuser of the brethren, the Devil, is a liar and the father of lies in whom there is no truth or light. He is described as cunning, subtle, and roaming like a lion seeking whom he may devour. (See John 10:10.)

Once Eve began thinking and believing the Devil's words over God's Word, her flesh took over. It was pleasant to the eyes... it was good for food... good to make one wise, disregarding that it would also make one... dead.

> *"Now the serpent was more cunning than any beast of the field which the* LORD *God had made. And he said to the woman, 'as God indeed said, "You shall not eat of every tree of the garden"?' And the woman said to the serpent, 'We may eat the fruit of the trees of the garden; but of the fruit of the tree which is in the midst of the garden, God has said, "You shall not eat it, nor shall you touch it, lest you die."' Then the serpent said to the woman, 'You will not surely die. For God knows that in the day you eat of it your eyes will be opened, and you will be like God, knowing good and evil.'"*
>
> **—Genesis 3:1-5, NKJV**

The first tactic the Devil uses to get believers from walking in the **Spirit of the law of life** and the truth of His Word and in their own flesh is to question it altogether as he did with Eve in the Garden of Eden. When Christians listen and adhere to voices that do not agree with His Word, they are siding with the devil. Those subtle thoughts or arguments will also steal life, blessing, and health and will lead to a path of death and curses.

What does Satan want to steal today? What he stole in the beginning. He wants to steal the truth of God's Word. When he succeeds, he sows death and destruction into what should be an abundant life bearing much fruit and glorifying the Father.

Once you understand the importance of knowing what the Word says, you can know what God's will is regarding blessing, being in good health, and receiving healing.

> *"Then you will know the truth, and the truth will set you free."*
>
> **—John 8:32, NIV**

The fierce battleground for seeds of thought, good or bad, is in the mind, and the believer's great weapon of combat is to be disciplined in thought life, guarding the precious Word of God. When we abide continually in the truth of His Word, and are doers of the Word, we also guard our soul, which is our mind, will, and emotions.

> *"Therefore I urge you, brethren, by the mercies of God, to present your bodies a living and holy sacrifice, acceptable to God, which is your spiritual service of worship. And do not be conformed to this world, but be transformed by the renewing of your mind, so that you may prove what the will of God is, that which is good and acceptable and perfect."*
>
> **—Romans 12:1-2, NASB**

In James 1:21 (NASB), James talked about receiving "the word implanted, which is able to save your souls." In 1:22-27, he goes on to emphasize doing the Word. In 1:22-24, he shows that hearing the Word without doing it leads to deception. He illustrates this in 1:26 with the man who claims to be religious, but who does not bridle his tongue. He deceives himself and his religion is worthless. In 1:25, he shows that hearing the Word accompanied by doing it, leads to blessing.

If the devil is allowed to get a foothold, then he can gain a stronghold. Strongholds come through areas of our **soul, mind, will, and emotions**. Although Jesus defeated the devil on the cross, His work was finished and we became His ambassadors to carry on the work. We do not run to Jesus for Him to save us from attacks from the devil. We are given the mandate, and have been given the authority in Jesus' name to pull down strongholds and have authority over demons.

> *"And these signs will follow those who believe: In My name they will cast out demons."*
>
> —**Mark 16:17a, NKJV**

> *"For though we walk in the flesh, we do not war according to the flesh. For the weapons of our warfare are not carnal but mighty in God for pulling down strongholds, casting down arguments and every high thing that exalts itself against the knowledge of God, bringing every thought into captivity to the obedience of Christ, and being ready to punish all disobedience when your obedience is fulfilled."*
>
> —**2 Corinthians 10:3-6, NKJV**

When God poured His wisdom onto Solomon, his earnest plea to a promise of having health and the issues of life was found in God's inspired Word, not through a lazy, haphazard reading the words in one's head while sorting through the day's agenda. It is giving it attention— focused time without interruption. It is a prescription for health to the flesh.

> *"My son, give attention to my words; Incline your ear to my sayings. Do not let them depart from your eyes; Keep them in the midst of your heart; For they are life to those who find them, And health to all their flesh. Keep your heart with all diligence, For out of it spring the issues of life."*
>
> **—Proverbs 4:20-23, NKJV**

The gospel is simple, and yet today—as it was in Paul's day—believers can be deceived by the Devil's subtle craftiness. The first step to producing real fruit and real life in the Spirit is to know and grow in God's Word.

A Seed Called "Sozo"

Jesus taught that as surely as God's Word is like a seed, the Devil comes to devour and feed.

> *"A sower went out to sow his seed. And as he sowed, some fell by the wayside; and it was trampled down, and the birds of the air devoured it... Now the parable is this: The seed is the word of God. Those by the wayside are the ones who hear; then the devil comes and takes away the word out of their hearts, lest they should believe and be saved."*
>
> **—Luke 8:5, 11-12, NKJV**

The Greek word "saved" is *sozo*[11]. The meaning goes deeper than "when you die, you go to heaven," although the most wonderful benefit for

---

[11] "G4982 - sōzō - Strong's Greek Lexicon (KJV)." Blue Letter Bible. Web. 24 Jun 2017.

believers is salvation and living in eternity with God. It also means made whole, healed, recovered and preserved, so you can also say, "the Devil comes and takes away the word out of their hearts, lest they should believe and be *sozo*, **healed and made whole."**

The powerful Word contains a storehouse of potential, as Jesus likened it unto a seed. The seed, which is the Word, is sowed, or heard. A person can read the gospel or hear it preached. The seed that falls onto rocky ground, among thorns or a wayside footpath has the same potential as the seed that falls onto good soil. Just like a seed, for God's Word to grow, it must also be tended to.

How people hear is not up to the preacher and it is not up to the seed. It is up to the person who hears and what they decide to do with it—to believe, abide, and understand, or to cast it aside as unimportant, choked by anxiety and pleasures, shriveled in the heat with no root, or trampled underfoot. The seed cast by the wayside will be stolen from the hearer's heart and devoured by the birds, which represent the Devil.

"IF" is one of the Most Powerful and Disregarded Words in the Bible.

Jesus understood this parable every time he opened his mouth to teach, sowing kingdom seeds on the ears of the people. In the next Scripture reference, note that Jesus spoke, and immediately, He was no longer speaking to the crowd, but only those who had responded in their hearts to believe and receive. Then, to those believers came an exhortation that *if* they would abide in the word that they believed, they would both understand and experience the life-changing promise of being made free.

*"As He spoke these words, **many believed** in Him. Then Jesus said **to those Jews who believed Him**, 'If you abide in My word, you are My disciples indeed. And you shall know the truth, and the truth shall make you free.'"*

—**John 8:30-33, NKJV**

The word "abide" in Greek is *meno*[12]. To get a fuller depth of the importance that Jesus put on His Word, the word "abide" includes: **remain, continue, stand, endure, tarry, and dwell.** It is more than a flippant glossing over of the Scriptures.

The progression to walking in faith and after the Spirit of life is this: **hear, believe, abide, or continue in Jesus' Word,** be a disciplined follower of Jesus, or disciple, knowing the truth, which shall make you free. It is the progression Jesus spelled out in John 8:30-32.

Jesus spoke.

Many believed.

To those who believed, He said,

"*If* you abide in my word you are my disciples

and **you** shall know the truth.

The truth shall make you free."

The first step in walking in the truth is to hear it first. The truth alone does not set anyone free. When Jesus spoke, His promises were only to those

---

[12] "G3306 - menō - Strong's Greek Lexicon (KJV)." Blue Letter Bible. Web. 24 Jun, 2017

who believed His word. The promises are contingent upon the hearer standing, continuing, and abiding in His word. **The truth revealed or known and acted upon shall make you free.**

The power of the Word of God remains powerless like a dormant seed until the hearer understands it, receives it with faith, speaks it out of his mouth, and stands or abides in that truth. Many Christians are not getting healed because of a lack of understanding on the truth of the Word regarding His will to bless with health and healing.

> *"It is written, 'I believed, and so I have spoken' (Psalm 116:10) We have that same spirit of faith. So we also believe and speak."*
>
> **—2 Corinthians 4:13, NIRV**

Hear + Receive + Believe + Speak + Abide + Act Upon = Receiving Your Healing

The Word of God is powerful when the hearer tends to it like a garden filled with life-giving fruit. In the area of receiving and maintaining God's healing, it is heaven's prescription for God's will being done. For the hundreds and thousands who have received a supernatural touch from the Lord, they also must hear what the Word says and how the Holy Spirit directs to align their thoughts and lifestyle to continue to walk in victory.

Just as there is a process for a seed to grow, there is a process for the Word to grow into a harvest of faith and good works and walking after the things of the Spirit that gives life. Jesus said:

> *"The kingdom of God is as if a man should scatter seed on the ground, and should sleep by night and rise by day, and the seed should sprout and grow, he himself does not know how. For the earth yields crops by itself: first the blade, then the head, after that the full grain in the head. But when the grain ripens, immediately he puts in the sickle, because the harvest has come."*
>
> **—Mark 4:26-29, NKJV**

Sprout + Growth + Blade + Head + Full Grain in the Head = Harvest

What kind of hearer are you? Do you believe, abide and tarry or meditate on God's Word? Do you allow it to permeate beyond your mind and tend to it with your whole heart, like acting upon the Word? What will you do when the lying voice of the Devil echoes through negative thinking, family, or friends? What is your response when church dogma and the traditions of religious men attempt to replace God's Word with man's whimsy doctrines?

> *"For anyone who hears the word but does not carry it out is like a man who looks at his face in a mirror, and after observing himself goes away and immediately forgets what he looks like. But the one who looks intently into the perfect law of freedom, and continues to do so—not being a forgetful hearer, but an effective doer—he will be blessed in what he does"*
>
> **—James 1:23-25, BSB**

Will you stand firm with the holy God, Creator of the universe, and His Word or will you entertain popular intellectualism or dead man's religious rituals and doctrines of the Devil's dogma? The Devil is cunning. He can be dressed in a suit and tie, packing a big Bible under his armpit. He can speak eloquently with a confident smile and swagger. But he has no power from the Holy One of Israel.

> *"Making the word of God of none effect through your tradition, which ye have delivered: and many such like things do ye."*
>
> **—Mark 7:13, KJV**

Are you ready to stand in agreement, speak in agreement, and be in divine alignment with the Word of God and choose to be the good soil that will bring forth fruit with patience and faith?

It is no wonder that in the parable of the sower Jesus names "wayside hearers" as those who have trampled the Word. They've heard it with little regard. It is under their feet and other things are more important. They allow the Devil to steal the powerful Word from their hearts lest they believe and be saved, healed, and made whole.

Back in the Garden of Eden, the Devil's first attack was against God's truth in Eve's mind. Although there were possibly hundreds or thousands of trees dangling lush fruit in the Garden, only one had the potential to make one wise. The Devil convinced Eve that God created her somehow inferior in her current state, promising a better life of being like God.

His mighty weapon of destruction and death was to simply coerce her to subtly buy into thoughts, opinions, vain imaginations, and lies that were contrary to the Word of God and His command. When Eve took a bite and convinced Adam to join her, their eyes were opened. They attempted to cover their nakedness, fear, guilt, and shame with aprons of leaves.

Breaking God's law created broken communion with Him, which brought a spiritual death that was a precursor to physical death.

Sword Fight in the Wilderness: Jesus the Swashbuckler

Fast-forward about 4,000 years when Jesus began His ministry at the Jordan River. After He was baptized, and the Spirit descended upon him like a dove, the Bible says He was led into the wilderness for one purpose—to be tempted. The fall of mankind after the Devil's temptation in the Garden of Eden was about to be turned upside down with Jesus taking up where Adam left off. It spelled the beginning of the end for the Devil, who attempted his same tactics on Jesus, the Son of God. A mighty battle ensued. Jesus drew his razor sharp two-edged sword, called the Word of God.

> *"Now when the tempter came to Him, he said, 'If You are the Son of God, command that these stones become bread.' But He answered and said, 'It is written, "Man shall not live by bread alone, but by every word that proceeds from the mouth of God."'"*
>
> **—Matthew 4:3-4, NKJV**

The Devil attempted to entice Jesus to use His Son-of-God power to turn rocks into bread and eat His fill. Jesus' bread was to do the will of the Father. He did only what He saw His Father doing, and He said only what He heard the Father saying so His response was directly from His Father, and that was to speak the Word. Jesus read, meditated on, and understood the Scriptures and his life was saturated in the Word. His time had come to speak the Word to resist the Devil's attack. Jesus spoke and the written Word was His authority.

The Law of the Spirit of Life

Undeterred, the Devil spoke again, this time tempting Him at the top of the pinnacle of the temple in Jerusalem, and quoting Scriptures out of context by leaving off half of the verse of Psalm 91:11.

> *"If You are the Son of God, throw Yourself down. For it is written: 'He shall give His angels charge over you,' and, 'In their hands they shall bear you up, Lest you dash your foot against a stone.' Jesus said to him, 'It is written again, "You shall not tempt the Lord your God."'"*
>
> **—Matthew 4:6-7, NKJV**

Then the Devil took Jesus up to an exceedingly high mountain and showed Him all the kingdoms of the world and their glory:

> *"And he said to Him, 'All these things I will give You if You will fall down and worship me.' Then Jesus said to him, **'Away with you, Satan! For it is written, "You shall worship the Lord your God, and Him only you shall serve."'***
>
> **—Matthew 4:9-10, NKJV**

Jesus commanded the Devil to leave... and he did...for a time, but he resurfaced repeatedly through the hard-hearted pompous religious leaders who were filled with pride, greed, lies, jealousy, and murder. I do believe they are the same spirits that we are battling today. See, the people loved Jesus—the multitudes came to His revival meetings—but the religious hated Him big-time.

It is the goal of the Devil to attack the mind, to steal the seed, the Word of God. He will speak subtle lies and attempt to plant doubts, which sow unbelief. He may even quote or twist bits and pieces of Scripture out of context as he did with Jesus.

The war is waged today as it was in the Garden of Eden and with Jesus in the wilderness, with the voices of temptation to waver in believing, standing on, and speaking the Word with authority. He works through planting thoughts that are contrary to the Word to deceive as he did with Eve in the Garden. He can entice through false church doctrine and traditions of men that sow unbelief. **Many people will believe first what some man says regarding a matter, regardless of what the Word says.**

The Devil can only steal the Word that he is allowed to steal. When he can coerce believers to side with him, and begin to speak the lie over the truth of the Word, he can keep believers from receiving "sozo" healing and being made whole.

> *"Dear friends, although I was eager to write you about the salvation we share, I found it necessary to write and exhort you to contend for the faith that was delivered to the saints once for all."*
>
> **—Jude 1:3, HCSB**

The foundation to walking after the law of the Spirit of life is built on God's Word. His Word is His will, which is for good, not evil. **It is for health, not sickness**. It is for blessing, not cursing. It's vitally important to know what the Word says for your situation and to have the strategy to stand and fight the good fight of faith speaking the Word of God. It is a two-edged sword against the wiles of Satan and can be used as Jesus showed us by example: **"It is written."** It becomes only as powerful as the ground it lands on and is tended to and is guarded against evil. We need to know what it says so when thoughts come or people speak against it, we can reject the lie and hold firm to the truth.

Some people set their minds on what they can see and feel, not on the truth of the Word. The fact might be a problem diagnosed by the doctor with symptoms, but the truth is what God's Word says about His provision for us to receive healing.

> *"Who his own self bare our sins in his own body on the tree, that we, being dead to sins, should live unto righteousness: by whose stripes ye were healed."*
>
> **—1 Peter 2:24, KJV**

The message that God is a good God who heals is a foreign concept for many coming out of some denominations that teach and pray things like, "If it be Thy will for You to heal Sister-So-and-So to not suffer," or, "Maybe, Lord, You can do something here, if You want to." If you don't read the Word or believe the Word, you can't pray the prayer of faith that heals the sick.

> *"Is anyone among you sick? He should call for the elders of the church, and they should pray over him after anointing him with olive oil in the name of the Lord."*
>
> **—James 5:15, HCSB**

> *"And the prayer offered in faith will make the sick person well; the Lord will raise them up If they have sinned, they will be forgiven."*
>
> **—James 5:15, NIV**

At the end of this book, I have listed many Scriptures regarding God's will for health, wholeness, and healing. Read and memorize them: tarry, remain, continue, stand, speak them out, dwell, abide, and meditate on them to get them from your head into your heart and spirit. Find one or several that speak to your heart, and memorize and speak them with authority. When the devil comes to steal the Word, stand and fight the good fight of faith, as Jesus did.

> *"Fight the good fight of faith, lay hold on eternal life, whereunto thou art also called, and hast professed a good profession before many witnesses."*
>
> **—1 Timothy 6:12, KJV**

How will you hear and what will you choose?

> *"I call heaven and earth as witnesses today against you, that I have set before you life and death, blessing and cursing; therefore choose life, that both you and your descendants may live."*
>
> **—Deuteronomy 30:19, NKJV**

1 to 25 Reasons Why Christians Are Not Being Healed

REASON #1: UNBELIEF

The biggest shock in my ministry is the one of unbelief in the churches. I probably spend about 85 percent of my entire time trying to convince people that God loves them and wants to heal them.

From 1996 to 1999, I was a staff evangelist of a large church in Phoenix, Arizona. One day the senior pastor called me into his office and showed me an article from a major Christian magazine. The editor had just completed a two-year survey of a hundred leading Charismatic, Pentecostal, and Word of Faith churches in America. They wanted to find out how many people were getting healed from the laying on of hands and anointing with oil, with the prayer of faith, according to **James 5:14-15**. The survey concluded that 97 percent of all people in those churches were not getting healed through this biblical method.

I believe this is where the Body of Christ is at today when it comes to people praying for and receiving healing by faith. We need to get rid of our unbelief and simply believe God's Word. **Isaiah 53:5, Matthew 8:17, and 1 Peter 2:24** declare that by His stripes we are healed. How many people are going to an early grave because they simply will not believe that God purchased their healing 2,000 years ago on the cross?

Jesus, the Son of God, marveled at people's unbelief; it was the reason no miracles happened when He visited his home country. His hometown folk were astonished at His wisdom. They had heard about the miracles He'd performed, and yet, in a spirit of unbelief, they discounted and scorned Him because they knew His family and His father's trade as a carpenter. Notice it doesn't say He *wouldn't* or *didn't* do any mighty work. **It says**

He *could do no mighty work*. Healing did not hinge on Jesus only; it was up to the sick if they wanted it or not. In the following account from Mark 6:1-6 (NKJV), He was able to heal only a few sick people.

> *"Then He went out from there and came to His own country, and His disciples followed Him. And when the Sabbath had come, He began to teach in the synagogue. And many hearing Him were astonished, saying, 'Where did this Man get these things? And what wisdom is this which is given to Him, that such mighty works are performed by His hands! Is this not the carpenter, the Son of Mary, and brother of James, Joses, Judas, and Simon? And are not His sisters here with us?' And they were offended at Him. But Jesus said to them, 'A prophet is not without honor except in his own country, among his own relatives, and in his own house. Now **He could do no mighty work there**, except that He laid His hands on a few sick people and healed them. And He marveled **because of their unbelief.**"*

When Jesus ministered to His home crowd and also to the multitudes away from home, didn't all hear the word? Faith comes by hearing, yes, but it also must be received and not doubted. Listeners heard His word, but only a few received it with expectant hearts. The word they heard, they also rejected. They nullified the power of God.

> *"If any of you lacks wisdom, [do you lack anything, including healing], you should ask God, who gives generously to all without finding fault, and it will be given to you. But when you ask, you must believe and not doubt, because the one who doubts is like a wave of the sea, blown and tossed by the wind. **That person should not expect to receive anything from the Lord.** Such a person is double-minded and unstable in all they do."*
>
> **—James 1:5-8, NIV**

Contrast that from the account in Luke 6:17-19 where a multitude came to Jesus. It says that **they came to hear and be healed.** They came expecting. What happened? He healed them all. The crowd came with faith, believing to receive healing. The only difference between these two accounts was the expectancy and faith of the people to receive. Jesus was the same. His desire to heal hadn't changed. However, not only was the second group hungry for a touch from Jesus, they sought to touch Him. They were passionate to receive Jesus Himself.

> *"A great multitude of people from all Judea and Jerusalem, and from the seacoast of Tyre and Sidon, who came to hear Him and be healed of their diseases, as well as those who were tormented with unclean spirits. And they were healed. And the whole multitude sought to touch Him, for power went out from Him **and healed them all.**"*
>
> **—Luke 7:16b-19, NKJV**

Hebrews 13:8 says that "Jesus Christ *is* the same yesterday, today, and forever," And we read in Malachi 3:6, "For I am the LORD, I change not."

If Jesus is the same yesterday, today, and forever, and if it was His will to heal all back then, it is **His will to heal all today**. But all do not receive healing as happened in the days of Jesus' ministry. Today people want to blame God when nothing happens. They say the preacher or evangelist is a fake, or the gifts of miracles or healing do not exist today.

Sometimes a crowd of people comes excited and expecting to receive and the atmosphere seems charged with faith. A tangible, corporate anointing can be felt as the presence of God is welcomed with the open hearts of believers. I have experienced the opposite as well, where the churches have chairs filled with skeptics and unbelief permeates the meeting. Maybe a few people get touched by the Holy Spirit and receive healing, but like Jesus' hometown folks, the unbelief of others hinders His anointing and power to heal and do miracles.

If the church's biggest problem from receiving healing is unbelief, then the answer is faith. How does faith come and grow? It's by hearing the Word and receiving the Word into the heart and expecting.

> *"So then faith comes by hearing, and hearing by the Word of God."*
>
> **—Romans 10:17, NKJV**

> *"My message and my preaching were not with wise and persuasive words, but with a demonstration of the Spirit's power, so that your faith might not rest on human wisdom, but on God's power."*
>
> **—1 Corinthians 2:4-5, NIV**

What is faith? Paul taught that *"now faith is the substance of things hoped for, the evidence of things not seen"* (Hebrews 11:1 KJV).

> *"While we look not at the things which are seen, but at the things which are not seen: for the things which are seen are temporal; but the things which are not seen are eternal."*
>
> **—2 Corinthians 4:18, KJV**

In English, the word "hope" connotes a sort of pie-in-the-sky wish. Maybe it will happen, maybe it won't. The Greek word used for hope actually means expect[13]. A pregnant woman is not hoping; she is expecting. We need to be pregnant with the healing promises of God, which we may not see. Our expectancy is the evidence. It is receiving by faith what is unseen.

One day Jesus and His disciples were coming out from Bethany, and He was hungry. He saw a fig tree in the distance and walked up to it, looking for something to eat. The tree bore leaves, but no fruit. The disciples overheard Jesus speaking to the tree.

> *"Let no one eat fruit from you ever again... Now in the morning, as they passed by, they saw the fig tree dried up from the roots. And Peter, remembering, said to Him, 'Rabbi, look! The fig tree which You cursed has withered away.' So Jesus answered and said to them, 'Have faith in God. For assuredly, I say to you, whoever says to this mountain, "Be removed and be cast into the sea," and does not doubt in his heart, but believes that those things he says will be done, he will have whatever he says.' Therefore I say to you, whatever things you ask when you pray, believe that you receive them, and you will have them."*
>
> **—Mark 11:14; 11:20-24, NKJV**

"If you believe, you will receive whatever you ask for in prayer" (Matthew 21:22 NIV). This includes the prayer for healing, does it not?

Another way of saying this is: When you ask, and have a full and confident expectancy to receive, you will have those things you request. They are received by faith, before they are seen. Have full confidence that

---

[13] "G1680 - elpis - Strong's Greek Lexicon (KJV)." Blue Letter Bible. Web. 25 Jun, 2017.

it is God's will to heal, that His Word is true, so when you do ask, you will also have a full confidence to receive.

Our hearing must be mingled with faith. We hear with our mind. First, we make the decision to believe the Word after hearing it; that is our will. When we stand in faith, our emotions change to an expectant hope, joy, and confidence. That is believing the Lord with all our heart and soul, and tilling fertile ground for the seeds of God's Word to take root and grow in our hearts.

> *"For indeed the gospel was preached to us as well as to them; but the word which they heard did not profit them, not being mixed with faith in those who heard it."*
>
> **—Hebrews 4:2, NKJV**

God does not bless unbelief. As an evangelist who has been called and anointed to preach and minister in the gifts of healings and miracles, when I pray for people with doubting, unbelieving hearts, it is like praying against a brick wall. As believers, we are expected to come to Him in faith with an open heart.

> *"...without faith it is impossible to please Him, for he who comes to God must believe that He is, and that He is a rewarder of those who diligently seek Him."*
>
> **—Hebrews 11:6, NKJV**

Some churches want nothing to do with the Holy Spirit and His gifts—**which means they want nothing to do with the real God of the Bible—**and the anointing which brings supernatural healing and miracles. The Lord will not force Himself onto a single person or church. He comes where He is welcomed and invited. Because of some church's traditions and doctrine, God blesses as much as He is welcomed. Some Christians only accept the Holy Spirit as Comforter but refuse His yoke-destroying anointing to break bondages of sickness and disease. (After all, isn't that what the Devil wants, a church with no movement of the Holy Spirit, no power, no signs and wonders, no healings, no miracles…Just men doing the same ol' same ol' thing every week. That's soooooo boring.

Following dead traditions of men can make the healing and miracle power of God to no effect as shown in Mark 7:13: *"Making the Word of God of none effect through your tradition, which ye have delivered: and many such like things do ye."*

God is in the healing business. He calls and anoints those whom He appoints to profit His church and to bring the unsaved to Him. The Word says that we are to desire spiritual gifts. They are manifestations of the Holy Spirit and He gives them as He wills. I thank God that the church my brother invited me to welcomed the Holy Spirit and His gifts of healings or I would've been sitting in a wheelchair on my way to hell, cursing God today.

> *"All these are the work of one and the same Spirit, and he distributes them to each one, just as he determines."*
>
> **—1 Corinthians 12:11, NIV**

> *"But in fact God has placed the parts in the body, every one of them, just as he wanted them to be."*
>
> **—1 Corinthians 12:18, NIV**

> *"Now to each one of us grace has been given proportionate to the measure of the Messiah's gift."*
>
> **—Ephesians 4:7, ISV**

> *"...and was affirmed by God through signs, wonders, various miracles, and gifts of the Holy Spirit distributed according to His will."*
>
> **—Hebrews 2:4, BSB**

When the church begins to believe the Word of God—that the Lord wants to bless and bring healing—then we will see greater healing and miracles and revival taking place. It is difficult for an individual who has been healed to go back to a church that sides with the Devil against the healing power of God. It is a wonderful testimony to God's wonderful love and healing power in those who believe.

> *"For our gospel did not come to you in word only, but also in power, and in the Holy Spirit and in much assurance, as you know what kind of men we were among you for your sake."*
>
> **—1 Thessalonians 1:5, NKJV**

> *"For the kingdom of God is not a matter of talk but of power."*
>
> **—1 Corinthians 4:20, NIV**

I've heard people say that they do not want the power of the Holy Spirit in their churches because it would bring division and God is not in division. Jesus said those who stand for the absolute truth of God's Word will always get persecuted by the religious Pharisees, who are like what Jesus said, "let the dead bury their own dead."[14]

> *"Do not think that I came to bring peace on earth. I did not come to bring peace but a sword. For I have come to 'set a man against his father, a daughter against her mother, and a daughter-in-law against her mother-in-law'; and 'a man's enemies will be those of his own household."*
>
> **—Matthew 10:34-36, NKJV**

When the power of God hits, it can be like a powerful blast of hot air from heaven, hitting the cold front of religious Pharisaical dead man's bones that are filled with total unbelief. Those who hold onto the gospel, which is in Word only, and discounts the anointing power **(see 1 Corinthians 4:20)** can create a storm of ridicule (they seem to love it so) and ruffled feathers for those who do believe in God's healing power. People's lives are flipped right-side-up, like mine was when I was healed and saved. The same can be true of Christians who have never been exposed to the fire of God when He shows up with a mighty anointing power to deliver and heal.

I have seen entire churches born when unbelievers and Christians from denominational churches began attending revival meetings. In one such case, a woman in a denominational church had been a member for many years. She had been very sick for a very long time with debilitating health

---

[14] Matthew 8:22

and overall weakness. The Lord did a marvelous work and she was healed and restored to complete health instantly, in Jesus' name.

She went back to her church and the people were shocked at the change in her health. The pastor had preached for almost two decades in that church against the gifts of the Holy Spirit. Word had spread about the big 2,000-seat tent revival and this pastor warned against charlatans like me who purported to lay hands on the sick and heal with the power of God.

After the woman in his church was apparently healed supernaturally, this pastor decided to take his pastoral staff and all of his elders to the tent revival one evening. The elders all sat about five rows from the front on my left side, alongside their pastor who was silently fuming with anger, his arms crossed at the so-called show. After the preaching, the Lord began speaking to me through a detailed word of knowledge. **I never knew who this pastor was, or who these people were that were with him until after the meeting.**

I said, "There is a man here, and you were in an accident when you were about eighteen to twenty years of age. You have pain in your right hip. As a matter of fact, that leg is two-and-a-half inches shorter than the other. You are wearing a special shoe with a sole that is thicker than the other to compensate for the difference in your legs. Where is that man?"

It was quiet as the large crowd waited, some looking around.

I said again, "When the Lord gives me a word of knowledge, I'm like a dog biting on a bone. You are here, and if you come forward, the Lord is going to heal you. Where is that man? You know who you are. You are wearing a special shoe on your right foot."

The pastor of that denominational church slowly stood to his feet. He glared at me, glanced across at his church staff, and then back toward me.

I said, "Yes, you! If you want to be healed, come down here and the Lord is going to do a mighty work in you now."

The pastor slowly began walking down the aisle. **I didn't know he was a pastor or why he was there; or where he was from.** What happened, though, was amazing. He was about halfway down the aisle and I felt the power of God come on me like a ball of fire and I threw my hand toward him. He was overwhelmed by the power of God and he hit the ground and flew backward about eight to ten feet. He spent some time on the ground, shaking under the power of God's awesome anointing as if someone were electrocuting him.

I said, "Praise the Lord. God is doing a mighty work in that man." About five minutes later he jumped to his feet, yelling, "I'm healed! God healed me!" He pointed to his church staff and yelled, "This is real! This is God! Look my right foot. It's the same length as the other one, and all the pain is gone from my body." He removed his special enlarged shoe to show the crowd and then he walked around back and forth normal. Then he said to his staff, "Get on down here, [Apparently a number of them had physical problems that needed healing] you can get healed too!"

In that case the Lord healed a pastor of a large church, who doubted the Holy Spirit. When I called him out with a word of knowledge, he could have refused. I didn't force him to come up. But I told him that if he did, that the Lord would heal him. He acted in faith, even though he'd come to discount God's healing power. He thought he was being righteous by preaching against the gifts of the Spirit, but he had a heart for God and for the truth; he was just deceived by the spirits of religion and unbelief.

He came wanting to know what was going on, and the Lord had mercy on him. He decided to follow Jesus in the Word and power, welcoming the Holy Spirit and His gifts into his church. He soon was no longer welcomed at his denominational church, as they fired him after nearly 18 years as senior pastor. So, he pioneered a new church, and I eventually preached for him at this church. Praise the Lord; God's healing power is real.

If you are a pastor, evangelist, preacher, teacher or Christian, I have a word for you: God heals. He is not moved by our tears and begging or whining. He is moved by our faith and expectancy. He is moved by a heart that hears His Word and believes and acts on it. If you have been a doubter and unbelief has kept you from being healed or for praying with the power of God for others to be healed, I challenge you to change your thinking to believe God and His Word.

REASON #2: UNCONFESSED SIN

Sin causes sickness. It may be said without fear of contradiction that, in a very real sense, *sin* is the cause for the existence of *sickness* in the world. There was no sickness in the Garden of Eden, and none of us expect to find either sin or infirmity in heaven. Until the day Eve yielded to the suggestion of Satan and took of the fruit, which God had forbidden her to eat, the human race was free from both sin and sickness. At that point, *sin entered into the world, and death by sin; and so death passed upon all men, for that all have sinned* (Romans 5:12 KJV). In this sense, all sickness is the result of sin.

> *"I will lead the blind by ways they have not known, along unfamiliar paths I will guide them; I will turn the darkness into light before them..."*
>
> **—Isaiah 42:16a, NIV**

Before we were Christians, if the answers to our prayers were dependent on our worthiness, then we would never have any prayers answered. Prayer is our way of communicating to God that we are sinful, needy people, in desperate need of divine intervention and salvation. Our initial prayer for salvation should never be based on our righteousness, but on His mercy and grace and what Jesus accomplished on the cross. He died for our sins so we would have a relationship with the Father and so we could walk in the light and have fellowship with Him.

But now that we are saved, we are instructed by the Lord to walk in the holiness that Christ has won for us on the cross. If we persist in the willful practicing of sin, which we know to be wrong, then we certainly have no right to expect our prayers to be answered.

> *"If we claim to have fellowship with him and yet [knowingly, willfully] walk in the darkness, we lie and do not live out the truth."*
>
> **—1 John 1:6, NIV**

> *"What shall we say then? Shall we continue in sin, that grace may abound? God forbid. How shall we, that are dead to sin, live any longer... [In sin]."*
>
> **—Romans 6:1-2, KJV**

> *"For sin shall not have dominion over you: for ye are not under law, but under grace. What then? Shall we sin, because we are not under the law, but under grace? God forbid."*
>
> **—Romans 6:14-15, ASV**

> *"As many as I love, I rebuke and chasten. Therefore, be zealous and repent."*
>
> —**Revelation 3:19, NKJV**

I once knew a pastor who committed adultery, and he became very sick. I asked the Lord about this man, and He said, "He hasn't truly repented; rather he was sorry he got caught." The Lord said to me, "He'll do it again," and he did, but this time, he had a major heart attack and he had to have a triple bypass. He nearly lost his life until he repented. He was on very shaky ground indeed!

> *"When I kept silent about my sin, **my body wasted away** through my groaning all day long."*
>
> —**Psalm 32:3, NASB**

There are several words for love in the New Testament. The Greek word used here is *phileo*. It means to be a friend of, fond sentiment and feeling.[15]

Part of our daily walk with Jesus requires us taking up our cross and following Him with humility. It requires a dying to ourselves and admitting when we are wrong. It is not in following some dogma of religious ritual and doctrines of men, but of following Jesus. It is more than just feeling sorry or bad for some thought or action. It is choosing to walk in fellowship and letting the effect of Jesus' blood have a continual work in our hearts. When we believed in Jesus, his blood cleansed us from

---

[15] "G5368 - philéō - Strong's Greek Lexicon (KJV)." Blue Letter Bible. Web. 28 Jun, 2017.

all of our sins. **We are saved by His grace and not by our works, lest any man should boast. (See Ephesians 2:8-9.)**

> *"All of us have become like one who is unclean, and all our righteous acts are like filthy rags; we all shrivel up like a leaf, and like the wind our sins sweep us away."*
>
> **—Isaiah 64:6, NIV**

In Jesus' great love and salvation for us, He wants us to grow and mature in humility, love, and grace. Part of His love includes chastisement. He loves us enough to tell us when we need to repent.

In the second and third chapter of Revelation, Jesus gave something like a state-of-the-union address to the seven churches through John. To all these churches, He began by saying, "I know your works."

The Lord knows our works. He let them know what they were doing right and what they were doing wrong. He told them to repent and what the consequences would be if they did not.

The "Jezebel spirit" has been used to describe certain undercurrents within churches for decades; however, she was an actual person in the church of Thyatira. The church was commended on their love, service, faith, patience, and works, which were on the upswing—the latter being greater than their first.

A woman named Jezebel had called herself a prophetess and she taught and seduced Christian believers in the church to commit sexual immorality and to eat things sacrificed to idols. **Jesus said that He gave her time to repent and she did not**. We don't know if He'd spoken through conviction of the Holy Spirit, or perhaps the leadership in the church had confronted her. What we do know is that the Lord cast her into a sickbed, along with all who had committed adultery with her. She and her children were going to die as a result.

> *"I know your works, love, service, faith, and your patience; and as for your works, the last are more than the first. Nevertheless I have a few things against you, because you allow that woman Jezebel, who calls herself a prophetess, to teach and seduce My servants to commit sexual immorality and eat things sacrificed to idols. And I gave her time to repent of her sexual immorality, and she did not repent. Indeed I will cast her into a sickbed, and those who commit adultery with her into great tribulation, unless they repent of their deeds. I will kill her children with death, and all the churches shall know that I am He who searches the minds and hearts. And I will give to each one of you according to your works."*
>
> **—Revelation 2:19-23, NKJV**

God's gift of salvation and grace is not a license to continue in sin. Jezebel was called out on her sin and given time to repent and change her ways. In God's grace, He gave her the opportunity to repent. She chose to follow the lusts of her flesh instead.

Receiving healing can be contingent on confessing our trespasses to one another. That may take great courage and humility. Confessing our trespasses is not just saying, "I'm sorry." Some people are not healed because they may need to confess with their mouth to brothers or sisters in the faith. It's not just praying, but confessing trespasses to one another.

> *"Confess your trespasses to one another, and pray for one another, that you may be healed."*
>
> **—James 5:16, NKJV**

In the passage below, Jesus calls to our attention that we are to leave our place of worship and giving to confess things we've done against another. We may come looking to Jesus for healing, but His prerequisite is to deal with our sin that we have committed against a brother. When the Lord speaks to us through His Holy Spirit regarding things we've done or said against another, we need to confess our faults and ask forgiveness. Then, our relationship with the Lord is restored. He is our Savior, but he wants to be Lord as well.

> *"If you bring your gift to the altar, and there remember that your brother has something against you, **leave** your gift there before the altar, and go your way. First be reconciled to your brother, and then come and offer your gift."*
>
> **—Matthew 5:23-24, NKJV**

When we have offenses that we haven't dealt with, it can feel like they are magnified under a bright light and a microscope when we come to church to worship or try to pray. We need to ask the Lord to forgive us, but we also need to ask forgiveness to those whom we have offended. If we attempt to ignore and bury sin that the Holy Spirit convicts us of, it hinders our walk in the Spirit. The Lord brings them to light because He wants us to walk in victory.

> *"He who covers his sins will not prosper, but, whoever confesses and forsakes them will have mercy."*
>
> **—Proverbs 28:13, NKJV**

> *"If I regard iniquity in my heart, the lord will not hear me."*
>
> **—Psalm 66:18, KJV**

> *"When I kept silent about my sin, my body wasted away through my groaning all day long."*
>
> **—Psalm 32:3, NASB**

> *"...He is faithful and just to forgive us our sins and to cleanse us from all unrighteousness."*
>
> **—1 John 1:9b, NKJV**

> *"Therefore confess your sins to each other and pray for each other so that you may be healed. The prayer of a righteous person is powerful and effective."*
>
> **—James 5:16, NIV**

Ongoing Repentance as a New Testament Christian

> *"I now rejoice, not that you were made sorrowful, but that you were made sorrowful to the point of repentance; for you were made sorrowful according to the will of God, so that you might not suffer loss in anything through us. For the sorrow that is according to the will of God produces a repentance without regret, leading to salvation, but the sorrow of the world produces death."*
>
> **—2 Corinthians 7:9-10, NASB**

> *"But I have this against you, that you have left your first love. Therefore remember from where you have fallen, and repent and do the deeds you did at first; or else I am coming to you and will remove your lampstand out of its place—unless you repent."*
>
> **—Revelation 2:4-5, NASB**

> *"So remember what you have received and heard; and keep it, and repent. Therefore if you do not wake up, I will come like a thief, and you will not know at what hour I will come to you."*
>
> **—Revelation 3:3, NASB**

The Lord convicts us of our sin because He loves us. He can bring about a godly sorrow that leads to repentance and restores fellowship with Him. If we ignore His promptings and refuse to humble ourselves and repent, then we begin to walk in a hardness of heart and broken fellowship with Him. His requirement lies on our willingness to confess sin to Him and to confess our faults with one another **that we may be healed by the power of the Holy Ghost in Jesus' name.**

REASON #3 UNFORGIVENESS

Bearing malice, hate, grudges, etc. Matthew 5:23-24 says, "Therefore if you bring your gift to the altar, and there remember that your brother has something against you, leave your gift there before the altar, and go your way. First be reconciled to your brother, and then come and offer your gift."

The big question is, why do we need to leave our gift at the altar first, before we make our prayer requests to God? Because unforgiveness will definitely hinder our prayers.

> *"But if you refuse to forgive others, your Father will not forgive your sins."*
>
> **—Matthew 6:15, NLT**

Unforgiveness is like poison. When you drink it, you expect the other person to die, but you only poison yourself. When we forgive others, we are released from the bitterness, sadness, and hardness of heart that becomes a stumbling block in our relationship with the Lord. Sometimes the feelings take time to catch up, but forgiveness itself is not a feeling. **It is a decision.**

I was preaching in a church in California one Sunday morning when the good Lord gave me a word of knowledge. I said, "There's a twenty-seven-year-old woman here in this congregation that has late stage emphysema and you've been given only a few months to live. You have been praying to God for your healing."

A woman stood up, quietly walked down the front of the church, and stood in front of me. "That's me," she said.

As I began to pray for her in the Spirit, I felt like I was bouncing off a brick wall. Usually, I can feel the anointing of the Holy Spirit flow when I pray for people, but it all seemed to stop cold and go nowhere. Then the Lord revealed to me that she had a blockage in her heart and mind. The Holy Spirit told me, "My Spirit is not able to bring healing to her, even though it's available."

Then the Lord showed me that the blockage was unforgiveness. I said to her, through revelation from the Lord, "You were raped seven years ago by your stepfather, and you have hated him very deeply ever since. Your hatred, bitterness, and unforgiveness have attracted a powerful spirit of infirmity to lodge in your lungs, which has produced this sickness. **If you will repent**, the good Lord will heal you. The Lord has also shown me that despite what the stepfather did, you need to go to him and tell him you forgive him for him raping you."

I continued, "This is a hard task in the natural, but God's Word requires it, and He will give you an anointing of grace and enabling power to do it."

I then prayed for her.

Eighteen months later I went back to that same church. That woman came up to me and said that she'd **repented** to God, and then went to her stepfather and told him she had forgiven him. She said, "He was so overwhelmed that he broke down and asked her to forgive him. **When I forgave him, he gave his life to Christ."**

> *"After this manner therefore pray ye: Our Father which art in heaven, Hallowed be thy name. Thy kingdom come, Thy will be done in earth, as it is in heaven. Give us this day our daily bread.* ***And forgive us our debts, as we forgive our debtors.*** *And lead us not into temptation, but deliver us from evil: For thine is the kingdom, and the power, and the glory, forever. Amen!"*
>
> **— Matthew 6:9-13, KJV**

Jesus showed the disciples what manner to pray—what we call the Lord's Prayer. In it He revisited the matter of forgiveness. The Father forgiving us is contingent on us forgiving men. Walking in the Spirit and not after the flesh means that when offenses come, we must forgive to continue to walk in blessing.

Our continual need to walk in forgiveness is recounted in Peter's question to Jesus.

> *"Then Peter came to Him and said, 'Lord, how often shall my brother sin against me, and I forgive him? Up to seven times?' Jesus said to him,* ***'I do not say to you, up to seven times, but up to seventy times seven.'"***
>
> **—Matthew 18:21-23, NKJV**

Jesus was saying that we need to forgive an infinite number of times. We shouldn't be counting. The Father forgives us our enormous debt, in comparison to the trespasses that happen between others and us.

> *"Then summoning him, his lord said to him, 'You wicked slave, I forgave you all that debt because you pleaded with me. 'Should you not also have had mercy on your fellow slave, in the same way that I had mercy on you?' And his lord, moved with anger, handed him over to the torturers until he should repay all that was owed him.* ***My heavenly Father will also do the same to you, if each of you does not forgive his brother from your heart.****"*
>
> —**Matthew 18:32-35, NASB**

Another young woman's life was swaying in the balance. **Her lifeline to live was to forgive.** She had issues with her heart at just 31 years old. She spent most of her time lying on the couch, and shuffling to the mailbox depleted her energy. She had always been very athletic, and had competed in track and field on a full scholarship a decade earlier, but now she suffered from continual arrhythmia and palpitations. The poor circulation led to tiredness and confusion. She could barely push a shopping cart and take care of the family.

She attended a Word of Faith church that believed in healing. After months and months of trying various prescriptions to regulate her heart, her doctor sent her to a heart specialist. That cardiologist told her that she had holes in her heart and would need to have surgery to correct the problem. If the surgery was not done, she was told that she would eventually die a premature death of an enlarged heart.

As she stood praying and believing for healing, the Lord revealed to her that she needed to forgive her sister. She'd grown up in a dysfunctional home and her older sister tormented her continually.

She said, "I asked my sister to forgive me for anything I've ever said or done to hurt or offend her. And I forgave her for anything she'd done or spoken that brought hurt and offense."

After being told what the problem was, **and forgiving her sister,** she spoke to her heart, like Jesus said to speak to the mountain. She said, "I command the holes in my heart that have caused problems to close. I command my electrical system in my heart to function properly. I speak that my heart is completely healed in Jesus' name."

The woman never called the heart doctor to schedule the operation. All of her heart problems ceased. Although she didn't feel well immediately, she never suffered another heart problem again. When she did go back to her doctor, she was told that the heart murmur that she'd had since birth had inexplicably disappeared.

If you feel bitterness in your heart toward a person or people, it can hinder the Lord's healing. The solution to rid ourselves of the poison that unforgiveness brings is to forgive others, and ask the Lord to forgive them. As we forgive, we will be released from the toxic emotions that keep us in bondage and turmoil and we can receive healing from the Lord.

How I Learned to Forgive From the Heart and not From the Emotions

I was brought up in a very dysfunctional home, where my stepfather and mother were very sadistically abusive to us eight kids. This caused us all to hate them both big-time with a vengeance. They were so abusive, that if they were to do that today, they would both go to jail for many years for their crimes.

Years later, after I become a Christian, I listened to many good preachers preach on the subject of forgiveness and, of course, I was touched by the word to forgive. I would get up and go down to the front of the church and I'd cry and forgive them both. Over a period of about four years, I did this forgiveness trip to the altar four different times, just to make sure I didn't miss anything or anyone that I needed to forgive. By this time, I was convinced beyond any shadow of a doubt that I'd cleaned it all out of my system for good.

I was in for a very big surprise of my life, however, and a real big lesson of truth worth remembering at how blinded we Christians can be until God opens our spiritual eyes to see the truth of His Word and have the blindness broken; to see clearly.

In 1980, five years after I became a Christian, I became a youth pastor for my brother, Ray, and later was promoted to Associate Pastor. One of my jobs was to lead the midweek prayer meeting. We would worship for about a half an hour. Then we'd all pray in the Holy Ghost (in tongues) for about two to three hours. In one of these prayer meetings, a woman called Beverly and her prayer partner, Irene, came over to me and said, "Dan, the Lord has shown us, in the Spirit, the reason you have been experiencing bad health for about a year is because you have unforgiveness in your heart towards your stepfather and your mother."

I was very indignant and said, "That is not so. I refuse to accept that as a word from the Lord." Then I shared with them about the four different times in the past when I'd gone down to the front of a large church in Adelaide, South Australia, and asked God to forgive me of unforgiveness.

Then they said, "Dan, you forgave from your emotions and not from your heart." I said, "That's a bunch of balderdash. I can't accept that, okay?"

Those ladies, in the Spirit, were like bulldogs. They weren't fazed one little bit at my denial. They pressed in and said, "Can we pray for you?" Politely, I said, "Okay, go ahead," and they prayed over me in tongues for about ten minutes. When they had finished, one said, "Show Dan the truth and open his eyes to see the truth, Lord, and break the blindness." Then they said, "Lord, fill him with the fire of God's glory."

All of a sudden I fell out under the power of the Holy Ghost, and as I lay on the floor with the Lord's glory on me, I heard Him say, "You forgave from your emotions and not from your heart." This was a very big surprise to me, because I thought I had definitely forgiven from my heart. **Obviously I was blinded in this area.** So, then, I asked the Lord to help me forgive from my heart, and not from my emotions, and He did. I then asked the Lord to heal me, and I was instantly and completely healed.

Consider this Bible text that the apostle had to pray over the Ephesian church, because they were spiritually blinded to certain biblical truths.

Ephesians 1:16-18 says, "Do not cease giving thanks for you, making mention [of you] at my prayers, that the God of our Lord Jesus Christ, the Father of glory, would give you [the] spirit of wisdom and revelation into the full knowledge of him, being enlightened in the eyes of your heart, so that ye should know what is the hope of his calling, [and] what the riches of the glory of his inheritance in the saints."

REASON #4 DISOBEDIENCE

"If you love Me, keep My commandments."

—**John 14:15, NKJV**

"If it does evil in My sight by not obeying My voice, then I will think better of the good with which I had promised to bless it."

—Jeremiah 18:10, NASB

"For if the word spoken through angels proved unalterable, and every transgression and disobedience received a just penalty."

—Hebrews 2:2, NASB

"Let no one deceive you with empty words, for because of these things the wrath of God comes upon the sons of disobedience."

—Ephesians 5:6, NKJV

"They profess to know God, but by their deeds they deny Him, being detestable and disobedient and worthless for any good deed."

—Titus 1:16, NASB

"Why do you call me, 'Lord, Lord,' and do not do what I say?"

—Luke 6:46, NASB

"You were running a good race. Who cut in on you to keep you from obeying the truth?"

—Galatians 5:7, NIV

"See how each of you is following the stubbornness of his evil heart instead of obeying me."

—Jeremiah 16:12, NIV

"I look on the faithless with loathing, for they do not obey your word."

—Psalm 119:158, NIV

"Streams of tears flow from my eyes, for your law [word]) is not obeyed."

—Psalm 119:136, NIV

"Anyone who runs ahead and does not continue in the teaching of Christ does not have God; whoever continues [this means to obey] in the teaching has both the Father and the Son."

—2 John 1:9, NIV

"Whoever [the man who] says, 'I know him,' but does not do what he commands is a liar, and the truth is not in him" **(1 John 2:4 NIV).** This means for us to obey the Word and the Holy Ghost.

"But if anyone obeys his word, God's love is truly made complete in him."

—1 John 2:5, NIV

"He who obeys instructions guards his life, but he who is contemptuous of his ways will die."

—Proverbs 19:16, NIV

"We must obey God rather than men!"

—**Acts 5:29b, ISV**

"...Walk in all the ways I command you, that it may go well with you."

—**Jeremiah 7:23b, TLV**

"If you fear the LORD and serve and obey him and do not rebel against his commands, and if both you and the king who reigns over you follow the LORD your God—good!"

—**1 Samuel 12:14, NIV**

"Oh, that their hearts would be inclined to fear me and keep all my commands always, so that it might go well with them and their children forever!"

—**Deuteronomy 5:29, NIV**

"Remember, therefore, what you have received and heard; hold it fast [obey it], and repent"

—**Revelation 3:3, NIV**

Jesus served, preached, ministered, and lived daily as a walking example of God's mercy, love, and kindness. With all the time that He spent with His disciples, He said that He still had many things to tell them, but He was going away.

The importance of obedience in the Old Testament is well understood. But I believe it is at least as important in the New Testament. There are differences in what we are to obey, but the motive for our obedience is just as great. As Paul puts it, we have a choice. We can be "slaves to sin" which leads to death, or to obedience which leads to righteousness.

> *"Do you not know that to whom you present yourselves slaves to obey, you are that one's slaves whom you obey, whether of sin leading to death, or of obedience leading to righteousness?"*
>
> **—Romans 6:16, NKJV**

> *"Children, obey your parents [God's children should obey their heavenly Father as well] in the Lord, for this is right. 'Honor your father and mother' (which is the first commandment with a promise), 'so that it may be well with you, and you may live long on the earth.'"*
>
> **—Ephesians 6:1-3, TLV**

God does not want us to submit to Him only for the benefits we hope to get. That was the issue in the book of Job, where God allowed Satan to test Job to see if he loved Him only because of what God had done for him. (See Job 1–2.)

God wants us to love Him and obey Him for who He is, and not just for what He does for us. Our relationship with God should be highly personal. God loves us, and we love Him. **When you love someone, you want to do what pleases them.**

The primary motive we have for obeying God is that we love Him and we want to do what pleases Him. We want to become like Him. Paul urges the church for Christians to walk in love and imitate God. His wrath comes upon the sons of disobedience and we are warned against being partakers along with them.

> *"Therefore be imitators of God as dear children. And walk in love, as Christ also has loved us and given Himself for us, an offering and a sacrifice to God for a sweet-smelling aroma. But fornication and all uncleanness or covetousness, let it not even be named among you, as is fitting for saints; neither filthiness, nor foolish talking, nor coarse jesting, which are not fitting, but rather giving of thanks. For this you know, that no fornicator, unclean person, nor covetous man, who is an idolater, has any inheritance in the kingdom of Christ and God. Let no one deceive you with empty words, for because of these things the wrath of God comes upon the sons of disobedience. Therefore do not be partakers with them, in disobedience"*
>
> **—Ephesians 5:1-7, NKJV**

We can be disobedient in tithing and giving, for example, when we believe we are to give and refuse to do so. If we love the Lord and follow Him, then we will also be faithful to give cheerfully.

Many say that they have made Jesus "Lord and Savior." But He is Lord only when we obey the things He tells us to do. When we are obedient to walk in love, to forgive, and to give, we are building a faith on the Rock, Jesus. When times come that we need healing, do we look at our lives as bearing fruit? When we are not walking in obedience, we cut ourselves off from Jesus, the Vine. Healing can't flow apart from the Vine, so when we walk in obedience, we walk in loving and pleasing God.

> *"But why do you call Me 'Lord, Lord,' and not do the things which I say? [people, that's disobedience]) Whoever comes to*

> *Me, and hears My sayings and does them, I will show you whom he is like: He is like a man building a house, who dug deep and laid the foundation on the rock. And when the flood arose, the stream beat vehemently against that house, and could not shake it, for it was founded on the rock. But he who heard and did nothing is like a man who built a house on the earth without a foundation, against which the stream beat vehemently; and immediately it fell. And the ruin of that house was great."*
>
> **—Luke 6:46-49 NKJV**

See, we are that house.

REASON #5: DISOBEDIENT MINISTERS

Jesus tells us in Mark 16:15, **"Go into all the world and preach the gospel..."** I believe that whether we are a local church, an international church, an evangelical preacher, or an evangelist, we all—**on a small or greater level**—should be reaching out to a hurting and lost world with the gospel. Most churches don't even reach out evangelistically anymore. To me, this is a terrible sin, and their blood will be on our heads on judgment day. So, let's all go and win some souls for Jesus.

> *"Not many of you should become teachers, my brothers, for you know that we who teach will be judged with greater strictness."*
>
> **—James 3:1, ESV**

> *"Preach the word; be ready in season and out of season; reprove, rebuke, and exhort, with complete patience and teaching. For the time is coming when people will not endure sound teaching, but*

having itching ears they will accumulate for themselves teachers to suit their own passions, and will turn away from listening to the truth and wander off into myths."

—**2 Timothy 4:2-4, ESV**

"How then will they call on him in whom they have not believed? And how are they to believe in him of whom they have never heard? And how are they to hear without someone preaching?"

—**Romans 10:14, ESV**

In May of 1993, I was called to preach in a church in Kansas. I'd never been to that church before, so I was excited to see what the Lord was going to do. Also, I'd never met the pastor other than speaking to him over the phone for about five minutes a few weeks earlier.

That Sunday morning I preached a message entitled, **"God, our Healer"**. Afterward, I said, "Let's pray to see what the good Lord's Spirit will do now." The Lord then gave me a word of knowledge for a man. I said, "There is a man here that's in a late stage of prostate cancer. Plus you have a wife who is home in bed with lung cancer who has a nurse looking after her."

The Lord continued to reveal to me problems in this family. I said, "You also have a daughter who is backslidden and is living with a guy in sin and she had his baby. Plus, you have a son who is doing jail time for selling drugs."

The pastor of the church stood up and said, "Brother Nolan, that's me and my family."

Then the anointing of the Holy Ghost came on me and I said to him, "This is what the Lord has shown me and what he wants you to do. He has shown me that over eleven years ago, the Holy Spirit told you to give up this church and go and minister on the mission field in Africa, along with your family.

"Your wife, your children, and four key members of this church fought against this. After a period of time, you became overwhelmed and exhausted by their persistent haggling and gave up the idea, so you stayed on as pastor. **Because of your disobedience,** you inadvertently brought a powerful curse on you, your family, and your church. Since that time, two of those key members of your church who opposed you have died of cancer. The third one left, and the other is here today, also very, very sick in body."

A few moments passed and I told him, "Repentance will give you the victory, but it's up to you now. **If you will all repent**, God will heal you and your wife, and your daughter will come back home and rededicate her life to the Lord. Your son will be released from jail early, and will come back home and go into the ministry where he has a calling."

About two months later, I received a phone call from the pastor. He was practically shouting over the phone, exclaiming what was happening in his family's life. He said, "Dan, the day after you left our church, I told my wife what you said. Then I called my daughter and then my son in jail to also tell them what you had said from God's Spirit."

He laughed with joy, and said, "We have all repented to the Lord. I have decided to give up the church and all the family is going with me to the mission field. After we made that decision, the Lord healed my wife and me. Then, my daughter came back home, and in three weeks, I will be picking up my son from the jail and bringing him home early, just like you prophesied."

I listened as this pastor continued to talk. "We are in negotiations with the head office, and they are putting together a deal for us to all go to the mission field in about five months!"

The pastor thanked me for being bold, and telling them the truth about how this foul curse of the law works when people don't walk in the Spirit, but in the flesh. He did not realize that his disobedience to follow God's plans would cause such a curse and sickness. He and his wife would have died prematurely and their children would not have come back to the Lord. But he did accept that word, and **he repented** and got back on track to what the Lord told him initially to do.

If you are a minister and it seems like your life is plagued with illness and a curse upon your family and ministry, I encourage you to seek the Lord to see if you are working in a "permissive will" or God's perfect will. Sometimes it may feel like you are doing your best, but something's just not quite right.

> *"And be not conformed to this world: but be ye transformed by the renewing of your mind, that ye may prove what is that good, and acceptable, and perfect, will of God."*
>
> **—Romans 12:2, KJV**

> *"That the God of our Lord Jesus Christ, the Father of glory, may give you the Spirit of wisdom and of revelation in the knowledge of him, having the eyes of your hearts enlightened, that you may know what is the hope to which he has called you, what are the riches of his glorious inheritance in the saints, and what is the immeasurable greatness of his power toward us who believe, according to the working of his great might that he worked in Christ when he raised him from the dead and seated him at his right hand in the heavenly places."*
>
> **—Ephesians 1:17-20, ESV**

Perhaps you are like the minister who gave in and gave up. I had times in my life when I was tempted by the easy path of being a salaried pastor with all of the perks and security. The Lord assured me that if I didn't follow Him in the direction he'd given me to take, that I was going to be on my own, without the anointing for the calling which He'd put on my life.

In Australia I was pastoring a very nice church. We were very comfortable with a lovely home on a beautiful flowing river, with fine furnishings. We had good cars to drive, and a good income. One day I was at my office desk, finishing up on a Monday morning with the church's bookkeeping, when the Lord's Spirit came on me big-time. He said, "Dan, it's time to go to America now." (Over the years, the Lord had shown me that I'd be going to America to live sometime to minister nationally as a healing evangelist.) I said, "Lord, I'm very comfortable here in Southern Queensland, pastoring and enjoying the good life." I really, really, did not want to go to America, period, and give up my comfort zone. The Lord said, "If you don't go, I'll give the mantle to someone else, and you will dry up like an old prune. You will still have a gift to preach, but no anointing, or movement of the Spirit as you have now." Then he said something that shocked me. "**Your disobedience** will bring a curse on you, and in time you will become very sick and may even die." I screamed out to God, "Lord, I'm sorry, please forgive me. I'll go."

I did go. I arrived in America 27 years ago, and I've been ministering here ever since with a powerful anointing, and signs, wonders, and miracles following the preaching of the Word. Through faith, the anointing is getting stronger. Thank You, Jesus. I love You, Lord, and I will obey you till death us do part.

The flip side of this disobedience among minister is when they do not walk in their calling. Others quit or retire before the Lord has finished His work through them.

> ***"He gave some, apostles, prophets, evangelists, pastors, teachers.** For the perfecting of the saints, for the work of the ministry, for the edifying of the body of Christ: Till we all come in the unity of the faith, and of the knowledge of the Son of God, unto a perfect man, unto the measure of the stature of the fullness of Christ: That we henceforth be no more children, tossed to and fro, and carried about with every wind of doctrine, by the sleight of men, and cunning craftiness, whereby they lie in wait to deceive."*
>
> **—Ephesians 4:11, KJV**

There was a pastor years ago who got a revelation on prayer. When he would teach or preach on prayer, people would be stirred up to pray. I believe, in a measure, he stood in the office of apostle.

The problem occurred when he thought he was an apostle (sent one) to the entire church world and left his church to travel and teach on prayer. He fell flat on his face and went from international prominence into obscurity. You don't hear of him anymore. I believe if he had stayed with his church and continued to teach on prayer you would still hear of him today. He got out beyond what the Lord had called and anointed him to do. We must make sure we stay within our calling.

I have personally known a number of ministers who got out of their calling and tried to operate in another office to which they were never called or anointed by the Lord. Like a pastor trying to operate as an evangelist when the calling and mantle to do that job was not given to him of the Lord, I've seen where evangelists grew tired of traveling and they took a church that was offered to them, but they soon got physically sick and couldn't do the job. They soon crashed because the anointing was not there in that office for them.

> *"For the one who sows to his own flesh will from the flesh reap corruption, but the one who sows to the Spirit will from the Spirit reap eternal life."*
>
> **—Galatians 6:8, NASB**

I got a revelation of this from the Lord by just watching what happens to these ministers, who get out of their calling and try to stand in an office that's not theirs. Several of them got very sick and died as young men. Others were so sick they couldn't do the job anymore, and they quit the ministry altogether. Others just retired young.

I believe that the protection of the Holy Ghost is on us to walk in the office and mantle that the Lord has given us. If we walk outside that protection, then we're in trouble with the Lord, and Satan messes up those people big-time. Stay with the calling and walk in the mantle that the Lord has given you, and do not retire until He says so.

> *"I call heaven and earth to record this day against you, that I have set before you life and death, blessing and cursing: therefore choose life, that both thou and thy seed may live."*
>
> **—Deuteronomy 30:19, KJV**

> *"Son of man, prophesy against the shepherds of Israel, prophesy, and say unto them, Thus saith the Lord God unto the shepherds; Woe be to the shepherds of Israel that do feed themselves! [lust for money and power)] should not the shepherds feed the flocks? Ye eat the fat, and ye clothe you with the wool, ye kill them that are fed: but ye feed not the flock. The diseased have ye not strengthened, [most ministers don't even pray for the sick anymore] neither have ye healed that which was sick, neither*

have ye bound up that which was broken, neither have ye brought again that which was driven away, neither have ye sought that which was lost; but with force and with cruelty have ye ruled them. And they were scattered, because there is no shepherd: and they became meat to all the beasts of the field, when they were scattered. My sheep wandered through all the mountains, [they go from church to church trying to find deep spiritual help to no avail] and upon every high hill: yea, my flock was scattered upon all the face of the earth, and none did search or seek after them. Therefore, ye shepherds, hear the word of the Lord; As I live, saith the Lord God, surely because my flock became a prey, [thousands of sheep in every city in America don't even go to church anymore] and my flock became meat to every beast of the field, because there was no shepherd, neither did my shepherds search for my flock, but the shepherds fed themselves, [big homes, cars lots of money, etc.] and fed not my flock; Therefore, O ye shepherds, hear the word of the Lord; Thus saith the Lord God; Behold, I am against the shepherds; and I will require my flock at their hand, and cause them to cease from feeding the flock; neither shall the shepherds feed themselves anymore; for I will deliver my flock from their mouth, that they may not be meat for them."

—**Ezekiel 34:2-10, KJV**

This false, seeker-friendly gospel [make me feel good, and please entertain me, preacher man], which has come on the scene in these last days, is killing God's people; and God himself will avenge.

Jesus said, *"follow me and I will make you fishers of men..."* (Matthew 4:19). If you are not following Jesus, who are you following and where will it take you? If you don't know where you are going, any road will get you there. **If God appoints, He will anoint.** When you follow Jesus, He will make you. He will take you. He will anoint you, and bless you big-time.

> *"[I always pray] that the God of our Lord Jesus Christ, the Father of glory, may grant you a spirit of wisdom and of revelation [that gives you a deep and personal and intimate insight] into the true knowledge of Him [for we know the Father through the Son]. And [I pray] that the eyes of your heart [the very center and core of your being] may be enlightened [flooded with light by the Holy Spirit], so that you will know and cherish the hope [the divine guarantee, the confident expectation] to which He has called you, the riches of His glorious inheritance in the saints (God's people), and [so that you will begin to know] what the immeasurable and unlimited and surpassing greatness of His [active, spiritual] power is in us who believe. These are in accordance with the working of His mighty strength."*
>
> **—Ephesians 1:17-19, AMP**

> *"Therefore I urge you, brothers and sisters, by the mercies of God, to present your bodies [dedicating all of yourselves, set apart] as a living sacrifice, holy and well-pleasing to God, which is your rational (logical, intelligent) act of worship. And do not be conformed to this world [any longer with its superficial values and customs], but be transformed and progressively changed [as you mature spiritually] by the renewing of your mind [focusing on godly values and ethical attitudes], so that you may prove [for yourselves] what the will of God is, that which is good and acceptable and perfect [in His plan and purpose for you]."*
>
> **—Romans 12:1-2, AMP**

So preachers, let this new Holy Ghost revival start with us.

REASON #6: A NEGATIVE CONFESSION WILL HINDER

> *"Death and life are in the power of the tongue, And those who love it will eat its fruit."*
>
> **—Proverbs 18:21, NKJV**

> "You have been trapped by what you said, ensnared by the words of your mouth."
>
> **—Proverbs 6:2, NIV**

> *"What goes into someone's mouth does not defile them, but what comes out of their mouth, that is what defiles them."*
>
> **—Matthew 15:11, NIV**

> *"There is one who speaks rashly like the thrusts of a sword, But the tongue of the wise brings healing."*
>
> **—Proverbs 12:18, NASB**

> "Whoso offereth praise glorifieth me: and to him that ordereth his conversation aright will I shew the salvation of God."
>
> **—Psalm 50:23, KJV**

"A man's belly shall be satisfied with the fruit of his mouth; and with the increase of his lips shall he be filled. Death and life are

> *in the power of the tongue: and they that love it shall eat the fruit thereof."*
>
> **—Proverbs 18:20-21, KJV**

We must not only claim God's Word, but we must also learn to speak or confess our faith in God's Word.

We must not confess lack, as the heavenly Father has given us everything we need. **We must not confess defeat**, as God has made us more than conquerors. **We must not confess doubt**, as God has given us His faith. **We are to speak the things that the Word of God declares as truth.** We easily quote what men have to say on a subject, and many times we believe them despite what the Word of God has to say about it. Yet we are often hesitant to quote what God says because the Devil tells us we would be lying. He causes us to look at our circumstances and the natural rather than the Word of God. Circumstances are subject to change, and one of the things that can cause them to do so is the confession of God's Word over a particular situation. In fact, the Word of God tells us to confess or talk about the things we are believing God to do in our lives and He will bring it to pass.

> *"He [Abraham] staggered not at the promise of God through unbelief; but was strong in faith, giving glory to God; And being fully persuaded that, what he had promised, he was able also to perform. And therefore it was imputed to him for righteousness."*
>
> **—Romans 4:20-22, KJV**

> *"(As it is written, I have made thee a father of many nations,) before him whom he believed, even God, who quickeneth the*

> *dead, and calleth those things which be not as though they were."*

—**Romans 4:17, KJV**

We are to say what God's Word says.

For instance, if we are in need of finances, the Devil will try to get us to confess such things as, "I guess we will just have to take bankruptcy since we cannot pay the bills," or "I don't know what we will do when we can't make the house payment." Instead, we need to align our confession with the Word of God.

> *"My God shall supply all your [my] need according to his riches in glory by Christ Jesus."*

—**Philippians 4:19, KJV**

> *"But seek ye first the kingdom of God, and his righteousness; and all these things shall be added unto you [me])."*

—**Matthew 6:33, KJV**

We should confess our faith and trust in the Lord by saying, "I don't know how the Lord is going to help us meet this need, but I confess that He will because He cares for us."

We bring evil and good things forth by what we speak. Jesus referred to this in **Matthew 12:34-37:**

> *"O generation of vipers, how can ye, being evil, speak good things? For out of the abundance of the heart the mouth speaketh. A good man out of the good treasure of the heart*

> *bringeth forth good things: and an evil man out of the evil treasure bringeth forth evil things. But I say unto you, That every idle word that men shall speak, they shall give account thereof in the day of judgment. For by thy words thou shalt be justified, and by thy words thou shalt be condemned."*

As Christians, we should never again confess any of the things that are against God's Word.

I've seen it time and time again. People speak negatively all the time saying things like, "God's not going to heal me," or "The doctors said I'm going to die, so, it's just a matter of time before the Lord takes me home." People can come forward for prayer, doubting in their heart, thinking, "I don't know if I believe in this healing stuff." I've heard pastors say that none of the folks in his church ever get healed. "It seems to work for others, but not for me. I guess it must not be God's will. It's in His hands."

Another great faith killer for starting and ending a prayer for the sick is, "If it be Thy will." That is doubt. Doubt does not receive the promises of God by faith. When nothing happens, people filled with negative thoughts and speeches throw it all on the good Lord, and not on their own unbelief.

> *"For as he thinketh in his heart, so is he: Eat and drink, saith he to thee; but his heart is not with thee."*
>
> **—Proverbs 23:7, KJV**

The words that we speak are like seeds with the power in them to create or destroy. Even saying, **"I'm sick and tired** of this or that" has the power to bring about lethargy and sickness. When we pronounce the sentence of sickness, we speak death over our situations. That is siding with the Devil.

When we side with the Word and proclaim the promises of healing and life, we sow seeds that bring forth life. We are created in God's image, and He brought about creation by speaking, and it was so.

A Christian woman I knew used to get bronchitis every year in the fall. She'd confess it over and over. "I will get bronchitis. I always do about October. It will probably turn into pneumonia." **And it did.** Every year coughing would commence, as did going to the doctor for antibiotics like an annual ritual. When she received teaching on the power of her negative confession, she quit saying that. Instead, she proclaimed the healing promises in God's Word that she walked in the blessings of God. She said that she never got bronchitis again.

People speaking doubt is probably one of the greatest faith killers. When a person comes forward for prayer and then says, "They prayed for me, but I don't feel like anything has changed," they will not receive. Their heart is filled with doubt and their faith is on what they see and feel, not on receiving by faith before they see the result. Jesus gives us very specific instructions on how to receive things in prayer in the Gospel of Mark. First, have faith in God. God is bigger than the mountains that you face. Proclaim Him and not the problem. Then when in faith, speak to the mountain and command it to move in Jesus' name.

We all have times when we face mountains in our life. What is your mountain? Is it illness? Speak to it in Jesus' name. Do not doubt in your heart. In other words, expect what you say and believe you will receive before you see what you are asking for. When we ask for healing, we know that we are asking according to His will because His Word says, that by His stripes we are healed. (See **1 Peter 2:24.**)

> *"So Jesus answered and said to them, 'Have faith in God. For assuredly, I say to you, whoever says to this mountain, "Be removed and be cast into the sea," and does not doubt in his heart, but believes that those things he says will be done, he*

will have whatever he says. Therefore I say to you, whatever things you ask when you pray, believe that you receive them, and you will have them."

—**Mark 11:22-24, KJV**

The promise of healing belongs to us.

"He is despised and rejected of men; a man of sorrows, and acquainted with grief: and we hid as it were our faces from him; he was despised, and we esteemed him not. Surely he hath borne our griefs, and carried our sorrows: yet we did esteem him stricken, smitten of God, and afflicted. But he was wounded for our transgressions, he was bruised for our iniquities: the chastisement of our peace was upon him; and with his stripes we are healed."

—**Isaiah 53:3-5, KJV**

"This was to fulfill what was spoken through the prophet Isaiah: "He took up our infirmities and bore our diseases."

—**Matthew 8:17, NIV**

"who Himself bore our sins in His own body on the tree, that we, having died to sins, might live for righteousness—by whose stripes you were healed."

—**1 Peter 2:24, NKJV**

"And in keeping with what is written: "I believed, therefore I have spoken," we who have the same spirit of faith also believe and therefore speak,"

—**2 Corinthians 4:13, BSB**

> *"To the law and to the testimony: if they speak not according to this word, it is because there is no light in them."*
>
> —Isaiah 8:20, KJV

When you have the Word and the Holy Spirit in you, then you will speak out the promises of God's word.... Try this: By His stripes I'm already healed. Therefore, I'm in the process of receiving that healing. Thank You, Jesus, and the Holy Spirit.

When we ask, we need to expect something is going to happen. That is faith.

When people asked Jesus to heal them, Jesus asked them if they believed He was able to do it. When He healed, it was "according to their faith."

> *"When Jesus departed from there, two blind men followed Him, crying out and saying, 'Son of David, have mercy on us!' And when He had come into the house, the blind men came to Him. And Jesus said to them, **'Do you believe that I am able to do this?'** They said to Him, 'Yes, Lord.' Then He touched their eyes, saying, **'According to your faith let it be to you.'**"*
>
> —**Matthew 9:27-30, NKJV**

Out of 19 of the most powerful miracles that Jesus did, 13 times He said, "Be it done unto you according to your faith."

You might say, "I had no idea the effect my words had on my health or receiving healing, and I have spent a lifetime of confessing negative things." Undoubtedly, many Christians are sick and they die before their time because of the seeds they have planted in their lives. They have spoken curses over themselves, and when it comes to praying for health, they can't receive because they undermine the blessing in progress **through their own words.**

"My people are destroyed from lack of knowledge..."

—Hosea 4:6a, NIV

"His divine power has given us everything we need for a godly life through our knowledge of him who called us by his own glory and goodness. Through these he has given us his very great and precious promises, so that through them you may participate in the divine nature, having escaped the corruption in the world caused by evil desires. For this very reason, make every effort to add to your faith goodness; and to goodness, knowledge; and to knowledge, self-control; and to self-control, perseverance; and to perseverance, godliness; and to godliness, mutual affection; and to mutual affection, love. For if you possess these qualities in increasing measure, they will keep you from being ineffective and unproductive in your knowledge of our Lord Jesus Christ."

—2 Peter 1:3-8, NIV

Ignorance of God's provision can be a catalyst for sickness and destruction. The good news is that ignorance and a lack of knowledge can be replaced with a life-changing decision based on the knowledge of God and His Word. **If we can be destroyed by a lack of knowledge, then we can be saved by understanding and knowledge.**

> *"Look to God's instructions and teachings! People who contradict his word or speak not according to his word, are completely in the dark."*
>
> —**Isaiah 8:20, NLT**

If you are guilty of negative confession, you probably can see the damaging effects of what you've believed and spoken. Quit speaking curses into existence. Begin to proclaim the truth of God's Word over your life and situation. Find scriptures that speak to your heart. Meditate on them and proclaim them with expectation, believing you receive what you say, regardless of how you feel or what things look like.

The confession of our mouths will eventually bring forth the things we speak if it's a promise from God's Word.

Try this for a confession: "1 Peter 2:24 says that by His stripes I am healed. Therefore, God has made total provision on the cross for my health and my healing. Thank You, Jesus, that as I stand on Your Word, I'm now a work in process, and Your Holy Spirit is bringing about this healing in my body now in Jesus' name."

> *"Lord, who shall abide in thy tabernacle? Who shall dwell in thy holy hill? He that walketh uprightly, and worketh righteousness,* ***and speaketh the truth in his heart.****"*
>
> —**Psalm 15:1-2, KJV**

If we continue to speak truth in our hearts, our mouths will soon begin to line up with our hearts. I would like to address an area that is related to this subject of watching our confessions. We should **not agree with**

negative things either spoken or written as this gives the enemy a doorway into our lives.

> *"Again I say unto you, That if two of you shall agree on earth as touching anything that they shall ask, it shall be done for them of my Father which is in heaven."*
>
> —**Matthew 18:19, ESV**

This is a perfect example of two agreeing before the answer to prayer can come to pass. My mouth and heart must agree to produce the answers to my prayers.

Instead of a negative confession, have a positive one.

Never again will I confess "I can't" for *"I can do all things through Christ which strengtheneth me"* (Philippians 4:13).

Never again will I confess lack, for *"My God shall supply all of my needs according to His riches in glory by Christ Jesus"* (Philippians 4:19).

Never again will I confess fear, for *"God hath not given us the spirit of fear; but of power, and of love, and of a sound mind"* (2 Timothy 1:7).

Never again will I confess doubt and lack of faith, for *"God hath dealt to every man the measure of faith"* (Romans 12:3).

Never again will I confess weakness, for *"The LORD is the strength of my life"* (Psalm 27:1). *"The people that know their God shall be strong and do exploits"* (Daniel 11:32).

Never again will I confess supremacy of Satan over my life, for *"Greater is He that is within me than he that is in the world"* (1 John 4:4).

Never again will I confess defeat, for *"God always causeth me to triumph in Christ Jesus"* (2 Corinthians 2:14).

Never again will I confess lack of wisdom, for *"Christ Jesus is made unto me wisdom from God"* (1 Corinthians 1:30).

Never again will I confess sickness, for *"With His stripes I am healed"* (Isaiah 53:5). *"Himself [Jesus] took my infirmities and bore my sickness"* (Matthew 8:17).

Never again will I confess worries and frustrations, for I am *"Casting all my cares upon Him, who careth for me"* (1 Peter 5:7). **In Christ I am "care-free."**

Never again will I confess bondage, for *"Where the Spirit of the Lord is, there is liberty"* (2 Corinthians 3:17).

Never again will I confess condemnation, for *"There is therefore now no condemnation to them which are in Christ Jesus"* (Romans 8:1). **I am in Christ; therefore, I am free from condemnation.**

Never again will I confess loneliness, for Jesus said, *"Lo, I am with you alway, even unto the end of the world"* (Matthew 28:20). *"I will never leave thee, nor forsake thee"* (Hebrews 13:5).

Never again will I confess curses or bad luck, for *"Christ hath redeemed us from the curse of the law, being made a curse for us...that the blessing of Abraham might come on the Gentiles through Jesus Christ; that we might receive the promise of the Spirit through faith"* (Galatians 3:13-14).

Never again will I confess discontent because *"I have learned, in whatsoever state [circumstances] I am, therewith to be content"* (Philippians 4:11).

Never again will I confess unworthiness because *"He hath made Him to be sin for us who knew no sin; that we might be made the righteousness of God in Him"* (2 Corinthians 5:21).

REASON #7: ENVY, BITTERNESS, HATE, AND GOSSIPERS

Roots that bring the wrong fruit.

> *"These six things the LORD hates, Yes, seven are an abomination to Him: A proud look, A lying tongue, Hands that shed innocent blood, A heart that devises wicked plans, Feet that are swift in running to evil, A false witness who speaks lies, And one who sows discord among brethren [gossipers]."*
>
> **—Proverbs 6:16-19, NKJV**

> *"A sound heart is life to the body, But envy is rottenness to the bones."*
>
> **—Proverbs 14:30, NKJV**

A negative, joyless mind and emotions can make you very sick.

Science is beginning to confirm what certain wise men have said at different points in history. King Solomon wrote about the wisdom of being cheerful:

> *"A merry heart does good, like medicine, But a broken spirit dries the bones."*
>
> **—Proverbs 17:22, NKJV**

Your mental and emotional states can have a profound effect on your physical body, your spiritual experience, and your quality of life. The mind, the body, and the spirit are all interconnected. When one is affected negatively, the other two suffer. If the mind is not healthy the other one cannot make up for the difference and can lead to physical ailments. **Negative emotions and thoughts— including worry, anger, jealousy, hate, ill will, grudges, vindictiveness, irritation, resentment, guilt, depression, despair and anxiety, and a lack of joy and happiness— have a negative effect upon the body and open the door for sickness and disease.**

One of the churches that I pastored in Australia was filled with people who had not been raised in Christian families or stable homes. Many of them grew up in loveless homes, steeped in neglect and abuse. One of these men who'd been raised in such an environment was active and serving in that church. When he became a Christian, he gave up his former way of life and turned away from his friendships that had fueled his life of sin. When he gave his life to Jesus, he was healed, made whole, and delivered from envy, bitterness, hate, perversion, lust, and drugs. He was walking in peace and joy and victory over his bondages and addictions from his former lifestyle.

He was doing fine for almost a year when some acquaintances from his past began to seek him out with the intent to pull him away from his new life as a Christian. They pursued him to bring him back to his former so-called "fun" lifestyle. They made him question his decision to follow Jesus and told him he'd become a sissy and a weakling; that he'd become one of those "Bible-thumping hypocrites." They ridiculed him for wasting his Sundays to become a church boy.

Their constant barrages of criticism made him begin to question his faith and his decision to believe in and follow Christ. The words hurt him deeply. Instead of giving his pain and burden over to the Lord and forgiving his old friends, he built up resentment against the church. He began to question the Christians and all the teaching he'd heard. In time, he succumbed to feelings of guilt and worthlessness.

Eventually he became completely overwhelmed with dealing with the taunting of his old companions who had convinced him that he belonged with them, not in church. He quit going to church, reading his Bible, praying in the Holy Ghost, believing the truth, and having any interest in following God's will.

He slipped back into his former lifestyle, joining his drug-abusing friends and again was living for the Devil. He refused counseling and cut himself off from the church and his Christian friends, choosing to turn his back on the law of life in the Spirit to follow after the law of sin and death, choosing sin over life in Christ.

The Bible talks about such people who backslide and become entangled again into their sinful, former way of life after becoming a Christian.

> *"While they promise them liberty, they themselves are slaves of corruption; for by whom a person is overcome, by him also he is brought into bondage. For if, after they have escaped the pollutions of the world through the knowledge of the Lord and Savior Jesus Christ, they are again entangled in them and*

> *overcome, the latter end is worse for them than the beginning. For it would have been better for them not to have known the way of righteousness, than having known it, to turn from the holy commandment delivered to them. But it has happened to them according to the true proverb: 'A dog returns to his own vomit,' and, 'a sow, having washed, to her wallowing in the mire.'"*
>
> **—2 Peter 2:19-22, NKJV**

The latter end is worse than the first. According to this passage, it would be better to not believe in Jesus at all than to believe and turn and walk away from Him. Why did he turn from his decision to follow Jesus? We find the answer in the parable of the sower.

> *"Then He spoke many things to them in parables, saying: 'Behold, a sower went out to sow. And as he sowed, some seed fell by the wayside; and the birds came and devoured them. Some fell on stony places, where they did not have much earth; and they immediately sprang up because they had no depth of earth. But when the sun was up they were scorched, and because they had no root they withered away... But he who received the seed on stony places, this is he who hears the word and immediately receives it with joy; yet he has no root in himself, but endures only for a while. For when tribulation or persecution arises because of the word, immediately he stumbles.'"*
>
> **—Matthew 13:3-6,20-21, NKJV**

Because of persecution from his friends on account of the Word, this Christian man endured for a while and later fell away. He gave in to the ridicule and began to feel embittered against the church, not having root in himself. The decision to continue to follow Jesus when temptations arise is on the believer. For this reason, I believe it is very important to pray for, mentor, and disciple new believers with grace and love in the church.

At the point where he chose to follow after the lust of the flesh—which was his former way of life—he was no longer "in Christ," or walking according to the law of the Spirit of life, but to the law of sin and death. He chose to walk away from the church with bitterness and hate in his heart. The last time I saw him he was selling drugs on the street. He was worse off than before he had given his life to Christ. He became very sick (he could not get healed, even by the doctors) and he eventually died, still being a young man.

Many would say he had never become a Christian. However, I knew his testimony of where he'd been and what the Lord had delivered him from. I knew him when he was following Jesus and serving in the church with fervent love. When I saw him back on the street, I could see that his life was a bigger mess than before he'd made the decision to become a Christian. His latter state was worse than his first. When we sweep our lives clean with receiving Jesus, we need to keep it filled with fellowship, the Word, and the Holy Spirit.

> *"When an unclean spirit goes out of a man, he goes through dry places, seeking rest, and finds none. Then he says, 'I will return to my house from which I came.' And when he comes, he finds it empty, swept, and put in order. Then he goes and takes with him seven other spirits more wicked than himself, and they enter and dwell there; and the last state of that man is worse than the first."*
>
> **—Matthew 12:43-45, NKJV**

What happens is that many people in our churches like this man are filled with bitterness, hate and unforgiveness, and they are diagnosed with all sorts of **sickness and terminal illness, like cancer**. Then they come to a revival meeting, in a backslidden state. Their heart might be cold against the Lord, with bitterness, anger, and hate in their hearts toward the church. Maybe someone in the church offended them. We call that getting burnt. It's sad and unfortunate, but it happens. Some people have walked away from the church wounded and fall away, but they need a miracle. The Lord loves the lost prodigal sons, and wants them back. He'll extend mercy to those who have walked away from the Lord and have fallen back into sin. God will heal the backslider if he will repent and come back to the Lord and live for him"

God's merciful purpose is to restore the backslider. From Isaiah 57:15b; 18, we read, "...*to revive the spirit of the humble, and to revive the heart of the contrite ones. I have seen his ways, and will heal him; / I will also lead him, / And restore comforts to him / And to his mourners."* God's merciful purpose to His people is to revive (v. 15b) and to restore (v. 18). He calls us back to Himself in a love relationship. We read our Lord's word to the church in Ephesus, *"Nevertheless I have this against you, that you have left your first love. Remember therefore from where you have fallen; repent and do the first works, or else I will come to you quickly and remove your lampstand from its place—unless you repent"* (Revelation 2:4-5). Jesus calls them to remember, repent, and repeat the first works. The humble and contrite ones enjoy the blessing of healing when there is backsliding. This is true for Christians individually and churches corporately.

I've prayed for many thousands of people over the years for this very problem. Over the decades, I have seen that these five negative attributes seem to run hand-in-hand: envy, anger, bitterness, hate, and unforgiveness.

Many times when I go to pray for a person, the Lord will give me a word of knowledge that their spiritual condition either brought about sickness or is preventing them from receiving healing as a result of envy, anger, bitterness, hate, and unforgiveness. Most people who are made aware that their physical ailments are a direct result of a spiritual condition make the decision to change. They repent and turn again to the Lord. They forgive the people and situations that brought about bitterness and hate and they repent of envy. They understand that the Lord loves and forgives them and they are ready to repent and walk away from their past behavior.

It is the Devil that is the accuser, telling Christians that they've committed some unpardonable sin, that they've crossed some line and the Lord will never want them back or cannot forgive them. When we ask Jesus to forgive us, He is faithful to forgive us and we can walk in restored fellowship with Him and with other believers.

I have prayed for people who had been healed and later became embroiled in envy, bitterness, and hate. The Devil knows if he can pull a believer into his slime pit away from walking in love and forgiveness, he can also strip away God's healing from their life. I have seen this thousands of times over. These people invariably get sick, and are unable to receive their healing—that's already been made available to them through the cross of Christ—until they deal with their deep spiritual poison and sickness first.

BITTERNESS

The Greek word for bitterness is *pikria* and also means (literally or figuratively speaking) "poison."[16] Bitterness is a poison in the soul. It poisons people who listen to somebody spewing negativity with a root of bitterness.

---

[16] G4088 - pikria - Strong's Greek Lexicon (KJV). Blue Letter Bible. Web. 12 Sep 2017.

> *"Pursue peace with all people, and holiness, without which no one will see the Lord: looking carefully lest anyone fall short of the grace of God; lest any root of bitterness springing up cause trouble, and by this many become defiled."*
>
> —**Hebrews 12:14-15, NKJV**

Defiled = To make filthy, dirty, polluted, unclean or unfit, and broken down.

We are told to pursue peace and holiness and to look carefully lest we fall short of the grace of God. If we are saved by grace and not by works, what does it mean to fall short of God's grace? Look at the cause and effect. The effect of falling short of God's grace can cause a root of bitterness. It's the decisions and thoughts that bring about the poison of bitterness. It could be a sadness that turns to sorrow and grief from a spirit of unbelief. It could be offenses that are not forgiven. When difficult things happen, we can meditate on the disparaging circumstances or we can turn our hearts to the Lord in faith. We can look to His Word for comfort and hope.

We will have less than perfect days, and will weather storms and troubles in this life. That's when the devil comes in with his tactics to discourage and kick a person when they are down. If we get sucked into negative thinking, we will get sucked into bitterness. What can we do? We can use the two-edged sword to combat the kind of thinking that keeps us from walking according to the Spirit of life in Christ. We can choose to forgive and pray for those who offend us.

Bitterness doesn't just affect the person wrapped in its tentacles. It oozes out and contaminates other people. When bitter people talk, their negative speech spills over to those who listen. Have you been on the listening end of a bitter person talking? It is a grime and mud-slinging session and you walk away feeling dirty when all you did was listen. Bitter people tend to backbite, slander, talk down, and complain. It's an anointing killer, because it grieves the Holy Spirit. It brings dissention, division, and doubt. For those reasons it hinders healing and affects the mind and body.

When things happen that we don't understand, we can call out to Jesus instead of getting bitter. He will never leave us or forsake us. Jesus said:

> *"Let your conduct be without covetousness; be content with such things as you have. For He Himself has said, 'I will never leave you nor forsake you.'"*
>
> **—Hebrews 13:5, NKJV**

> *"... and lo, I am with you always, even to the end of the age.' Amen"*
>
> **—Matthew 28:20b, NKJV**

HATE

> *"You have heard that it was said, 'You shall love your neighbor and hate your enemy.' But I say to you, love your enemies, bless those who curse you, do good to those who hate you, and pray for those who spitefully use you and persecute you, that you may be sons of your Father in heaven; for He makes His sun rise on the evil and on the good, and sends rain on the just and on the unjust."*
>
> **—Matthew 5:43-45, NKJV**

God loved the world. He gave us His only begotten Son, Jesus, who died for all who believe on Him and love Him, as well as those who hate Him. When we walk according to the law of the Spirit of life, we can walk in love to people who might be deserving of hatred. How is that possible? Hate is a feeling, but the love we are to walk in is an action of selfless humility. When we are patient and kind toward others, we show God's love.

1 Corinthians 13 is known as the love chapter, God's *agape* love. Walking in the love of God in word and action is following after the Spirit of life in Christ Jesus. It is following Jesus. Deciding to put away or cast off hate and to walk in love and forgiveness is taking up Jesus' yoke, which is easy. Hate is a heavy weight that brings torment and sleepless nights. It can tie one's stomach in knots and bring anxiety.

Even in the church, we are told to forebear one another in love. That means to put up with.

The Holy Spirit yearns to bring God's people back to serving the Lord with joy and gladness. How grieved heaven must be to witness the wet blanket of despair and sadness that has fallen upon multitudes of believers. When we decide to forgive and to serve the Lord with gladness, we can cast off the darkness and negative thoughts and emotions that keep us from receiving healing and walking in health.

ENVY

Money and possessions in themselves are not evil. We need money to live. Many people think that money is the root of all evil, but it is the *love* of it. When Christians continually think about what they don't have and what they wish they had, and begin to want what others have, it is covetousness and leads to envy. Envy can become all-consuming and can bring about sickness. A person cannot be filled with envy and be happy. The two are contradictory.

In the church, Christians might envy another person's gifts or ministry. God gives the gifts. We need to pursue Him and be faithful to use the gifts He has given.

> *"...useless wranglings of men of corrupt minds and destitute of the truth, who suppose that godliness is a means of gain. From such withdraw yourself. Now godliness with contentment is great gain. For we brought nothing into this world, and it is certain we can carry nothing out. And having food and clothing, with these we shall be content. But those who desire to be rich fall into temptation and a snare, and into many foolish and harmful lusts which drown men in destruction and perdition. For the love of money is a root of all kinds of evil, for which some have strayed from the faith in their greediness, and pierced themselves through with many sorrows."*
>
> **—1 Timothy 6:5-10, NKJV**

God's Word has an answer for bitterness, hate, and envy. It is choosing forgiveness, deciding to love, and having godliness with contentment.

> *"And let the peace of God rule in your hearts, to which also you were called in one body; and be thankful."*
>
> **—Colossians 3:15, NKJV**

REASON #8: SINS OF THE FOREFATHER OR GENERATIONAL CURSES

> *"As he passed by, he saw a man blind from birth. And his disciples asked him, "Rabbi, who sinned, this man or his parents, that he was born blind?" Jesus answered, "It was not that this man sinned, or his parents, but that the works of God might be displayed in him..."*
>
> —John 9:1-3, ESV

Although this man's sin wasn't a generational curse, nevertheless, the reason the disciples mentioned it to Jesus is because all through the Bible this generational curse is apparent.

> *"And God spake all these words, saying, I am the LORD thy God, which have brought thee out of the land of Egypt, out of the house of bondage. Thou shalt have no other gods before me. Thou shalt not make unto thee any graven image, or any likeness of anything that is in heaven above, or that is in the earth beneath, or that is in the water under the earth. Thou shalt not bow down thyself to them, nor serve them: for I the LORD thy God am a jealous God, visiting the iniquity of the fathers upon the children unto the third and fourth generation..."*
>
> —Exodus 20:1-5, KJV

> *"Christ hath redeemed us from the curse of the law, being made a curse for us: for it is written, Cursed is every one that hangs on a tree"*
>
> —Galatians 3:13, KJV

By the power of the cross, in Jesus' name we have been set free!

> *"And you will know the truth, and the truth will set you free."*
> —**John 8:32, ESV**

> *"My people are destroyed for lack of knowledge; because you have rejected knowledge, I reject you from being a priest to me. And since you have forgotten the law of your God, I also will forget your children."*
> —**Hosea 4:6, ESV**

Sins of the Forefathers

Example #1 of how this generational curse works.... From 1991 to 1994 I pastored a Pentecostal church in Tulsa, Oklahoma. A woman came into one of our meetings for prayer who was dying of breast cancer. She had about three months to live. After I laid hands on her, the Lord spoke to me and said, "This is a **generational curse**, passed down through her family."

So I said to her, "Tell me about your family history of this breast cancer." She said that her great grandmother, grandmother, mother, and two of her sisters had all died in their mid- to late- 50's with this same cancer. (She was 55-years-old.) **My, how the Holy Ghost teaches us true theology that supersedes people's arguments.**

I prayed for her and cursed that generational family curse. She was made perfectly whole and healed by the power of God. She later came to our church with her whole family, bringing a doctor's report to declare what the good Lord had done for her. Her husband became a Christian as a result. Thank You, Jesus!

Example #2 of how this generational curse works…. When I pastored in Tulsa, in the early nineties, I prayed for a girl with a serious lung problem, and as I laid hands on her, the Holy Spirit said, "It's a generational curse." So I asked the young lady about her family and if they were sick or had been sick with this same ailment. She said that her three sisters, her mother, her grandmother, and great-grandmother **(who were all good solid Bible-believing Christians for all those generations)** all had the same problem with their lungs. This was undoubtedly, beyond any shadow of a doubt, a family curse, or generational curse. Even the doctors know this. When you go to the doctors for treatment, the first thing you will hear them ask is: "Do any other members of your family have these problems?"

See! Even the doctors know about these things, family generational curses. The doctors actually call it "generational family sickness" but it means the same thing.

Over the years, I have prayed for thousands of these types of cases where generational family curses were the cause of their sickness. **The common denominator was this:** none of these people were able to receive their healing until I dealt with their spiritual sickness **first.** Then healing was able to flow. When I first started out in the ministry about 39 years ago (8 years part-time and 31 years full-time), I used to just pray for everyone, no matter what their sickness was. I found out the hard way that very few people were receiving their healing. That's when the good Lord started to teach me about some of these hindrances to healing. Later when I pastored in Tulsa (1991–1994) the good Lord got me to go much deeper into the hindrances to healing.

More on Generational Curses and Their Effects on People

Have you ever seen a family where the father has a problem with uncontrollable anger, the grandpa had the same problem, and his son seems to have inherited it? Or have you noticed that not only do you suffer from persistent irrational fears or depression, but your mother and father also suffered from it as well?

Many people today are living under bondage that the sins of their forefathers brought them under. My own family **(five generations back)** all had severe learning problems, and I dropped out in my second year of high school. Ten months after I became a Christian, I was prayed over by a pastor and he said this is a family curse **(he didn't know anything about my family)** and then he broke that stronghold over me in Jesus' name and I was set free. I later went back to school to get my GED, then I went to building college, and then to business college. Still later, I went all the way through to get my masters in theology. So, I have proven beyond any shadow of a doubt that there are such things as a family curse and how one can be set free of them.

> *"Keeping mercy for thousands, forgiving iniquity and transgression and sin, and that will by no means clear the guilty; visiting [punishing] the iniquity of the fathers upon the children, and upon the children's children, unto the third and to the fourth generation."*
>
> **—Exodus 34:7, KJV**

"Our fathers have sinned, and are not; and we have borne [been punished for] their iniquities."

—**Lamentations 5:7, KJV**

This is beyond learned behavior. Many children learn to be messy if their parents are messy. This is a spiritual bondage that is passed down from one generation to another. Some symptoms of a generational curse include a continual negative pattern of bad behavior that all the males in the family have. Maybe they all ended up in lots of trouble and even jail. Something being handed down from generation to generation is easy to detect. Often people who are adopted end up with the same characteristics as their birth parents—not because they were around their birth parents to learn how they behaved, but because they inherited their spiritual bondage.

Some other common symptoms of generational curses are family illnesses and diseases that seem to just walk from one person down to the next. **(Cancer is a common physical manifestation of a spiritual bondage.)** Others are continual financial difficulties **(they continually hit roadblocks in their finances and never seem to be able to get ahead in life),** mental problems, and persistent irrational fears and depression. Anything that seems to be a persistent struggle or problem that was handed down from one generation to another may very well be a generational curse. One Christian family I knew all had very bad back problems. Another family I knew all had heart problems. Another family I knew all had arthritis through every member of that family. Still another family I knew all had bad stomach and digestive bowel problems.

The price for generational curses has been paid!

Christ was made a curse for us, so we can be freed from the curse that sin—**all our sins and those future sins**—has brought us. **Galatians 3:13 says that, "Christ hath redeemed us from the curse of the law, being**

made a curse for us: for it is written, Cursed is every one that hangeth on a tree."

Jeremiah 31:29-30 says, "In those days they shall say no more, The fathers have eaten a sour grape, and the children's teeth are set on edge. But every one shall die for his own iniquity: every man that eateth the sour grape, his teeth shall be set on edge." Wow! But the good news is, that Jesus Christ died for our sins once and for all. The price is paid by his blood.

So why are there so many believers who seem to be living under a generational curse? This puzzled me before I understood how it worked. What is needed to be dealt with, though, is any bondage that was already passed down to you before you came into covenant with God. The legal grounds are certainly paid for on the cross and therefore broken. The only thing left to do is break the fleshly curse and cast out any spirits that have gained entrance before you accepted Jesus.

Nonbelievers are Still Affected

Even after Jeremiah 31:29-30 makes it clear that believers are redeemed from generational curses, the next chapter in Jeremiah (32:18) clearly says, "Thou shewest lovingkindness unto thousands, and recompensest the iniquity of the fathers into the bosom of their children after them: the Great, the Mighty God, the LORD of hosts, is his name." Apparently, generational curses are still in effect, but for who is the big question.

Ezekiel 18:2-3 tells us, "What mean ye, that ye use this proverb concerning the land of Israel, saying, The fathers have eaten sour grapes, and the children's teeth are set on edge? As I live, saith the Lord GOD, ye shall not have occasion any more to use this proverb in Israel." (Note the keywords "in Israel." This is referring to those who are in covenant with God, which are we believers, not the rest of the world.)

Obviously, generational curses are alive and well in the lives of those who are outside the New Covenant with God (nonbelievers).

Triggering the Effects of a Generational Curse

It is possible for demons to enter a child before he accepts Jesus, then remain dormant or hidden in that child's life until some time later in his or her life when it manifests (or makes itself known). Sometimes when a person heads for the ministry, it seems like the Devil kicks up his ugly heels and causes havoc for that person. Other times, a line of fear runs in the family tree, but isn't manifested in a person's life until they get themselves involved in something fearful, such as watching a demonic movie. All of a sudden, the spirits in that person's life "come alive" so to speak, and make themselves known. They were there all along, but just now they have come out into the open. The solution is to break them and cast them out, in Jesus' name.

If you have involved yourself in any sin or opened any doors in your own life while awakening or triggering the spirits, then it's important that you clear up any legal grounds (or strongholds) that you gave the enemy in your own life relating to the bondage. For example, if you went to see a demonic movie before you were a Christian, or you were involved in tarot card reading, teacup reading, Ouija board games, or any other witchery, this will trigger spirits of fear, occult, and other devils in your life that were handed down to you. It's important to repent, renounce all those evil doings, then cast out the spirits in Jesus' name.

I believe unforgiveness is a great way to trigger generational spirits, so I would be on the lookout for any bitterness or unforgiveness in your heart as well. A common sight is when a spirit of cancer is running down the family tree, and I believe hate and bitterness are great ways to trigger those spirits. Unforgiveness is a serious sin that blocks the forgiveness of your own sins (Matthew 6:15), which creates ample legal grounds for the enemy in your life. Unforgiveness in itself puts us into the enemy's hands (Matthew 18:23-35), to say nothing about awaking any evil spirits in us already!

The Curse May be Canceled, but the Demons May Remain

Just as other demons don't automatically leave at the time of salvation, neither do the demons that you get from your ancestors automatically leave you.

Let's say that you accept Jesus at age 15. Because you were born a sinner and outside of God's covenant, you were still living under the curses handed down to you and demons can enter you through those curses. Once you've accepted Jesus, the curse of sin is broken automatically and you are a new creation in Christ Jesus. However, the old fleshly family curses and the demons that entered into you before you accepted Jesus might still need to be broken and the spirits cast out.

Then we can pray for their healing in Jesus' name. Healing is ours, so accept it and walk free in Jesus name. Amen!

REASON #9: NOT DISCERNING THE LORD'S TABLE

Paul recounted he'd received instruction from the Lord regarding taking communion. The bread signified His body and the cup, the new covenant in His blood. We are to partake of the bread and cup in remembrance of Him, proclaiming the Lord's death until he returns.

The communion service is a reminder for Christians that the Lord gave His body and shed His blood for the remission of our sins. (See 1

Corinthians 11:23-26). It has no meaning for people who aren't Christian because they haven't accepted His death as payment for their sins. Many believers have been deeply wounded by well-meaning but biblically incorrect Christians who tell them they're not worthy to celebrate the fact that the Lord died for their sins. None of us is worthy in ourselves, but that's not the issue. The issue is our belief in the Lord's death as payment for our sins. **This passage above must be one of the most abused and misunderstood passages in the entire Bible. It is regularly used to deny communion to those who need it.**

I hold that the bread and wine are symbols (not "just" symbols or "mere" symbols, but symbols full of deep spiritual meaning which serve several purposes), as taught by Christ and Paul (and even James indirectly). However, there is power in the *act*, or in the taking. Why do I say this? Because one can eat and drink *temporary* damnation, or rather rendered judgment (in the Greek; *krima*), or sickness on themselves, according to Paul. Eating and drinking without remembering Jesus and His sacrifice leads to this.

"This do in remembrance of me." With these words ringing in our ears, we regularly celebrate communion. As we drink the cup and eat the bread, we reflect on Christ's sacrifice and look forward to His return.

Yet communion is more than a memorial. Our continued participation in this powerfully symbolic ceremony molds our thinking and brings to life deeply spiritual truths in very concrete ways. It shapes our identity as a people of God and provides the truly blessed assurance that we have been redeemed by the blood of the Lamb. The message of communion is important and deserves our full attention.

Jesus said to them, *"I tell you the truth, unless you eat the flesh of the Son of Man and drink his blood, you have no life in you. Whoever eats my flesh and drinks my blood has eternal life, and I will raise him up at the last* *day. For my flesh is real food and my blood is real drink. Whoever eats my flesh and drinks my blood remains in me, and I in him" (John 6:53-56 NLT).*

Because some of the Christians in Corinth had not examined themselves in taking the bread and the cup, they had not discerned the Lord's body and they ate and drank judgment upon themselves. Paul warns that whoever eats the bread and cup signifying the Lord's shed blood and body in an unworthy manner will be guilty of the body and blood of the Lord.

From the written account, they were eating bread to their fill and drinking to the point of drunkenness, and not judging themselves. Because of that judgment and chastening came upon them in the form of weakness, sickness, and premature death.

> *"For I received from the Lord that which I also delivered to you: that the Lord Jesus on the same night in which He was betrayed took bread; and when He had given thanks, He broke it and said, 'Take, eat; this is My body which is broken for you; do this in remembrance of Me.' In the same manner, He also took the cup after supper, saying, 'This cup is the new covenant in My blood. This do, as often as you drink it, in remembrance of Me. For as often as you eat this bread and drink this cup, you proclaim the Lord's death till He comes. Therefore whoever eats this bread or drinks this cup of the Lord in an **unworthy manner** will be guilty of the body and blood of the Lord. But let a man examine himself, and so let him eat of the bread and drink of the cup. For he who eats and drinks in an unworthy manner eats and drinks judgment to himself, not discerning the Lord's body. **For this reason many are weak and sick among you, and many sleep.** For if we would judge ourselves, we would not be judged. But when we are judged, we are chastened by the Lord, **that we may not be condemned with the world.** Therefore, my brethren, when you come together to eat, wait for one another.' But if*

anyone is hungry, let him eat at home, lest you come together for judgment. And the rest I will set in order when I come."

—1 Corinthians 11:23-34, NKJV

When we take of the Holy Communion, the Lord's Supper, we need to deeply consider what the blood of Jesus has truly done for us. We need to stop and reflect regarding the significance of the bread and what it speaks to us. Jesus is our healer. When we eat and drink in a worthy manner **(considering the whole work of the cross),** God's grace and healing power will be in it.

Many Christians don't stop to examine themselves and discern how powerful the shed blood of Jesus is, and what it has accomplished for them. The bread and the cup also signifies healing that is provided through the stripes that Jesus took on His body.

> *"Who Himself bore our sins in His own body on the tree, that we, having died to sins, might live for righteousness—by whose stripes you were healed."*
>
> —1 Peter 2:24, NKJV

If Christians don't understand or believe that healing is a part of the atonement of Jesus, then they won't receive healing or walk in health. As a result, Christians will remain weak and sickly, or even die.

If you have sinned in eating and drinking of the Lord's Table in an unworthy manner, the answer is to ask for forgiveness before taking communion, and begin to examine yourself and reflect on what Jesus actually did on the cross.

> *"If we confess our sins, He is faithful and just to forgive us our sins and to cleanse us from all unrighteousness."*
>
> **—1 John 1:9, KJV**

There is much discussion throughout the body of Christ, about what it means to take the bread and cup "**in an unworthy manner**." These are the six **main different interpretations** that are floating around the body of Christ today.

It could be that those taking the communion elements need to be fully aware that they represent the sacrifice of Christ by which we are redeemed from sin. Therefore, to participate in communion while not understanding this would be to take it in an unworthy manner.

Another possibility is that taking the supper with willful, unconfessed sin would be in an unworthy manner.

The earlier context of 1 Corinthians 11 seems to suggest that taking communion in an unworthy manner means to do so while you have a problem with another Christian with whom you are not reconciled.

Another view is that some Corinthians were using the communion supper as an opportunity for self-indulgence, which is why Paul mentioned in verse 21 about how some got drunk.

The fifth view is that *both* elements (bread *and* wine) must be taken, not just one (bread *or* wine) since Christ commanded that both be taken. This would, incidentally, invalidate the Roman Catholic practice of taking the wafer only.

The final view is that the person taking communion must be worthy in order to take it. This view, however, is dangerous because no one is worthy to take the communion supper. Our worthiness comes from Christ, not ourselves. In conclusion: As we can see from the above, there are many different views in the body of Christ as to what it means to take the communion unworthily.

One of my own personal views is as follows: *Although we **were** all sinners saved by grace, we are no longer sinners, because Jesus washed away all our sins. Period. So now, friends, we can all come to the table of the Lord, knowing that **we are all worthy to take communion and celebrate Jesus' death until He comes.** But again, only because of His finished work on the cross is this possible. Amen!*

But I believe there is another side to this story that we all need to consider big-time.

Hebrews 12:15-19 states, "Looking diligently lest any man **[This is talking to us believers in Christ] fail** of the grace of God; lest any root of bitterness springing up trouble you, and thereby many be defiled **[spiritual poison].** Lest there be any fornicator, or profane or filthy person. [You could say also, adulterers and perverts.]

Sadly, these people are **Christians**, and they know what is the right thing is to do, and how they should live, but they are angry and rebellious against God. They are walking in outright, deliberate, and blatant sin, even though they know the truth of the blood that has cleansed them.

> *"What shall we say then? Shall we continue in sin, that grace may abound? God forbid. How shall we, that are dead to sin, live any longer therein? Know ye not, that so many of us as were baptized into Jesus Christ were baptized into his death? Therefore we are buried with him by baptism into death: that like as Christ was raised up from the dead by the glory of the Father, **even so we also should walk in newness of life.** For if we have been planted together in the likeness of his death, we shall be also in the likeness of his resurrection: Knowing this, that our*

*old man is crucified with him, that the body of sin might be destroyed, **that henceforth we should not serve sin [anymore].** For he that is dead is freed from sin. Now if we be dead with Christ, we believe that we shall also live with him. Knowing that Christ being raised from the dead dieth no more; death hath no more dominion over him. For in that he died, he died unto sin once: but in that he liveth, he liveth unto God. Likewise reckon ye also yourselves to be dead indeed unto sin, but alive unto God through Jesus Christ our Lord. **Let not sin therefore reign in your mortal body**, that ye should obey it in the lusts thereof. **Neither yield ye your members as instruments of unrighteousness unto sin**: but yield yourselves unto God, as those that are alive from the dead, and your members as instruments of righteousness unto God. **For sin shall not have dominion over you: for ye are not under the law, but under grace."***

—Romans 6:1-14, KJV

If we are walking in the grace of God, we have ceased from sin. If we say, we are under grace, but deliberately, willfully, knowingly, defiantly resist the Holy Spirit, and continue in that sin, then we are out of grace and we are living on dangerous ground, and may even sin unto death.

*"If any man see his brother sin a sin which is not unto death, he shall ask, and he shall give him life for them that sin not unto death. **But there is a sin unto death: I do not say that he shall pray for it**. All unrighteousness is sin: and there is a sin not unto death. We know that whosoever is born of God sinneth not; but he that is begotten of God keepeth himself, and that wicked one toucheth him not... [If you won't keep yourself from sin, **meaning you will not stop it and repent**, the wicked one will touch you]."*

—1 John 5:16-18, KJV

"What then? shall we sin, because we are not under the law, but under grace? **God forbid.** *Know ye not, that to whom ye yield yourselves servants to obey, his servants ye are to whom ye obey;* **whether of sin unto death, or of obedience unto righteousness?** *But God be thanked, that ye were the servants of sin, but ye have obeyed from the heart that form of doctrine which was delivered you. Being then made free from sin,* **ye became the servants of righteousness.** *I speak after the manner of men because of the infirmity of your flesh: for as ye have yielded your members servants to uncleanness and to iniquity unto iniquity; even so now yield your members servants to righteousness unto holiness. For when ye were the servants of sin, ye were free from righteousness. What fruit had ye then in those things whereof ye are now ashamed? for the end of those things is death. But now being made free from sin, and become servants to God, ye have your fruit unto holiness, and the end everlasting life. For the wages of sin is death; but the gift of God is eternal life through Jesus Christ our Lord."*

—Romans 6:15-23, KJV

"Be not deceived; God is not mocked: for whatsoever a man soweth, that shall he also reap. For he that soweth to his flesh shall of the flesh reap corruption; but he that soweth to the Spirit shall of the Spirit reap life everlasting **[This is talking to Christians, not unbelievers]."**

—Galatians 6:7-8, KJV

"But he who is joined to the Lord is one spirit with Him. **Flee sexual immorality.** *Every sin that a man does is outside the body, but he* **who commits sexual** *immorality sins against his own body. Or do you not know that your body is the temple of the Holy Spirit who is in you, whom you have from God, and you are not your own? For you were bought at a price; therefore glorify God in* **your body** *and in your spirit, which are God's."*

—1 Corinthians 6:17-20, NKJV

"Therefore, 'Come out from smong them And be separate, says the Lord. Do not touch what is unclean, And I will receive you.' 'I will be a Father to you, And you shall be My sons and daughters, Says the Lord Almighty."

—2 Corinthians 6:17-18, MEV

Luke 15:11-22 (NIV) — The Parable of the Lost Son

Jesus continued: "There was a man who had two sons. The younger one said to his father, 'Father, give me my share of the estate.' So he divided his property between them.

"Not long after that, the younger son got together all he had, set off for a distant country and there squandered his wealth in wild living.

After he had spent everything, there was a severe famine in that whole country, and he began to be in need.

So he went and hired himself out to a citizen of that country, who sent him to his fields to feed pigs.

*He longed to fill his stomach with the pods that the pigs were eating, but no one gave him anything. [He **repented to God first and asked His forgiveness and then he went to his earthly father to seek forgiveness for his sin as well.**].*

"When he came to his senses, he said, 'How many of my father's hired servants have food to spare, and here I am starving to death!

I will set out and go back to my father and say to him: **Father, I have sinned against heaven and against you.**

I am no longer worthy to be called your son; make me like one of your hired servants.'

So he got up and went to his father. "But while he was still a long way off, his father saw him and was filled with compassion for him; he ran to his son, threw his arms around him and kissed him.

"The son said to him, 'Father, I have sinned against heaven and against you. I am no longer worthy to be called your son.'

*"But the father said to his servants, 'Quick! Bring the best robe and put it on him. Put a ring on his finger and sandals on his feet **[This prodigal son didn't just flippantly say, "Oh well, the grace of God will cover my sin." No, he repented, and then called to God for mercy and forgiveness…. Then he also went to his earthly father, and did the same]**.*

We have been made holy (in the Spirit only) because of the blood of Christ. Now we are challenged to walk and live a life worthy of that calling, free from fleshly sin. If we won't live a holy life, we will pay the consequences. God wants to heal us completely in this life. So live right, and don't hinder the Holy Spirit from doing His work to make you completely whole. Thank You, Jesus, and the Holy Ghost.

REASON #10: A BROKEN SPIRIT OR BROKEN EMOTIONS

Over the years, I have prayed for multiple thousands of people with wounds, rejection, deep hurts, pain, sorrow, and utter brokenness that has caused physical sickness in their bodies. When I brought them to a place of total surrender to God's grace and power in worship, and laying their burdens on Him, then I prayed over them and they were healed of their physical sickness as well.

It is God's will for us to prosper and be healthy in body, mind, will, and emotions. To prosper means to succeed in reaching. How does one prosper in their soul? We are all wired differently with different motivations and personalities. However, the Lord has made each of us and He wills for us to be successful and healthy in matters **of our mind, will, and emotions.**

> *"Beloved, I pray that you may prosper in all things and be in health, just as your soul prospers."*
>
> —3 John 1:2, NKJV

> "May God himself, the God of peace, sanctify you through and through. May your whole spirit, soul and body be kept [complete] blameless at the coming of our Lord Jesus Christ."
>
> —1 Thessalonians 5:23, NIV

I have found these proverbs to be true in ministering over the decades. It is difficult to break through for a person to receive healing for a physical condition when they are spiritually sick or broken down emotionally. The Lord wants to bind up and heal brokenheartedness and emotions that open the doors to physical healing.

> *"The spirit of a man will sustain him in sickness, But who can bear a broken spirit [Crushed, hurt, and wounded emotions]?"*
>
> —Proverbs 18:14, NKJV

> *"A merry heart makes a cheerful countenance, But by sorrow of the heart the spirit is broken."*
>
> —Proverbs 15:13, NKJV

Some people have had a lifetime of oppression and sadness, or a calamity or a string of events that come their way. It may be because of poor decisions or circumstance. Sometimes people come up for prayer for a sickness and the biggest problem is the shackles of despair, hurt, wounds, and rejection that come from a broken spirit which hinders them from receiving by faith.

The Lord is merciful to those who have a broken heart.

> *"The LORD is near to those who have a broken heart, And saves such as have a contrite spirit."*
>
> **—Psalm 34:18, NKJV**

Emotions are from the Lord. Negative emotions are the ones we feel when we are down. We have times when we go through sadness and pain. Sometimes, however, people can get stuck in their pain. It might be from things that happened in childhood or as an adult. When a person is weighed down with continual anxiety, sadness, and depression, it can lead to brokenness in the spirit and it will affect *your* physical health. The Bible says that it dries the bones. It can lead to sickness and can also hinder getting well and receiving healing from the Lord.

Proverbs 14:30 (NIV) says that "A heart at peace gives life to the body, but envy rots the bones." Add the reverse to that scripture; A heart that is not at peace will bring sickness to the body. Do you see it?

The problem comes when we carry our burdens and do not give them to the Lord. Jesus gave us the solution. When He began His preaching ministry, He began by proclaiming His mission that the Holy Spirit had spoken to the prophet Isaiah about the coming Messiah. (See Luke 4:18-19.)

> *"The Spirit of the Lord is upon Me, Because He has anointed Me To preach the gospel to the poor; He has sent Me to heal the brokenhearted, To proclaim liberty to the captives And recovery of sight to the blind, To set at liberty those who are oppressed; To proclaim the acceptable year of the Lord."*
>
> **—Luke 4:18-19, NKJV**

Further down, Isaiah had also written that He came:

> *"To console those who mourn in Zion, To give them beauty for ashes, The oil of joy for mourning, The garment of praise for the spirit of heaviness; That they may be called trees of righteousness, The planting of the LORD, that He may be glorified."*
>
> **—Isaiah 61:1-3, NKJV**

***Years ago*, when I was pastoring in Australia**, a young man came into my office and asked me to pray away his heaviness, pain, and sadness. So I leaned over and grabbed my guitar and said, "Let's praise the Lord for about an hour." He looked at me in astonishment and said, "What's that got to do with my heaviness and oppression?" I said, "Everything." That's when I gave him the above scripture to read, and then we worshiped the Lord for about an hour. When I felt in my spirit that the spirit of heaviness was broken, I prayed over him, and he lay on the floor under the power of God's Holy Spirit and fire. When he finally got up, he said, "It's all gone, preacher." "See," I said, "that's how you get rid of that heaviness, sadness, and pain**, and mental oppression."**

We need Heaven's oil of joy. The garment of praise is something **we need to put on** to break the spirit of heaviness. God does not need for us to wait until Sunday morning to hear our praise. We can thank Him as we go about our daily lives. We can lift up our hands, dance, jump, sing, whisper or shout to Him, because He is worthy to receive the fragrant perfume of our praise that comes from our brokenness. When we take Jesus' hand in faith, He brings healing, wholeness, and joy into our lives as we look to Him and walk after His Spirit and not after the things of our flesh and of this world.

The Gospel of Mark recounts that after a long day of the disciples ministering next to Jesus, evening had come. Jesus told them that they were going to get in a boat and cross over to the other side. When Jesus was asleep on the boat with the disciples, a great windstorm began to bear down on them. The disciples became distraught and they woke Jesus up with a question:

"Teacher, do You not care that we are perishing?" (Mark 4:35-39 NKJV.)

Even with Jesus with them, they became overwhelmed, thinking they were going to perish. When storms hit, we need to know that Jesus is on the boat. He's not worried. When Jesus tells you to cross over to the other side, He will get you to the other side.

In times of trouble, instead of having thoughts and feelings that go around and around in circles and thinking, "I'm going under," this is the time to stop and go to Jesus. We need to take thoughts captive.

Some people get comfortable in their bad circumstances and pain, and stay in those thoughts and emotions. To continue to dwell on and speak about troubles and trials is digging a pit deeper and deeper. We don't need to get stuck on a merry-go-round of continuous sadness and brokenness. We don't need to pretend like the emotions don't exist, but there is a way to move on toward healing. We need to take Jesus by the hand and He will walk with us through the valleys before us. He can take us through the times of pain to a place of rest, wholeness, and healing. In His presence is peace and joy.

We are not to set up a permanent home in the valley of the shadow of death. We are to walk through it. When we do, we will emerge with strength and a deepening trust in Jesus. Jesus tells us:

> *"Come to Me, all you who labor and are heavy laden, and I will give you rest. Take My yoke upon you and learn from Me, for I am gentle and lowly in heart, and you will find rest for your souls. For My yoke is easy and My burden is light."*
>
> **—Matthew 11:28-30, NKJV**

We need to take our burdens that bring grief and heaviness and give them to Jesus, and then take His yoke upon us, which is light. We need to learn of Him. We learn of Him when we spend time talking to Him and waiting upon Him and seeking Him in the Word.

Peace and refreshing joy come from being in His presence. As we wait upon Him, we will renew our strength.

> *"He gives power to the weak, And to those who have no might He increases strength... But those who wait on the LORD shall renew their strength; They shall mount up with wings like eagles, They shall run and not be weary, They shall walk and not faint."*
>
> **—Isaiah 40:29, 31, NKJV**

If you are brokenhearted, you can look to Jesus to heal your emotions. He said that we can ask the Father in His name to receive whatever we need. He came that we could be healed and He would be glorified.

In this world we will have tribulation. Jesus said so. We can have tribulation with or without Jesus, but how much better if we go to Him. When we realize that He will never leave us or forsake us, and that He will go with us through the trials of life, we can have hope. We may be brokenhearted, but we don't have to stay broken hearted.

Nehemiah said, "This day is holy to our Lord. Do not grieve, for the joy of the LORD is your strength" (Nehemiah 8:10 NIV).

> *"You will show me the path of life; In Your presence is the fullness of joy; At Your right hand are pleasures forevermore."*
>
> **—Psalm 16:11, NKJV**

> *"May God himself, the God of peace, sanctify you through and through. May your whole spirit, soul and body be kept blameless at the coming of our Lord Jesus Christ."*
>
> **—1 Thessalonians 5:23, NIV**

Jesus said that whatever we ask the Father in His name, He will give it. (See John 16:24.) We can ask for the oil of joy and healing for our mind and emotions. As we learn of Jesus and wait upon the Lord, coming into His presence with praise, He will bring refreshing. He will strengthen and He will lift us up. In His presence is the fullness of joy.

REASON #11: UNHEALTHY LIFESTYLE

The greatest asset you have in this earthly life is your body.

In 31 years of full-time ministry, I've preached thousands of sermons in nearly 500 different churches all over Australia, America, the Islands of the sea, plus many other countries and places I've visited. I'm convinced that the greater percentages of God's people are treating their bodies no different than the world does.

Improper eating, resting, and exercise will eventually lead to the body getting sick, and folks may even die before their time.

> *"Don't be excessively wicked, and don't be foolish. Why should you die before your time?"*
>
> —Ecclesiastes 7:17, CSB

> *"Now may the God of peace Himself sanctify you completely, and may your spirit and soul and body be preserved, entirely [completely] blameless at the coming of our Lord Jesus Christ."*
>
> —1 Thessalonians 5:23, BLB

That word "blameless" means, perfect, faultless, very sound.

> *"Beloved, I pray that you may prosper in all things and be in health, just as your soul prospers"* **(3 John 1:2 NKJV).**

A woman came into one of my revival meetings, who was terribly overweight and had blown out knee joints, whereby she could barely walk, even with a walker. As I lay hands on her to receive healing, the Holy

Spirit said, "I will heal her, but you must tell her (from Me) that she needs to get her weight down so it doesn't come back and get worse." So I did, and she promised to go on a diet and obey the Lord's word. Then I prayed for her, and she was instantly healed and was able to bend her knees, walk, and move around without a walker. A real genuine miracle had just happened.

About a year later, I visited that same church to do a week's revival. Guess what? That same woman—who was healed from very bad knees—was there in the front row in a wheelchair all crippled up. When it came time to pray for the people, I said to her, "Obviously, you didn't obey the Lord in getting your weight down." She said, "No I didn't bother, as I was already healed." I said to her, "But the Lord's word to you was that if you didn't do it, you would end up worse, and that's what has happened to you now." She was very sad. This time when I prayed for her, nothing happened, and she remained crippled in her wheelchair.

In this day and age of electronic information, information on healthy lifestyle is at our fingertips. Magazines and books on the benefits of diet, exercise, sleep, and well-being fill magazine racks and bookstores. Television programs hosted by doctors and nutritionists expound on the benefits of good nutrition and lifestyle.

The Lord wants us to glorify Him in our physical bodies so that we may be His witnesses without hindrances resulting from poor diet and lifestyle. Much of the sickness and disease that people suffer from stem from unhealthy eating, drinking, and lifestyle habits. The others are bad lifestyle habits like smoking, overworking, and not enough rest and exercise. The Lord will help deliver us from those things that are hurting and defiling our body, which the Scriptures say is the temple of the Holy Spirit.

> *"Do you not know that your body is a temple of the Holy Spirit who is in you, whom you have received from God? You are not your own; you were bought at a price. Therefore glorify God with your body."*
>
> —1 Corinthians 6:19-20, BSB

In John 14:23 (KJV), Jesus introduces the basis for this concept to illustrate the closeness of our relationship with God: *"If anyone loves Me, he will keep My word; and My Father will love him, and We will come to him and make Our home with him."*

> *"Know ye not that ye are the temple of God, and that the Spirit of God dwelleth in you? If any man defile the temple of God, him shall God destroy; for the temple of God is holy, which temple are ye."*
>
> —1 Corinthians 3:16-17, KJV

Did you know that 30.5 percent of the population in every state in America is obese? And 50 million people worldwide will die this year from chronic diseases due to bad eating habits and being overweight. **The most recent survey (2015) among American adults, 64.5 percent were overweight, 30.5 percent were obese, and 6.7 percent were severely obese.**

Your physical health is an important part of making your life count. I want to look at the right motivation for getting healthy—what Gods says about the importance of your body in 1 Corinthians 6:12.

God expects me to manage my body. *"Everything is permissible for me, but not everything is beneficial...I will not be mastered by anything..."* (v. 12). Your body is a gift from God. **He loans it to you and it's your**

responsibility to manage it well. What are you doing with what He's given you?

During a series of revival meetings, I called a man out with a word of knowledge, "There is a man here who has blockages in the arteries in his heart. You've been experiencing chest pain and the doctor wants to schedule surgery for you."

The man came forward. When I laid my hands on him and prayed, I knew that the Lord had done a miraculous, instant work. The doctor's report confirmed what the Lord had done. The man was over 50, and probably well over 100 pounds overweight. His health problem arose from his poor eating habits and lack of exercise. The Lord can heal and do a work in a person regardless of their weight, **but it is up to the person to make changes that will result in a continuing healthy life.**

We can ask God to show us what He wants us to change regarding these areas. Eating healthy can help give the body the nutrition it needs to have a strong immune system needed to stay healthy. If we really desire to become an overcomer, we will bring our bodies into subjection to the Holy Spirit as Paul did in 1 Corinthians 9:24-27 (NKJV):

> *"Do you not know that those who run in a race all run, but one receives the prize? Run in such a way that you may obtain it. And everyone who competes for the prize is temperate in all things. Now they do it to obtain a perishable crown, but we for an imperishable crown. Therefore, I run thus: not with uncertainty. Thus I fight: not as one who beats the air. But I discipline my body and bring it into subjection, lest, when I have preached to others, I myself should become disqualified."*

I knew of one man who seemed to be pretty healthy in diet, exercise, and lifestyle, but he felt prodded by the Lord regarding his sugar intake. For years and years, he's had two or three cups of coffee or tea in the morning with large amounts of sugar. He admittedly was a sugar addict. He ate cookies, candy, and cakes in excess; however, he kept his weight down because of a very active lifestyle. When he felt like the Lord was leading him to stop consuming sugar, he'd nearly panicked at the thought.

He said that he prayed, believing if the Lord were leading, He would also give the direction as to how to make the changes. It started with the tea in the morning. It would not be a specific diet, but a lifestyle change of how to drink the tea. He had a cup of tea with no sugar, but added cinnamon for flavor. It tasted bitter and terrible at first, but it was just the first baby step in cutting out the sugar. Over the weeks and months, the cravings subsided. He also lost the extra 10 pounds he'd struggled to lose.

As believers in Jesus, as we follow Him in all areas of our life, such as eating habits, He will lead us in ways that bring abundant life. Though we have weaknesses, we can exercise discipline in what we eat and drink and how much. We are to glorify Jesus in our body and spirit. He wants our life here to be abundant in health, but it is up to us what we put into it.

1 Corinthians 10:31 sums it up beautifully:

> *"Whether therefore ye eat, or drink, or whatsoever ye do, do all to the glory of God."*

It's no glory to God when people abuse their bodies with junk food and no exercise, and then they wonder why God's healing power isn't working in their lives.

The apostle Paul practiced being disciplined when it came to eating. His reasoning was that his body was bought with a price, and that he should become disqualified as one who has preached to others. In other words, how could he preach to others about being disciplined if he was not living a disciplined life?

> *"Do you not know that those who run in a race all run, but one receives the prize? Run in such a way that you may obtain it. And everyone who competes for the prize is temperate in all things. Now they do it to obtain a perishable crown, but we for an imperishable crown. Therefore I run thus: not with uncertainty. Thus I fight: not as one who beats the air. But I discipline my body and bring it into subjection, lest, when I have preached to others, I myself should become disqualified."*
>
> **—1 Corinthians 9:24-27, NKJV**

> *"Or do you not know that your body is the temple of the Holy Spirit who is in you, whom you have from God, and you are not your own? For you were bought at a price; **therefore glorify God in your body and in your spirit**, which are God's."*
>
> **—1 Corinthians 6:19-20, NKJV**

Some practical guidelines include:

(1) Eat God's approved foods listed in the Bible:

A good guideline would be to eat "living foods." The natural, living foods are fresh vegetables, fruits, grains, meats and dairy products. The "dead foods" are those that are highly refined. They are not only expensive, but also in most instances have little nutrition. Many people are tired, run down, and sick because a large part of their diets are made up of "dead" junk, overly-processed food.

I've listed of some of God's approved foods with scripture references to help people get started on the road to proper eating.

Barley—Ruth 2:23

Bread—Luke 22:19

Butter—Isaiah 7:22

Corn—Ruth 2:14; 1 Samuel 17:17

Cheese—1 Samuel 17:18

Dates—Genesis 3:2

Eggs—Job 6:6

Figs—-Numbers 13:23; 1 Samuel 25:18

Fruits (all)—Genesis 1:29

Herbs (leafy plants) and vegetables—Genesis 1:29

Honey—Deuteronomy 8:8

Meats—(beef, fish, lamb, poultry, venison) Deuteronomy 14; Leviticus 11

Milk—Isaiah 7:21-22

Nuts—Genesis 43:11

Olives and Olive Oil—Leviticus 2:4; Deuteronomy 8:8

Salt—Leviticus 2:13

Wheat (bread, cereal, pasta)—Psalm 81:16

The apostle Paul said in Philippians 3:19 that many walk as enemies of the cross, "whose end is destruction, whose god is their belly, and whose glory is in their shame, who mind earthly things." Eating has become a god for some people. As believers we need to eat to the glory of the Lord. Although there is no diet that is set in stone, we can be led by the Holy Spirit and by our own consciences to lead a disciplined life in regard to eating.

REST

If we do not take time to rest, it will eventually catch up with us. God did not create us to work seven days a week. In his letter to the Romans, Paul spoke to the church regarding the Sabbath and of eating. His point comes back to our personal walk with the Lord Jesus Christ and how the Holy Spirit leads us in regard to our daily living, working, and eating. We don't live and die to ourselves, but to the Lord.

We are all in different places in our maturity in the Lord, as we are in our strength and stamina, along with our physical age. The Lord will lead and guide us into all truth; not just in spiritual matters, but in practical, everyday matters, like what and how much we eat and drink, and how much we work, exercise, rest, and sleep. In all these matters, He is the Good Shepherd and will lead us.

We don't know much about the apostle Paul's friend in the ministry, Epaphroditus, from the letter to the Philippians except that he did not regard his own life and literally worked himself sick and almost to death. He pulled out of his sickbed by the mercy of God, and later continued in the ministry.

> *"For indeed he was sick almost unto death; but God had mercy on him, and not only on him but on me also, lest I should have sorrow upon sorrow. Therefore, I sent him the more eagerly, that when you see him again you may rejoice, and I may be less sorrowful. Receive him therefore in the Lord with all gladness, and hold such men in esteem; because for the work of Christ he came close to death, not regarding his life, to supply what was lacking in your service toward me."*
>
> **—Philippians 2:27-30, NKJV**

When it comes to matters of health, we can use common sense. If we don't eat a proper diet, don't exercise, don't get enough rest, or push ourselves with no rest, we tax our physical bodies. If you ask the Lord, He can help direct your personal habits to lead a longer, healthier life. He created our bodies, and we need to look after them. Amen!

REASON #12: NOT WALKING IN LOVE

This principle is based on the scripture in Peter regarding husbands and wives walking in love toward each other.

> *"Likewise, husbands, live with your wives in an understanding way, showing honor to the woman as the weaker vessel, since they are heirs with you of the grace of life, **so that your prayers may not be hindered.**"*
>
> **—1 Peter 3:7, ESV**

> *"Enjoy life with the wife whom you love, all the days of your vain life that God has given you under the sun...."* (**Ecclesiastes 9:9a ESV**). Amen!

If we are not walking in the love of God towards others, this will grieve the Holy Spirit, and our prayers will be hindered.

> *'If I speak in the tongues of men or of angels, but do not have love, I am only a resounding gong or a clanging cymbal. If I have the gift of prophecy and can fathom all mysteries and all knowledge, and if I have a faith that can move mountains, but do not have love, I am nothing. If I give all I possess to the poor and give over my body to hardship that I may boast, **but do not have love, I gain nothing**. Love is patient, love is kind. It does not envy, it does not boast, it is not proud. It does not dishonor others, it is not self-seeking, it is not easily angered, it keeps no record of wrongs. Love does not delight in evil but rejoices with the truth. It always protects, always trusts, always hopes, always perseveres. Love never fails. And now these three remain: faith, hope and love. But the greatest of these is love."*
>
> —1 Corinthians 13:1-13, NIV

God is love, and if we are not walking in the love of God, we are not walking in God, period.

1 John 4:8 (NIV) states, "Whoever does not love does not know God, because God is love. If someone does not love, they do not know God." Wow! That says it all. No wonder thousands of people in our churches are not being healed, no love for others. So, let's love God and love others, so our prayers will not be hindered. Amen!

"Husbands, love your wives, as Christ loved the church and gave himself up for her, that he might sanctify her, having cleansed her by the washing of water with the word, so that he might present the church to himself in splendor, without spot or wrinkle or any such thing, that she might be holy and without blemish. In the same way husbands should love their wives as their own bodies. He who loves his wife loves himself."

—**Ephesians 5:25-28, ESV**

"Husbands, love your wives, and do not be harsh with them."

—**Colossians 3:19, ESV**

"Now concerning the matters about which you wrote: "It is good for a man not to have sexual relations with a woman." But because of the temptation to sexual immorality, each man should have his own wife and each woman her own husband. The husband should give to his wife her conjugal rights, and likewise the wife to her husband. For the wife does not have authority over her own body, but the husband does. Likewise the husband does not have authority over his own body, but the wife does. Do not deprive one another, except perhaps by agreement for a limited time, that you may devote yourselves to prayer; but then come together again, so that Satan may not tempt you because of your lack of self-control."

—**1 Corinthians 7:1-5, ESV**

The Lord speaks to us through David, warning us of the danger of misdirected love when He says: *"O sons of men, how long will my honor become a reproach? How long will you love what is worthless and aim at deception?"* **(Psalm 4:2 NASB).**

> *"And this I pray, that your love may abound still more and more in real knowledge and all discernment, so that you may approve the things that are excellent, in order to be sincere and blameless until the day of Christ;"*
>
> **—Philippians 1:9-10, NASB**

This passage instructs us that our love needs knowledge and discernment. If our love does not have knowledge and discernment we will approve things that will condemn us. "Happy is he who does not condemn himself in what he approves" (Romans 14:22 NASB).

So That Your Prayers May Not be Hindered...

While preaching in one church, the good Lord gave me a word of knowledge for an older man who had a brain tumor and the doctors had given him just a few months to live. Well, a man got up and came down the front of the church and said, "That's me." He said he wears a hat because all the chemotherapy treatment he had caused his hair to fall out. The pastor of that church said to me, "Everyone has prayed for him and we don't know why the Lord is not healing him."

I said to the whole congregation, "The Lord has already taken care of all of our healing on the cross. According to 1 Peter 2:24, by His stripes we are healed."

As I went to pray for him, the Lord said to me, "The sick man before you doesn't love his wife. That's why he is sick and why he hasn't been able to receive his healing."

I repeated to this man what the Lord had told me, and he said, **"Not so, preacher. I do love my wife."**

I was taken aback and stood silent before the congregation, which seemed to be holding their breath.

I said, "Let's see what the Lord says."

Suddenly the fire of the Holy Spirit fell on that man and he fell to the floor shaking under the power of the Holy Ghost, crying, and saying, "The preacher is right, the preacher is right, I don't love my wife; I lied."

He was so much under the anointing that he couldn't stand up. He crawled back to his seat and hugged his wife and said, "God forgive me!" He then pleaded for his wife to forgive him as he wept and cried under the conviction of the Holy Spirit.

I then felt in my spirit that he was now free of the breach in the spirit between him and God and, of course, his wife, so I asked him to come down to the front again to pray for his healing. He walked to the front of the church again and I prayed over him. About 12 months later, I was asked to preach in that same church again and found that man had been completely healed and restored as a loving husband.

Cultivating the love of God in your life and sharing it with others is the key to experiencing the fullness of His power. Without love, the gifts of God are useless. The word used for Christians to love one another is the Greek word *agape*. It is not contingent upon a feeling, as we typically think. It is both a decision *and* an action. When we walk in love toward one another we can facilitate the blessings of the Lord, including receiving our healing.

Praise the Lord for His chastening when we are not walking in love. He wants to mature who we are in Him. When we pursue a life of walking after the Spirit of life, love is the first fruit of the Spirit that will be evident in our lives.

Walk in Love

The phrase "walk in love" expresses our entire relationship with God and mankind. (See Matthew 22:37-40.)

Paul says: *"Therefore be followers of God as dear children. And walk in love, as Christ also has loved us and given Himself for us, an offering and a sacrifice to God for a sweet-smelling aroma"* (Ephesians 5:1-2 NASB).

Those who love God are followers (imitators) of God as His dear (beloved, dearly loved) children. The phrase "as beloved children" denotes that we are following God because of His love for us. And because God loved us, we love Him (1 John 4:19). Therefore, we imitate Him as dear children.

Now take a moment and think about God. Think about His goodness and mercy toward mankind. Think about His kindness, love, and grace. Think about His love to give Jesus as a sacrifice for our sins. And think about Jesus' love for us to die on the cross. To imitate God is to be like God thus to love (Matthew 5:43f); God is love (1 John. 4:16); Jesus left an example for us (1 Peter 2:2); and Paul commands us to imitate him as he imitates Christ (1 Corinthians 11:1) whereby we imitate God.

And note that we are to love as children. Think about the trusting love a young child has for his parents. John says that we are either children of God or children of the Devil (1 John 3:10). Those who are children of the Devil are children of wrath (Ephesians 2:3) but the children of God are children of light (Ephesians 5:8), saved by grace through faith and created in Christ (Ephesians 2:8-10).

Jesus is our example of walking in love. He emptied Himself to come to earth in the form of a servant and in the likeness of man was obedient even to the point of death on the cross (Philippians 2:5f). Love is giving one's self as a servant in obedience to God which is an offering and sacrifice to

Him. We must be a living sacrifice to God (Romans 12:1) as we serve Him by faith (Hebrews 11:4) in offering the sacrifice of praise to Him, giving thanks to His name, and sharing (Hebrews 13:15-16). Therefore the church offers up spiritual sacrifices acceptable to God through Jesus (1 Peter 2:5).

The result of a sacrificial walk in love is a sweet-smelling aroma to God. But note that what is sweet smelling to God is not necessarily sweet smelling to the world. As burning flesh of Old Testament sacrifices were horrible smelling to men, it was sweet smelling to God when performed by faith. Therefore, we cannot rely on the judgments of men as to what is sweet smelling and thus pleasing to God. We cannot allow ourselves to be deceived by those teaching human doctrines (Ephesians 5:6-7; Colossians 2) nor may we be partakers with them in evil deeds.

We have a grave responsibility to walk in love. A walk in love is not dictated by the doctrines and emotions of men but by God, thus imitating Him.

Are you walking in love as a beloved child of God? If not, whose child are you?

> *John 13:34-35 "A new commandment I give to you, that you love one another: just as I have loved you, you also are to **love one another**. By this all people will know that you are my disciples, if you have love for one another."*
>
> **—John 13:34-35, ESV**

> *"But the fruit of the Spirit is love, joy, peace, longsuffering, kindness, goodness, faithfulness, gentleness, self-control. Against such there is no law. And those who are Christ's have crucified*

the flesh with its passions and desires. If we live in the Spirit, let us also walk in the Spirit."

—**Galatians 5:22-25, NKJV**

In the last days, the love of many will grow cold. (See Matthew 24:4-12 AMP.)

Many people, including Christians, are abandoning the "love realm" in order to operate in the "sense realm." Many are convinced that walking in love is useless because of the sinful and lawless times they are living in. Your vertical relationship with God will determine the effectiveness of your horizontal relationship with others. By perfecting your love walk with others, you ultimately perfect your love walk with God. When you choose not to love others, you allow fear to affect you, thereby giving Satan access to your life.

Love enables you to live as a conqueror in the world. How can you perfect your love? Always keep God as the focal point of everything that you do. Pray in tongues in order to keep yourself in the love of God (Jude 1:20-21). Practice loving everyone, especially those of your own household, which includes your wife. God has called us to love each other, but when we cut off our love to others, we are actually cutting ourselves off from God, because God is love, and He commands us to love each other.

Healing for our bodies has been paid for by the work of the cross. Thank You, Jesus. But as Christians, we **can hinder** that flow from heaven when we are unloving, uncaring, unappreciative, unkind, unjust, unfriendly, unsympathetic, uncompassionate, and just plain lukewarm. Here's the big question: Are these types of people real Christians?

REASON #13: THE THING I FEARED HAS COME ON ME

Job said, "For the thing I greatly feared has come upon me, And what I dreaded has happened to me."

—Job 3:25, NKJV

"When I am afraid, I will trust in thee. In God I will praise his word, in God I have put my trust; I will not fear what flesh can do unto me."

—Psalm 56:3-4, ESV

It is a well-known fact that, when a good physician starts to work on a case, the first step is to find out, if possible, the cause of the sickness. Then he works to eliminate that cause. So it is, when we come to God for healing. We find that He deals not so much with symptoms as with causes. In this case, we are dealing with fear that hinders our healing.

The opposite of faith is fear. Fear is the fruit of unbelief, and it opens the door of your life to the Devil. Sixty-three times in the Bible, the Lord uses the phrase, "Fear not."

"Take heed, brethren, lest there be in any of you an evil heart of unbelief, in departing from the living God" (Hebrews 3:12 KJV). **If people are in fear, they are in unbelief, and if they are in unbelief, they have inadvertently cut themselves off from God's help. That being the case, how can such people receive healing from the Lord?**

"If any of you lacks wisdom [or you could say, whatever your need is], you should ask God, who gives generously to all without finding fault, and it will be given to you. But when you

ask, you must believe and not doubt, because the one who doubts is like a wave of the sea, blown and tossed by the wind. **That person should not expect to receive anything from the Lord. Such a person is double-minded and unstable in all they do."**

—James 1:5-8, NIV

Unbelief will get us nothing from the Lord, and healing comes under the topic of anything...so, let's get rid of the unbelief and the fear will go, and we will receive our healing from the Lord. Amen!

Job said, *"For the thing I greatly feared has come upon me, And what I dreaded has happened to me"* **(Job 3:25 NKJV).**

David wrote in the Psalms, *"Yea, though I walk through the valley of the shadow of death, I will fear no evil; For You are with me; Your rod and Your staff, they comfort me."* **(Psalm 23:4 NKJV).**

"Behold, I have given you authority to tread on serpents and scorpions, and over all the power of the enemy, ***and nothing shall hurt you."***

—Luke 10:19, ESV

Evil includes sickness. When people dwell in fear about sickness and disease, they can open a door. When thoughts are consumed with fear of sickness, then the next step to follow is confessing. Remember that words we speak are powerful seeds that will produce a harvest of life and death.

The answer to fear is to meditate on Jesus, our Shepherd and the truth of His Word. When we walk in His love, and walk after the Spirit, bearing the fruit of love, fears will have no place.

> *"There is no fear in love; but perfect love casts out fear, because fear involves torment. But he who fears has not been made perfect in love."*
>
> **—1 John 4:18, NKJV**

> *"I sought the LORD, and he answered me and delivered me from all my fears."*
>
> **—Psalm 34:4, ESV**

> *"Humble yourselves, therefore, under the mighty hand of God so that at the proper time he may exalt you, casting all your anxieties on him, because he cares for you."*
>
> **—1 Peter 5:6-7, ESV**

> *"Say to those who have an anxious heart, 'Be strong; fear not! Behold, your God will come with vengeance, with the recompense of God. He will come and save you.'"*
>
> **—Isaiah 35:4, ESV**

Fear carries with it the bondage of anxiety. We will feel what we give our minds to. The Word of God has the answer to our problem of fear and anxiety, and how it is replaced with God's peace.

"Be anxious [do not fear] for nothing, but in everything by prayer and supplication, with thanksgiving, let your requests be made known to God; and the peace of God, which surpasses all understanding, will guard your hearts and minds through Christ Jesus. Finally, brethren, whatever things are true, whatever things are noble, whatever things are just, whatever things are pure, whatever things are lovely, whatever things are of good report, if there is any virtue and if there is anything praiseworthy--meditate on these things. The things which you learned and received and heard and saw in me, these do, and the God of peace will be with you."

—Philippians 4:6-9, NKJV

"*Fear thou not; for I am with thee: be not dismayed; for I am thy God: I will strengthen thee; yea, I will help thee; yea, I will uphold thee with the right hand of my righteousness.*"

—Isaiah 41:10, KJV

"*I sought the LORD, and he heard me, and delivered me from all my fears.*"

—Psalm 34:4, KJV

"*Ye are of God, little children, and have overcome them: because greater is he that is in you, than he that is in the world.*"

—1 John 4:4, KJV

"*Now the God of hope fill you with all joy and peace in believing, that ye may abound in hope, through the power of the Holy Ghost.*"

—Romans 15:13, KJV

"God is not a man, that he should lie; neither the son of man, that he should repent: hath he said, and shall he not do it? or hath he spoken, and shall he not make it good?"

—Numbers 23:19, KJV

"And Moses said unto the people, Fear not: for God is come to prove you, and that his fear may be before your faces, that ye sin not [unbelief is sin]."

—Exodus 20:20, KJV

"O LORD, I have heard thy speech, [and] was afraid: O LORD, revive thy work in the midst of the years, in the midst of the years make known; in wrath remember mercy."

—Habakkuk 3:2, KJV

"Fear not, for I am with you; be not dismayed, for I am your God; I will strengthen you, I will help you, I will uphold you with my righteous right hand."

—Isaiah 41:10, ESV

"Do not be anxious about anything, but in everything by prayer and supplication with thanksgiving let your requests be made known to God. And the peace of God, which surpasses all understanding, will guard your hearts and your minds in Christ Jesus."

—Philippians 4:6-7, KJV

"When I am afraid, I put my trust in you."

—**Psalm 56:3, ESV**

"For God gave us a spirit not of fear but of power and love and self-control."

—**2 Timothy 1:7, ESV**

"Be strong and courageous. Do not fear or be in dread of them, for it is the Lord your God who goes with you. He will not leave you or forsake you."

—**Deuteronomy 31:6, ESV**

"I sought the Lord, and he answered me and delivered me from all my fears."

—**Psalm 34:4, ESV**

"Therefore I tell you, do not be anxious about your life, what you will eat or what you will drink, nor about your body, what you will put on. Is not life more than food, and the body more than clothing? Look at the birds of the air: they neither sow nor reap nor gather into barns, and yet your heavenly Father feeds them. Are you not of more value than they? And which of you by being anxious can add a single hour to his span of life? And why are you anxious about clothing? Consider the lilies of the field, how they grow: they neither toil nor spin, yet I tell you, even Solomon in all his glory was not arrayed like one of these."

—**Matthew 6:25-29, ESV**

"Humble yourselves, therefore, under the mighty hand of God so that at the proper time he may exalt you, casting all your anxieties on him, because he cares for you."

—1 Peter 5:6-7, ESV

"Have I not commanded you? Be strong and courageous. Do not be frightened, and do not be dismayed, for the Lord your God is with you wherever you go."

—Joshua 1:9, ESV

"Casting all your anxieties on him, because he cares for you."

—1 Peter 5:7, ESV

"Say to those with fearful hearts, "Be strong, and do not fear, for your God is coming to destroy your enemies. He is coming to save you."

—Isaiah 35:4, NLT

*"I prayed to the L*ORD*, and he answered me. He freed me from all my fears."*

—Psalm 34:4, NLT

"He said to his disciples, "Why are you so afraid? Do you still have no faith?'"

—Mark 4:40, NIV

"...Jesus told him, "Don't be afraid; just believe."

—**Mark 5:36b, NIV**

"Even though I walk through the darkest valley, I will fear no evil, for you are with me."

—**Psalm 23:4, NIV**

"Do not be afraid of anyone, for judgment belongs to God."

—**Deuteronomy 1:17b, NIV**

"Do not be afraid of them; the LORD your God himself will fight for you."

—**Deuteronomy 3:22, NIV**

"The LORD is my light and my salvation— whom shall I fear? The LORD is the stronghold of my life— of whom shall I be afraid?"

—**Psalm 27:1, NIV**

If we meditate on those things that bring fear, then we open the door for attacks from the Devil, including sickness. Meditate on the things of the Lord, and speak His Word. **His perfect love casts out fear. Then we can receive our healing, by faith through prayer.**

REASON #14: THE SPIRIT OF INFIRMITY

Jesus laid hands on the sick and prayed for them to be healed, but many times He had to cast out an evil spirit first, then they were healed.

The term *spirit of infirmity* occurs in Luke 13:11, specifically in the King James Version. Here, a woman who had been crippled for eighteen years is healed by Jesus on the Sabbath day. Luke says she had a "spirit of infirmity" or a "disabling spirit" (ESV), a "sickness caused by a spirit" (NASB), or is "crippled by a spirit" (NIV). Quite simply then, this "spirit of infirmity" is a *demon* that caused the woman to be crippled for eighteen years

The Bible is clear that spiritual warfare exists. Ephesians 6:12 says, *"For our struggle is not against flesh and blood, but against the rulers, against the authorities, against the powers of this dark world and against the spiritual forces of evil in the heavenly realms."* And from Luke 13, it is clear that evil spirits can sometimes cause physical sicknesses, diseases, ailments, and bodily malfunctions.

Many people are not healed when we lay hands on them, until the spirit of infirmity is broken. I have prayed for tens of thousands of deliverances over the years, and when the demonic power is broken, I then pray for their healing, and they are healed.

Demons can be responsible for feebleness of body or mind, disease, infirmity, sickness, and weakness to name a few.

I was preaching in a church I'd never been to before, and I had a word of knowledge that there was a man in his late fifties who had a bad heart for about thirty years. Over the years it had gotten worse, and now this man's doctors have scheduled him for a triple bypass operation for the next Tuesday. A tall white-headed man got up and came down to the front of the church and said to me, "That's my condition, and yes, the doctors want to do a triple bypass on my heart this coming Tuesday."

I closed my eyes, laid my hands on him to pray, and God gave me a vision of his heart. I saw—like a movie screen—a small chimp-like animal-looking thing inside of his heart that obviously had caused this heart problem—a spirit of infirmity that he had. I took authority over that spirit of infirmity in Jesus' name, and commanded it to leave. The spirit screamed and left his body, and then I prayed for his healing in Jesus' name, and he went out under the power of the Holy Ghost.

A week later, he came back to the church (I was doing an ongoing revival in that church) with a doctor's report saying he had a normal heart, and needed no medication or surgery. A year later, I went back to that same church, and that man come and told me that since he'd received prayer, he's had no pain or any problems with his heart.

Another Testimony About the Spirit of Infirmity

Years ago, I was preaching in a church in Florida (I'd never been to that church before either) when the Lord gave me a word of knowledge about a woman who had a serious back and neck problem, whereby her neck was all locked up with very little movement. Also, she could hardly bend over more than about 30 percent. The pastor's wife stood up and came down to the front and said, "That's me, Dan." As I closed my eyes to pray for her, I saw a vision of her spine, and entwined around her spine—from top to bottom—was a three-cord rope. As I looked closer, I saw it was really three little snakes entwined around her spine, which the Holy Spirit said were spirits of infirmity. I took authority over those spirits of infirmity and told them to go in Jesus' name, and they did, and then I prayed for her healing. The pastor's wife fell out under the powerful Holy Spirit and fire, and lay on the floor.

About five minutes later, she got up off the floor, and she was crying, shouting, and praising the Lord big-time. She could bend over and touch the floor and move her neck back and forth without pain. She had total freedom and movement for the first time since she was a little girl.

See, it's the truth, people. Over the years I've been led by the Holy Spirit to cast out thousands of these spirits of infirmities, and then I'd pray for their healing after they were delivered.

> *"Now, He was teaching in one of the synagogues on the Sabbath. And behold, there was a woman who had a spirit of infirmity eighteen years, and was bent over and could in no way raise herself up."*
>
> **—Luke 13:10-11, NKJV**

When ministering in the Spirit, the Lord will reveal when a person is in bondage to a demonic oppression. Jesus ministered to a child with epilepsy. When Jesus rebuked the demon, the child was cured that hour.

> *"And when they had come to the multitude, a man came to Him, kneeling down to Him and saying, 'Lord, have mercy on my son, for he is an epileptic and suffers severely; for he often falls into the fire and often into the water. So I brought him to Your disciples, but they could not cure him.' Then Jesus answered and said, 'O faithless and perverse generation, how long shall I be with you? How long shall I bear with you? Bring him here to Me.' And Jesus rebuked the demon, and it came out of him; and the child was cured from that very hour."*
>
> **—Matthew 17:14-18, NKJV**

And in that same hour he cured many of their infirmities and plagues, and of evil spirits; and unto many that were blind he gave sight.

> *"When the even was come, they brought unto him many that were possessed with devils: and he cast out the spirits with his word, and healed all that were sick:"*
>
> **—Matthew 8:16, KJV**

> *"And he called unto him the twelve, and began to send them forth by two and two; and gave them power over unclean spirits;"*
>
> **—Mark 6:7, NKJV**

> *"And they were all amazed, and spake among themselves, saying, What a word is this! for with authority and power he commandeth the unclean spirits, and they come out."*
>
> **—Luke 4:36, KJV**

> *"Then goeth he, and taketh to him seven other spirits more wicked than himself; and they enter in, and dwell there: and the last state of that man is worse than the first."*
>
> **—Luke 11:26, KJV**

> *"For unclean spirits, crying with loud voice, came out of many that were possessed with them: and many taken with palsies, and that were lame, were healed."*
>
> **—Acts 8:7, KJV**

"And in that same hour he cured many of their infirmities and plagues, and of evil spirits; and unto many that were blind he gave sight."

—Luke 7:21, KJV

"And certain women, which had been healed of evil spirits and infirmities, Mary called Magdalene, out of whom went seven devils,"

—Luke 8:2, KJV

"So that from his body were brought unto the sick handkerchiefs or aprons, and the diseases departed from them, and the evil spirits went out of them."

—Acts 19:12, KJV

Types of Spirits Found in the Old Testament:

"And the spirit of jealousy [qinah = jealousy, envy] come upon him, and he be jealous of his wife, and she be defiled: or if the spirit of jealousy come upon him, and he be jealous of his wife, and she be not defiled...Or when the spirit of jealousy [qinah = jealousy, envy] cometh upon him, and he be jealous over his wife, and shall set the woman before the Lord, and the priest shall execute upon her all this law."

—Numbers 5:14, 30, KJV

"Then God sent an evil spirit [ra = evil, bad] between Abimelech and the men of Sechem; and the men of Shechem dealt treacherously with Abimelech:"

—**Judges 9:23, KJV**

"And Hannah answered and said, No, my lord, I am a woman of a sorrowful spirit [qasheh = sorrowful, sharp, hard]: I have drunk neither wine nor strong drink, but have poured out my soul before the LORD."

—**1 Samuel 1:15 KJV**

"But the Spirit of the LORD departed from Saul, and an evil spirit [ra = evil, bad] from the LORD troubled him."

—**1 Samuel 16:14, KJV**

"And it came to pass on the morrow, that the evil spirit [ra = evil, bad] from God came upon Saul, and he prophesied in the midst of the house: and David played with his hand, as at other times: and there was a javelin in Saul's hand."

—**1 Samuel 18:10, KJV**

"And the evil spirit [ra = evil, bad] from the Lord was upon Saul, as he sat in his house with his javelin in his hand: and David played with his hand."

—**1 Samuel 19:9, KJV**

*"There came forth a **spirit**, and stood before the LORD, and said, I will persuade him. And the LORD said unto him, Wherewith? And he said, I will go forth, and I will be a lying spirit [sheqer = lie, falsehood)]in the mouth of all his prophets. And he said, Thou shalt persuade him, and prevail also: go forth, and do so. Now therefore, behold, the Lord hath put a **lying spirit** (sheqer = lie, falsehood) in the mouth of all these thy prophets, and the Lord hath spoken evil concerning thee."*

—1 Kings 22:21-23, KJV

"Then there came out a spirit, and stood before the LORD, and said, I will entice him. And the LORD said unto him, Wherewith? And he said, I will go out, and be a lying spirit [sheqer = lie, falsehood] in the mouth of all his prophets. And the LORD said, Thou shall entice him, and thou shalt also prevail: go out, and do even so. Now therefore, behold, the LORD hath put a lying spirit [sheqer = lie, falsehood] in the mouth of these thy prophets, and the LORD hath spoken evil against thee."

—2 Chronicles 18:20-23, KJV

"Pride goeth before destruction, and an haughty spirit [gobah = haughty, lofty, to soar, proud, raise up great height, upward] before a fall."

—Proverbs 16:18, KJV

"A merry heart doeth good like a medicine: but a broken spirit [nake = broken, smitten, wounded, afflicted] drieth the bones."

—Proverbs 17:22, KJV

"The spirit of a man will sustain his infirmity; but a wounded spirit [nake = wounded, broken, smitten, broken] who can bear?"

—Proverbs 18:14, KJV

"And the spirit of Egypt shall fail in the midst thereof; and I will destroy the counsel thereof: and they shall seek to the idols, and to the charmers [ittim = to charm, fascinate, secret], and to them that have familiar spirits [ob = to mumble, ventriloquist], and to wizards [yiddeoni = a knowing one, conjure, a ghost]..."

—Isaiah 19:3, KJV

"The LORD hath mingled a perverse spirit [ivim =perverse, wicked, crooked, iniquity] in the midst thereof: and they have caused Egypt to err in every work thereof, as a drunken man staggereth in his vomit."

—Isaiah 19:14, KJV

"For the LORD hath called thee as a woman forsaken and grieved in spirit [atsab = to grieve, hurt, pain], and a wife of youth, when thou wast refused, saith thy God."

—Isaiah 54:6, KJV

"To appoint unto them that mourn in Zion, to give unto them beauty for ashes, the oil of joy for mourning, the garment of praise for the spirit of heaviness [kehah = heaviness, weakness, feeble]; that they might be called trees of righteousness, the planting of the Lord, that He might be glorified."

— Isaiah 61:3, KJV

"Behold, my servants shall sing for joy of heart, but ye shall cry for sorrow of heart, and shall howl for vexation [sheber=a breaking, destruction] of spirit."

—Isaiah 65:14, KJV

*"My people ask counsel at their stocks, and their staff declareth unto them: for the **spirit of whoredoms** [zenunim = fornication], adultery, play the harlot) hath caused them to err, and they have gone a whoring from under their God."*

—Hosea 4:12, KJV

*"They will not frame their doings to turn unto their God: for the **spirit of whoredoms** [zenunim = fornication, adultery, play the harlot] is in the midst of them, and they have not known the Lord."*

—Hosea 5:4, KJV

*"And it shall come to pass in that day, saith the Lord of hosts, that I will cut off the names of the idols out of the land, and they shall no more be remembered: and also I will cause the prophets and the **unclean spirit** [tumah =defile, filthy, impure] to pass out of the land."*

—Zechariah 13:2, KJV

Types of Spirits Found in the New Testament:

> *"When the even was come, they brought unto him many that **were possessed with demons:** and **he cast out the spirits** with his word, and healed all that were sick:"*
>
> **—Matthew 8:16, KJV**

> *"And when he had called unto him his twelve disciples, he gave them power against **unclean spirits** [akethartos = unclean, impure, foul, lewd], to cast them out, and to heal all manner of sickness and all manner of disease."*
>
> **—Matthew 10:1, KJV**

> *"Then was brought unto him one **possessed with a demon, blind, and dumb**: and he healed him, insomuch that the blind and dumb both spake and saw. And all the people were amazed, and said, is not this the son of David? But when the Pharisees heard it, they said, This fellow doth not **cast out demons**, but by Beelzebub the prince of demons. And Jesus knew their thoughts, and said unto them, Every kingdom divided against itself is brought to desolation; and every city or house divided against itself shall not stand: And **if Satan cast out Satan**, he is divided against himself; how shall then his kingdom stand? And if **I by Beelzebub cast out demons**, by whom do your children **cast them out**? Therefore they shall be your judges. But **if I cast out demons by the Spirit of God, then the kingdom of God is come unto you**. Or else how can one enter into a strong man's house, and spoil his goods, except he first bind the strong man? And then he will spoil his house. He that is not with me is against me; and he that gathereth not with me scattereth abroad."*
>
> **—Matthew 12:22-30, ASV**

*"And there was in their synagogue a man with an **unclean spirit** [alatjartps = unclean, impure, foul, lewd]; and he cried out, saying, Let us alone; what have we to do with thee, thou Jesus of Nazareth? Art thou come to destroy us? I know thee who thou art, the Holy One of God. And Jesus rebuked him, saying, Hold thy peace, and come out of him. And when the **unclean spirit** had torn him, and cried with a loud voice, he came out of him. And they were all amazed, insomuch that they questioned among themselves, saying, What thing is this? What new doctrine is this? For with authority commandeth he even the unclean spirits [akathartos = unclean, impure, foul, lewd], and they do obey him."*

—**Mark 1:23-27, KJV**

"For he [Jesus] said unto him, Come out of the man, thou unclean spirit [akathartos = unclean, impure, foul, lewd]."

—**Mark 5:8, KJV**

"When Jesus saw that the people came running together, he rebuked the foul spirit [akathartos = foul, unclean, impure, lewd]), saying unto him, Thou dumb and deaf spirit, I charge thee, come out of him, and enter no more into him."

—**Mark 9:25, KJV**

"And, behold, there was a woman which had a spirit of infirmity [astheneia = weakness, frailty, feebleness of body or mind] eighteen years, and was bowed together, and could in no wise life up herself. And when Jesus saw her, He called her to Him, and said unto her, Woman, thou art loosed from thine infirmity [estheneia = weakness, frailty, feebleness of body or mind]. And He laid His hands on her: and immediately she was made straight, and glorified God."

—**Luke 13:11-13, KJV**

"Now the Spirit speaketh expressly, that in the latter times some shall depart from the faith, giving heed to seducing spirits [apoplanao = to lead away, astray, deceiver, imposter], and doctrines of devils..."

—**1 Timothy 4:1, KJV**

"For God hath not given us the spirit of fear [deilia = timidity, fearful, faithless]; but of power, and of love, and of a sound mind."

—**2 Timothy 1:7, KJV**

"Beloved, believe not every spirit, but try [dokimazo = test, examine, determine, to prove] the spirits whether they are of God: because many false prophets are gone out into the world. Hereby know ye the Spirit of God: Every spirit that confesseth that Jesus Christ is come in the flesh is of God: And every spirit that confesseth not that Jesus Christ is come in the flesh is not of God: and this is that spirit of antichrist, whereof ye have heard that it should come; and even now already is it in the world."

—**1 John 4:1-3, KJV**

"We are of God: he that knoweth God heareth us; he that is not of God heareth not us. Hereby know we the spirit of truth, and the spirit of error [plane = wandering, straying, deceit]."

—**1 John 4:6, KJV**

"And I saw three unclean spirits [akathartos = impure, lewd, foul] like frogs come out of the mouth of the dragon, and out of the mouth of the beast, and out of the mouth of the false prophet. For they are the spirits of demons [daimon = a deified spirit,

devil], working miracles, which go forth unto the kings of the earth and of the whole world, to gather them to the battle of that great day of God Almighty."

—**Revelation 16:13-14, KJV**

"And he cried mightily with a strong voice, saying, Babylon the great is fallen, is fallen, and is become the habitation of devils, and the hold of every foul spirit [akathartos = unclean, impure, lewd], and a cage of every unclean and hateful bird. For all nations have drunk of the wine of the wrath of fornication, and the kings of the earth have committed fornication with her, and the merchants of the earth are waxed rich through the abundance of her delicacies. And I heard another voice from heaven, saying, **Come out of her, my people, that ye be not partakers of her sins, and that ye receive not her plagues."**

—**Revelation 18:2-4, KJV**

REASON #15: CURSING AND BAD LANGUAGE

"As he clothed himself with cursing like as with his garment, so let it come into his bowels like water, and like oil into his bones" (Psalm 109:18, KJV). **This means you actually poison your own body, with a filthy foul mouth.**

"His mouth is filled with cursing and deceit and oppression; under his tongue are mischief and iniquity."

—**Psalm 10:7, ESV**

> *"It is not what enters into the mouth that defiles the man, but what proceeds out of the mouth, this defiles the man."*
>
> —Matthew 15:11, NASB

In over 39 years of ministry, I've seen and experienced this hundreds of times, where people were not being healed, after I laid hands on them. The Holy Spirit would say to me, "They have a foul, filthy, perverted and unclean mouth, and son, this is holding up their healing. They need to repent and I will heal them now."

> *"But now you yourselves are to put off all these: anger, wrath, malice, blasphemy, filthy [foul] language out of your mouth"*
>
> —Colossians 3:8, NKJV

> *"If anyone thinks himself to be religious, and yet does not bridle his tongue but deceives his own heart, this man's religion is worthless."*
>
> —James 1:26, NASB

> *"You shall not take the name of the LORD your God in vain, for the LORD will not leave him unpunished who takes His name in vain."*
>
> —Exodus 20:7, NASB

> *"And there must be no filthiness [or unclean] and silly talk, or coarse jesting, which are not fitting, but rather giving of thanks."*
>
> —Ephesians 5:4, NASB

"For, 'The one who desires life, to love and see good days, must keep his **tongue** from evil and his lips from speaking corruption and deceit'" (1 Peter 3:10 NASB). Do you want a good life and see good days?

> *"With it we bless our Lord and Father, and with it we curse men, who have been made in the likeness of God; from the same mouth come both blessing and cursing. My brethren, these things ought not to be this way. Does a fountain send out from the same opening both fresh and bitter water?"*
>
> **—James 3:9-12, NASB**

Of all the creatures on this planet, only man has the ability to communicate through the spoken word. The power to use words is a unique and powerful gift from God.

Words have real power. In the beginning of creation, God spoke the worlds into being by the power of His *rhema*, or spoken word. God spoke, "Let there be…and it was so." Hebrews 11:3 states that words were the invisible force of bringing the worlds into existence.

> *"By faith we understand that the worlds were framed by the Word of God, so that the things which are seen were not made of things which are visible"*
>
> **—Hebrews 11:3, NKJV**

The Lord wants to heal and bring blessing, but sometimes His work is hampered because of our cursing and bad language. He does not bless disobedience. He does not pour out healing when we grieve the Holy Spirit by what we speak.

> *"Let no corrupt [foul or filthy] word proceed out of your mouth, but what is good for necessary edification, that it may impart grace to the hearers. **And do not grieve the Holy Spirit of God**, by whom you were sealed for the day of redemption. Let all bitterness, wrath, anger, clamor, and evil speaking be put away from you, with all malice."*
>
> **—Ephesians 4:29-31, NKJV**

We can grieve the Holy Spirit by our words and actions. The Holy Spirit is not some fleeting wisp of a vapor. He is God. Just like one can bring sorrow on a person by ill-spoken words, the Holy Spirit—the third Person of the Trinity—can be saddened by what we speak. **The word "grieve" means to shrink back or withdraw oneself. The word in the Greek means heavy sorrow.**[17]

When Christians cuss, swear, use foul, filthy, and vulgar language, it grieves the Holy Ghost and He is heavily sorrowed and withdraws Himself. Do you really want to be healed? Then repent and cleanse yourself, and He will heal you. He loves you, and healing is available to you, as a free gift, just like salvation—only don't hinder it.

> *"Therefore, since we have these promises, dear friends, let us purify [and cleanse] ourselves from everything that contaminates body and spirit, perfecting holiness out of reverence for God."*
>
> **—2 Corinthians 7:1, NIV**

---

[17] "G3076 - lypeō - Strong's Greek Lexicon (KJV)." Blue Letter Bible. Web. 17 Jul. 2017

From the Abundance of the Heart

Words are the external fruit of what is inside a person's heart. What is inside is what is going to come out. Jesus said that we are going to be judged by our words to be justified or condemned.

> *"...out of the abundance of the heart the mouth speaks. A good man out of the good treasure of his heart brings forth good things, and an evil man out of the evil treasure brings forth evil things. But I say to you that for every idle word men may speak, they will give account of it in the day of judgment. For by your words you will be justified, and by your words you will be condemned."*
>
> **—Matthew 12:34b-37, NKJV**

"The tongue has the power of life and death, and those who love it will eat its fruit" (Proverbs 18:21 NIV). If you have a foul mouth, you will eat the fruit thereof and that may well be a terrible sickness.

> *"If anyone thinks he is religious and does not bridle his tongue but deceives his heart, this person's religion is worthless."*
>
> **—James 1:26, ESV**

> *"Whoever keeps his mouth and his tongue keeps himself out of trouble."*
>
> **—Proverbs 21:23, ESV**

"But avoid irreverent babble, for it will lead people into more and more ungodliness,"

—**2 Timothy 2:16, ESV**

"Let the words of my mouth and the meditation of my heart be acceptable in your sight, O Lord, my rock and my redeemer."

—**Psalm 19:14, ESV**

"Set a guard, O Lord, over my mouth; keep watch over the door of my lips!"

—**Proverbs 141:3, ESV**

"The good person out of the good treasure of his heart produces good, and the evil person out of his evil treasure produces evil, for out of the abundance of the heart his mouth speaks."

—**Luke 6:45, ESV**

"Put away from you crooked speech, and put devious talk far from you."

—**Proverbs 4:24, ESV**

"A worthless person, a wicked man, goes about with crooked speech,"

—**Proverbs 6:12, ESV**

"Do not be conformed to this world, but be transformed by the renewal of your mind, that by testing you may discern what is the will of God, what is good and acceptable and perfect."

—Romans 12:2, ESV

"Let your speech always be gracious, seasoned with salt, so that you may know how you ought to answer each person."

—Colossians 4:6, ESV

"His mouth is filled with cursing and deceit and oppression; under his tongue are mischief and iniquity."

—Psalm 10:7, ESV

"Husbands, love your wives, just as Christ also loved the church and gave Himself for her, that He might sanctify and cleanse her with the washing of water by the word,"

—Ephesians 5:25-26, NKJV

Before I was a Christian, I was one of the worst foul-mouth persons you'd want to meet. When I got saved, my heart was touched and changed. Immediately I was talking differently than I had before. Even so, the Lord revealed to me when I first got saved and began my walk of faith and following Jesus, that when I said things that grieved Him, I felt grieved in my spirit. As I grew in the faith, my cursing ceased. The Lord is my Savior. He is also my Friend. Jesus told His disciples that He no longer called them servants. He called them friend.

> *"Greater love has no one than this, than to lay down one's life for his friends. You are My friends if you do whatever I command you. No longer do I call you servants, for a servant does not know what his master is doing; but I have called you friends, for all things that I heard from My Father I have made known to you."*
>
> **—John 15:13-15, NKJV**

The Lord had delivered me from a great pit of darkness, and I was so thankful that when I said something I knew grieved Him, I was quick to say, "I'm sorry, Lord. Please forgive me. Please help deliver me and work in me." Correction from the Lord through His Holy Spirit is never condemnatory, but rather convicting, and the Word cleanses. See, I was washed by the spoken *rhema* word from the Holy Ghost, which does not bring condemnation, but a godly repentance to be more like Jesus. Amen!

When we are filled with His forgiveness and thankfulness, walk in humility, and love others as we have been forgiven and loved, we can usher in His kingdom into our lives. His kingdom is righteousness, peace, and joy in the Holy Ghost. Do not let circumstances dictate what you speak. Let what you speak dictate your circumstances.

We can't escape times of tribulation in this life, and when trouble happens, it is not the time to curse and use coarse foul language. Jesus' answer was to be of good cheer because He has overcome the world (see John 16:33). If we could get ahold of that one concept, we wouldn't get down in the mouth and dragged into depression and anxiety every time things go wrong. Sometimes, our world comes unraveled and seems to blow apart all at once. What is the answer? Is it to gripe, moan, curse, cuss, and complain when nothing is going right? Jesus said for us to be of good cheer.

> *"These things I have spoken to you, that in Me you may have peace. In the world you will have tribulation; but be of good cheer, I have overcome the world."*
>
> **—John 16:33, NKJV**

> *""Rejoice in the Lord always: and again I say, Rejoice. Let your moderation be known unto all men. The Lord is at hand. Be careful for nothing; but in every thing by prayer and supplication with thanksgiving let your requests be made known unto God. And the peace of God, which passeth all understanding, shall keep your hearts and minds through Christ Jesus. Finally, brethren, whatsoever things are true, whatsoever things are honest, whatsoever things are just, whatsoever things are pure, whatsoever things are lovely, whatsoever things are of good report; if there be any virtue, and if there be any praise, think on these things."*
>
> **—Philippians 4:4-8, KJV**

When things are going right or things are going wrong, we are to rejoice always, because God is working a good work. Notice it doesn't say *for* everything give thanks, but *in* everything. When the storms are raging and things look the worst, speaking praise and thanksgiving to the Lord is the ultimate display of faith.

> *"See that no one renders evil for evil to anyone, but always pursue what is good both for yourselves and for all. Rejoice always, pray without ceasing, in everything give thanks; [no more foul or abusive language]) for this is the will of God in Christ Jesus for you."*
>
> **—1 Thessalonians 5:15-18, NKJV**

While cursing grieves the Lord and bad language hampers God's blessing, praise has the power to open prison doors. Is your prison sickness? What are your shackles? Are they depression and anxiety? Whatever pain has held you, it can't bear the glory that comes when the Lord hears the sweet sound of praise in our darkest midnight hour.

The Lord inhabits our praises. Praising has the power to change our circumstances in our midnight hour. Thank Him for His healing power and the blood that saves. When Paul and Silas were thrown into a dark and filthy prison, shackled with chains, in the midnight hour they began praying and singing hymns to God, loud enough for the other prisoners to hear.

> *"But at midnight Paul and Silas were praying and singing hymns to God, and the prisoners were listening to them. Suddenly there was a great earthquake, so that the foundations of the prison were shaken; and immediately all the doors were opened and everyone's chains were loosed."*
>
> **—Acts 16:25-26, NKJV**

Praising and Giving Thanks Brings His Light

When bitterness is replaced by forgiveness, and when wrath and anger are replaced with humility and longsuffering, bitter and hateful speaking and cursing will cease.

The word "clamor" is a combination of tumult and crying. Today we might define it as loud, continuous, negative whining. When clamor is replaced by joy and thankfulness, then language that praises the Lord will break the atmosphere of doom and gloom, sickness and despair created by continual complaining.

> *"And they overcame him by the blood of the Lamb and by the word of their testimony, and they did not love their lives to the death."*
>
> **—Revelation 12:11, NKJV**

Sickness comes from the Devil. When we curse and use bad language, we glorify him and open the door for him. When we submit our heart, mind and mouth to the Word and to Jesus and proclaim our victory in Him and speak of His goodness in our lives, we put the Devil under our feet. Jesus provided us His blood and we proclaim His truth. By these two things, it says in the book of Revelation that the Devil is overcome. We can praise Him and proclaim thanks for the power of His blood.

REASON #16: INTEGRITY IN BUSINESS (which includes pastors and their money dealings)

God said to Ezekiel that the pastors were feeding themselves with the very best, yet the sheep, were going without food and proper comfort and care.

> *"The word of the LORD came to me: "Son of man, prophesy against the shepherds of Israel; prophesy and say to them:* ***'This is what the Sovereign LORD says: Woe to you shepherds of Israel who only take care of yourselves!*** *Should not shepherds take care of the flock? You eat the curds, clothe yourselves with the wool and slaughter the choice animals, but you do not take care of the flock. You have not strengthened the weak or healed the sick or bound up the injured. You have not brought back the strays or searched for the lost. You have ruled them harshly and brutally. So they were scattered because there was no shepherd, and when they were scattered they became food for all the wild animals. My sheep wandered over all the mountains and on every high hill. They were scattered over the whole earth, and no one searched or looked for them. Therefore, you shepherds, hear*

the word of the LORD: As surely as I live, declares the Sovereign LORD, because my flock lacks a shepherd and so has been plundered and has become food for all the wild animals, and because my shepherds did not search for my flock but cared for themselves rather than for my flock, therefore, you shepherds, hear the word of the LORD: This is what the Sovereign LORD says: I am against the shepherds and will hold them accountable for my flock. I will remove them from tending the flock so that the shepherds can no longer feed themselves. I will rescue my flock from their mouths, and it will no longer be food for them."

—**Ezekiel 34:1-10, NIV**

"Woe to the shepherds who are destroying and scattering the sheep of My pasture!" declares the Lord. 2Therefore thus says the Lord God of Israel concerning the shepherds who are tending My people: "You have scattered My flock and driven them away, and have not attended to them; behold, I am about to attend to you for the evil of your deeds," declares the Lord."

—**Jeremiah 23:1-2, NASB**

Paul warned Timothy about such men.

These men of "corrupt mind" supposed godliness was a means of gain and their desire for riches was a trap that brought them "into ruin and destruction" (1 Timothy 6:9). The pursuit of wealth is a dangerous path for Christians and one that God warns about: "For the love of money is a root of all kinds of evil. Some people, eager for money [fame and wealth] have wandered from the faith and pierced themselves with many griefs" (1 Timothy 6:10). If riches were a reasonable goal for the godly, Jesus would have pursued it, but He did not. Paul said covetousness is idolatry (Ephesians 5:5) and instructed the Ephesians to avoid anyone who brought a message of immorality or covetousness (Ephesians 5:6-7).

God is watching Christian businessmen too!

I once knew a Christian businessman who was involved in some shady business dealings. I knew in my spirit that he would not repent, because about 5 million dollars was involved. The Lord showed me in the Spirit that a powerful curse had come on him because of it. He soon became very sick, as did his wife. His family fell apart and he ended up divorced. He lost most of his money and he never did get healed from his sickness.

Over the years, I have personally known seven ministers of the gospel who were involved in shady business dealings. I tried to warn them, but invariably, they all ended up in ruin, losing all their money. Plus, they all ended up very sick, and three died young. You choose who you are going to follow—the god of this world or Jesus.

*"He who is greedy for gain troubles his own house, But he who **hates bribes** will live"* (Proverbs 15:27 NKJV). If you don't **hate bribes,** you will not live.

*"So are the ways of **everyone** who is greedy for gain; It takes away the life of its owners"* (Proverbs 1:19 NKJV). Repent or it will take away your life.

> *"For the love of money is the root of all evil: [sickness is an evil] which while some coveted after, they have erred from the faith, and pierced themselves through with many sorrows."*
>
> **—1 Timothy 6:10, KJV**

When a Christian person in business becomes ensnared in greed and dishonest dealings, the curse that he brings upon his house can include sickness. When the business is run honestly, the Lord can bring blessings.

When wealth comes from the Lord, the Word says that he adds no sorrow with it.

> *"The blessing of the LORD makes one rich, And He adds no sorrow with it."*
>
> **—Proverbs 10:22, NKJV**

If you run a business through shady and dishonest dealings motivated by greed, this can bring the curse of sickness. **The answer is to do all work as unto the Lord with integrity.**

REASON #17: THE CURSE OF SIN UNTO DEATH

The "sin unto death" is brought on by willful, continuous, unrepentant sin.

By His stripes we are already healed. Therefore, God does not put sickness or diseases on people, nor does He withhold healing from anyone. but some people do terrible things and won't repent, whereby placing themselves under a curse. If they would only repent, it would lift off them, but God did not do it; they brought it on themselves.

> *"What shall we say then? Shall we continue in sin [this means willfully sinning] that grace may abound? Certainly not! [The Greek word means God forbids it]. How shall we who died to sin live any longer in it? Or do you not know that as many of us as were baptized into Christ Jesus were baptized into His death? Therefore we were buried with Him through baptism into death, that just as Christ was raised from the dead by the glory of the Father, even so we also should walk in newness of life...*

> *Therefore, do not let sin reign in your mortal body, that you should obey it in its lusts. And do not present your members as instruments of unrighteousness to sin, but present yourselves to God as being alive from the dead, and your members as instruments of righteousness to God.* ***For sin shall not have dominion over you, for you are not under law but under grace."***
>
> —**Romans 6:1-4, 12-14, NKJV**

When we are under grace, we have ceased from sin. Willful continuous sinning pulls people from out of the protection zone of grace and puts them under the curse. God doesn't do it, but rather they do it to themselves.

One Sunday I was preaching in a church revival meeting on the subject of God's unconditional grace and how we've been blessed from heaven with the free gift of salvation. I said that means there's nothing we can do to merit salvation. After I finished, a young man came up to me and said, "We're under grace and God will cover all my sins—past, present, and future, right?" I replied, "When Jesus shed His blood on the cross, yes, He paid for all our sins forever." "But..." I said, "that doesn't give us a license to sin." He then said to me, "I was taught in a big church that if I sin, I don't have to repent for the sin, because it's already taken care of."

I said, "Have you read the book of Revelation, where eleven times God tells His people to repent? Three of those warnings were given to the seven New Testament churches, and once to Jezebel who was a false teacher in the church. Jesus said to His churches, *'If you don't repent, I'll remove your candlestick.'*" "No," I said, **"You have been taught a lie.** If you sin, God's word said repent. Yes, the blood will cover and wash away your sin, but you need to repent of that sin."

1 John 1:9 (NIV) says, "If we confess our sins, he is faithful and just and will forgive us our sins and purify us from all unrighteousness."

> *"Pursue peace with all people, and holiness, without which no one will see the Lord: looking carefully **lest anyone fall short of the grace of God**; lest any root of bitterness springing up cause trouble, and by this many become defiled; lest there be any fornicator or profane person like Esau, who for one morsel of food sold his birthright."*
>
> **—Hebrews 12:14-16, NKJV**

> *"If you see any brother or sister commit a sin that does not lead to death, you should pray and God will give them life. I refer to those whose sin does not lead to death. There is a sin that leads to death. I am not saying that you should pray about that."*
>
> **—1 John 5:16, NIV**

Compare this verse to what happened to Ananias and Sapphira in Acts 5:1–10 (see also 1 Corinthians 11:30). The "sin unto death" is willful, continuous, deliberate unrepentant sin. God has called His children to holiness (1 Peter 1:16), and He corrects them when they sin. We are not "punished" for our sin in the sense of losing salvation or being eternally separated from God, yet we are disciplined. "The Lord disciplines the one he loves, and he chastens everyone he accepts as his son" (Hebrews 12:6 NIV).

1 John 5:16 says there comes a point when God can no longer allow a believer to continue in unrepentant sin. When that point is reached, God may decide to take the life of that willfully stubborn sinful believer. The "death" is physical death. God at times purifies His church by removing

those who deliberately disobey Him. The apostle John makes a distinction between the "sin that leads to death" and the "sin that does not lead to death." Not all sin in the church is dealt with the same way because not all sin rises to the level of the "sin that leads to death."
In Acts 5:1–10 and 1 Corinthians 11:28–32, God dealt with intentional, calculated sin in the church by taking the physical life of the sinner. This is perhaps also what Paul meant in 1 Corinthians 5:5 by "the destruction of the flesh.".

John says that we should pray for Christians who are sinning, and that God will hear our prayers. However, there comes a time when God decides to cut short a believer's life due to willful unrepentant sin. Prayers for such an unheeding person will not be effective.

God is loving, good, and just, and He will eventually make us "a radiant church, without stain or wrinkle or any other blemish, but holy and blameless" (Ephesians 5:27). To further that end, God chastens His children by allowing the curse to work. May the Lord preserve us from the hard-heartedness that would cause us to commit the "sin unto death."

A Powerful Personal Testimony

Many years ago. I was preaching in a large church I'd never been to before. When I started to pray for the sick, a woman was brought to me in a wheelchair who was dying of cancer and was crippled. When I laid hands on her, the Holy Spirit said to me, "I refuse you to pray for her." I said, "Lord, how could that be?" And I went to pray for her again, and again the Lord said, "Get your hands off her. Don't pray for her because she has sinned unto death."

Up until that time I had only encountered this from the Lord once before. After the service that night, I asked the pastor about the woman, telling him what the Lord had said to me about her, and not to pray for her, because she had sinned unto death.

I learned that her first husband divorced her because she committed adultery with a man in this church. She then married her new lover and they were married for just a few years before that husband divorced her too, because she committed adultery with another man in this church. She then married her new lover (her third marriage now) and she was still married to him, except she has committed adultery two more times with different men from this city.

She refused to be counseled or corrected in any way (she was a very stubborn woman) and no one could help her. Just about a year ago, she fell very sick, and later fell and smashed her spine. Now she's a cripple in a wheelchair, and dying with cancer. **The pastor said, "She'll be gone soon."** He then added, "Wow! So that's why none of us were able to pray her through to healing." Then he said, "This is her life's history for the past twenty years. She's been married three times, and destroyed all those people's lives, and never repented."

Jesus came, not to condemn the world, but to save it. He loved us enough to lay down His life for us. Once we believe in Him, belong to Him, He loves us where we are at, but loves us enough to mold us into what he wants us to become when we continue to follow Him. He said, "If you love Me, keep my commandments" (John 14:15 NKJV).

Part of Jesus' love for us is chastisement to bring repentance and warning us regarding the consequences of willfully continuing in sin. This He told to the church at Laodicea. He can speak to us through His Word and by His Spirit.

Chastening from the Lord is proof that we belong to Him and that He loves us as a Father. He corrects and chastens us because He loves us as His legitimate children and wants us to glorify Him and bear good fruit.

> *"My son, do not despise the chastening of the LORD, Nor detest His correction; For whom the LORD loves He corrects, Just as a father the son in whom he delights."*
>
> **—Proverbs 3:11-12, NKJV**

> *If you endure chastening, God deals with you as with sons; for what son is there whom a father does not chasten? But if you are without chastening, of which all have become partakers, then you are illegitimate and not sons."*
>
> **—Hebrews 12:7-8, NKJV**

> *"As many as I love, I rebuke and chasten. Therefore be zealous and repent."*
>
> **—Revelation 3:19, NKJV**

Jesus had healed a man at the well of Bethesda who'd been stricken with an infirmity and unable to walk for 38 years.

> *"Afterward Jesus found him in the temple, and said to him, "See, you have been made well. Sin no more, lest a worse thing come upon you."*
>
> **—John 5:14, NKJV**

We don't know what the sin was, but Jesus gave him a warning that if he decided to continue in sin, a worse thing could come upon him. If he repented and turned away from his sin, then he was safe from the "curse of something worse" which Jesus spoke of. Walking in continued healing was up to him.

When Jesus told the man to sin no more, it didn't mean he'd never sin again, but there was a particular willful sin that He was addressing.

If you are struggling with a particular sin in your life, then you need to continue to look to the Lord to overcome it in the power of His might and through the saving power of Jesus' blood. Decide or *will* that you will not continue in sin when the Lord convicts you in your spirit.

> *"No temptation has overtaken you except such as is common to man; but God is faithful, who will not allow you to be tempted beyond what you are able, but with the temptation will also make the way of escape, that you may be able to bear it."*
>
> **—1 Corinthians 10:13, NKJV**

We might think that we are the only person in our church struggling with a certain sin. The Bible says that all temptation is common to man. The Lord loves us enough to bring to our attention sin that causes broken fellowship. He gives us the solution, which is to repent, make a decision to change direction, and ask forgiveness.

Sound doctrine will address sin with mercy and love to bring about repentance, as Paul did in telling the church to confront the man with the sin of sexual immorality. (See 1 Corinthians 5:1-5.) Before the report that he had repented, Paul told the church to turn the man over to Satan for the destruction of his flesh. We know from the second letter to the Corinthians (2 Corinthians 2:5-11) the man had repented and the church was then told to receive him back with love. **Had he not repented,** he was in the Devil's hand to destruction. **That would have been a sickness unto death.**

> *"It is actually reported that there is sexual immorality among you, and such sexual immorality as is not even named among the Gentiles--that a man has his father's wife!*
>
> *And you are puffed up, and have not rather mourned, that he who has done this deed might be taken away from among you. For I indeed, as absent in body but present in spirit, have already judged (as though I were present) him who has so done this deed. In the name of our Lord Jesus Christ, when you are gathered together, along with my spirit, with the power of our Lord Jesus Christ, deliver such a one to Satan for the destruction of the flesh, that his spirit may be saved in the day of the Lord Jesus."*
>
> **—1 Corinthians 5:1-5, NKJV**

I've listed several scripture references for dealing with sin in the church. If a person will not listen to the conviction of the Holy Spirit, the Lord may bring people in for correction. If the person refuses to repent, then they are subject to chastisement of the Lord. At some point, they will be turned over to the destruction of the flesh that they may be saved in the day of the Lord Jesus.

> *"Brethren, if a man is overtaken in any trespass, you who are spiritual restore such a one in a spirit of gentleness, considering yourself lest you also be tempted."*
>
> **—Galatians 6:1, NKJV**

> *"Therefore take heed to yourselves and to all the flock, among which the Holy Spirit has made you overseers, to shepherd the church of God which He purchased with His own blood."*
>
> **—Acts 20:28, NKJV**

In 1 Corinthians 10:1-13, Paul recounts the judgment, which befell their forefathers when Moses led them out of Egypt, saying that those things became our examples. It was written for our admonition, summing up a warning for us, the church. "Therefore let him who thinks he stands take heed, lest he fall."

The listed sins and repercussions are that 23 thousand people died in one day because of committing sexual immorality. Those who tempted Christ were destroyed by serpents. Those who complained were destroyed by the destroyer. God scattered most of their bodies in the wilderness.

> *"But with most of them God was not well pleased, for their bodies were scattered in the wilderness. Now these things became our examples, to the intent that we should not lust after evil things as they also lusted. And do not become idolaters as were some of them. As it is written, 'The people sat down to eat and drink, and rose up to play.' Nor let us commit sexual immorality, as some of them did, and in one day twenty-three thousand fell; nor let us tempt Christ, as some of them also tempted, and were destroyed by serpents; nor complain, as some of them also complained, and were destroyed by the destroyer. Now all these things happened to them as examples, and they were written for our admonition, upon whom the ends of the ages have come."*
>
> **—1 Corinthians 10:5-11, NKJV**

The Lord will give grace to the humble in matters of sin and overcoming sinful habits, but He will resist the proud. Those who think they can play with fire and not get burned are not fooling the good Lord. He will convict us of our sin, and if we refuse to repent, then we take ourselves out of the Lord's perfect will of the blessings of health and healing and are **subjected to sickness, illness, and dying before our time.**

Judgment can come when a believer willfully decides to commit and continue in sin.

A young man wanted to talk with me after I finished preaching one night. He said, "If I go out and sleep with my girlfriend tonight, then God will forgive my sin, right?" I said, "You are playing with fire, because that's not grace you're dealing with, but rather judgment." I gave him the following scriptures to read:

Believers Are Dead to Sin and Alive to God

Now what is our response to be? Shall we sin to our heart's content and see how far we can exploit the grace of God? What a ghastly abhorrent thought!

> *"What shall we say [to all this]? Should we continue in sin and practice sin as a habit so that [God's gift of] grace may increase and overflow? Certainly not! How can we, the very ones who died to sin, continue to live in it any longer? Or are you ignorant of the fact that all of us who have been baptized into Christ Jesus were baptized into His death? We have therefore been buried with Him through baptism into death, so that just as Christ was raised from the dead through the glory and power of the Father, we too might walk habitually in newness of life [abandoning our old ways]. For if we have become one with Him [permanently united] in the likeness of His death, we will also certainly be [one with Him and share fully] in the likeness of His resurrection. We know that our old self [our human nature without the Holy Spirit] was nailed to the cross with Him, in order that our body of sin might be done away with, so that we would no longer be slaves to sin. For the person who has died [with Christ] has been freed from [the power of] sin. "Now if we have died with Christ, we believe that we will also live [together] with Him, because we know [the self-evident truth] that Christ, having been raised from the dead, will never die again; death no longer has power over Him. For the death that He died, He died*

> to sin *[ending its power and paying the sinner's debt] once and for all; and the life that He lives, He lives to [glorify] God [in unbroken fellowship with Him]. Even so, consider yourselves to be dead to sin [and your relationship to it broken], but alive to God [in unbroken fellowship with Him] in Christ Jesus. Therefore do not let sin reign in your mortal body so that you obey its lusts and passions. Do not go on offering members of your body to sin as instruments of wickedness. But offer yourselves to God [in a decisive act] as those alive [raised] from the dead [to a new life], and your members [all of your abilities —sanctified, set apart] as instruments of righteousness [yielded] to God. For sin will no longer be a master over you, since you are not under Law [as slaves], but under [unmerited] grace [as recipients of God's favor and mercy]. What then [are we to conclude]? Shall we sin because we are not under Law, but under [God's] grace? Certainly not! Do you not know that when you continually offer yourselves to someone to do his will, you are the slaves of the one whom you obey, either [slaves] of sin, which leads to death, or of obedience, which leads to righteousness (right standing with God)?"*
>
> **—Romans 6:1-16, AMP**

The solution to this **"curse of sin unto death"**—which can bring sickness and hinder healing even unto death—is for us to **repent** of the sin, then commit to following Jesus and His Word. **To love Jesus is to obey His commandments. (See John 14:15.)** When He convicts us of sin in our lives, we need to repent and turn from satisfying the lusts of our flesh and walk after the Spirit of life in Christ Jesus. **He may be your Savior, but you need to make Him Lord over your life, then healing and all the blessings of God will flow freely.**

REASON #18: NOT PUTTING ON THE WHOLE ARMOR GOD

People who do not put on the whole armor of God will not be able to stand against the wiles of the Devil…one of those wiles of the Devil is sickness and disease.

Sickness and disease come from the Devil. We have a sure defense against him in putting on the armor of God. It tells us to be strong in the Lord and the power of His might, and by what means.

The first piece of armor is truth.

> *"As He spoke these words, many believed in Him. Then Jesus said to those Jews who believed Him, 'If you abide in My word, you are My disciples indeed. And you shall know the truth, and the truth shall make you free.'"*
>
> —**John 8:30-32, NKJV**

We hear and believe. Faith comes by hearing the Word. Jesus said that if we continue and abide in His Word, we are His disciples, coming to knowing the truth, which shall make us free.

> ***Put on the whole armor of God****, that you may be able to stand against the wiles of the devil. For we do not wrestle against flesh and blood, but against principalities, against powers, against the rulers of the darkness of this age, against spiritual hosts of wickedness in the heavenly places. **Therefore, take up the whole armor of God, that you may be able to withstand in the evil day, and having done all, to stand. Stand therefore, having girded your waist with truth, having put on the breastplate of righteousness, and having shod your feet with the preparation***

of the gospel of peace. Above all, taking the shield of faith with which you will be able to quench all the fiery darts of the wicked one. And take the helmet of salvation, and the sword of the Spirit, which is the Word of God;"

—**Ephesians 6:11-17, NKJV**

"What is the full armor of God?"

The phrase "the full armor of God" comes from Ephesians 6:13-17 (ESV): "Therefore put on the full armor of God, so that when the day of evil comes, you may be able to stand your ground, and after you have done everything, to stand. Stand firm then, with the belt of truth buckled around your waist, with the breastplate of righteousness in place, and with your feet fitted with the readiness that comes from the gospel of peace. In addition to all this, take up the shield of faith, with which you can extinguish all the flaming arrows of the evil one. Take the helmet of salvation and the sword of the Spirit, which is the Word of God."

Ephesians 6:12 clearly indicates that the conflict with Satan is spiritual, and therefore no tangible weapons can be effectively employed against him and his minions. We are not given a list of specific tactics Satan will use. However, the passage is quite clear that when we follow all the instructions faithfully, we will be able to stand, and we will have victory regardless of Satan's strategies.

The first element of our armor is *truth* (verse 14). This is easy to understand, since Satan is said to be the "father of lies" (John 8:44). Deception is high on the list of things God considers to be an abomination. A "lying tongue" is one of the things He describes as "detestable to Him" (Proverbs 6:16-17). We are therefore exhorted to put on truth for our own sanctification, deliverance, and victory in life. If we do not know the truth about our healing that has already been paid for by Jesus **(by his**

stripes we are healed—Isaiah 53:5; He took our infirmities and bare our sicknesses on Himself—Matthew 8; by His stripes we were healed —1 Peter 2:24), then we will be double-minded on this issue of "does God still heal today". If we are double-minded, we will not receive anything from God (read James 1:1-8), even though it is His will to heal us.

Also in verse 14, we are told to put on the *breastplate of righteousness*. A breastplate shielded a warrior's vital organs from blows that would otherwise be fatal. This righteousness is not works done by men. Rather, this is the righteousness of Christ, imputed by God and received by faith, which guards our hearts against the accusations and charges of Satan and secures our innermost being from his attacks.

Verse 15 speaks of the preparation of the feet for spiritual conflict. In warfare, sometimes an enemy places dangerous obstacles in the path of advancing soldiers. The idea of the preparation of the *gospel of peace* as footwear suggests what we need to advance into Satan's territory, aware that there will be traps, with the message of grace so essential to winning souls to Christ. Satan has many obstacles placed in the path to halt the propagation of the gospel.

The *shield of faith* spoken of in verse 16 makes Satan's sowing of doubt about the faithfulness of God and His Word ineffective. Our faith—of which Christ is "the author and perfecter" (Hebrews 12:2)— is like a golden shield, precious, solid, and substantial, and is able to sustain us through all battles.

The *helmet of salvation* in verse 17 is protection for the head, keeping viable a critical part of the body. We could say that our way of thinking needs preservation. The head is the seat of the mind which—when it has laid hold of the sure gospel hope of eternal life—will not receive false doctrine or give way to Satan's temptations. **To say that God doesn't heal today is a doctrine of devils and demons.**

The Helmet of Salvation

A helmet protects the head, which is a picture of covering for the mind. We received salvation because of a decision we made. We receive the things of God because we make a choice to hear, believe, and abide in all the blessings of God.

We can't control every thought that comes into our head, but we can control what we do with every thought. If we give place to wrong thinking by mulling over and over those things that are contrary to the Word of God, it will affect the emotions. The Devil will speak lies to us in regard to our situations that will always be contrary to God's Word.

When we make a decision to meditate on the Scriptures with our minds and hearts, we bring them from our head down into our hearts where they produce the fruit of faith. When the Devil speaks his lies, we can combat him with the truth of the Word as Jesus did when He was tempted of the Devil after fasting forty days. When our heart is filled with the Word, we will be speaking it out of the abundance in our heart, mingled with faith.

Verse 17 interprets itself as to the meaning of the sword of the Spirit—it is the Word of God. While all the other pieces of spiritual armor are defensive in nature, the *sword of the Spirit* is the only offensive weapon in the armor of God. It speaks of the holiness and authoritative power of the Word of God. A greater spiritual weapon is not conceivable. In Jesus' temptations in the desert, the Word of God was always His overpowering response to Satan. When we are attacked by the Devil in the area of healing ("Does God still heal today?"), what a blessing that the same Word is available to us! We can say, **"Devil, by Jesus' stripes I am already healed, and now I'm standing in faith and waiting for the natural breakthrough in my life."**

> *"Fight the good fight of faith, lay hold on eternal life, whereunto thou art also called, and hast professed a good profession before many witnesses."*
>
> **—1 Timothy 6:12, KJV**

> *"So we look not at the things which are seen, but at the things which are unseen; for the things which are visible are temporal [just brief and fleeting], but the things which are invisible are everlasting and imperishable."*
>
> **—2 Corinthians 4:18, AMP**

In verse 18, we are told to pray in the Spirit—that is, with the mind of Christ, with His heart and His priorities—in addition to wearing the full armor of God. We cannot neglect prayer, as it is the means by which we draw spiritual strength from God. Without prayer, without reliance upon God, our efforts at spiritual warfare are empty and futile. **The full armor of God—truth, righteousness, the gospel, faith, salvation, the Word of God, and prayer**—are the tools God has given us, through which we can be spiritually victorious, overcoming Satan's attacks and temptations and **receive our healing from the Lord that has already been won for us on the cross.**

When some people come up for prayer, I know that they are not putting on the whole armor of God and they are being defeated in many areas of their lives, **including sickness and diseases**. The Devil comes in like a flood, and they are not able to raise up a standard in the Lord's power and Word against him. **They fail to stand their ground, and they often get sick. Healing doesn't come their way until they get the Word of God into them to strengthen them in their weakness of faith. So, put on the whole armor of God, so you can stand in the evil day. God has called you to be a winner.**

REASON #19: DO YOU WANT TO BE HEALED?

Some people do not want to be healed, even though they may go down to the front of a church for prayer.

I've dealt with this problem many hundreds of times in my ministry.

Now, that may sound like a strange spiritual quagmire, but it's the truth. Some people may say that they are believing for their healing, but secretly in their heart they are just playing along with the game. Some are happy to wallow in their misery, because they are looking for emotional support from a spouse, and others simply do not want to **lose disability or insurance benefits**. Sometimes the person's spouse doesn't want them to be healed for the same reason. How sad, when the dollar is more important than their healing and health.

I once was ministering in a church in California, when the Holy Ghost began to move powerfully and many people were being healed. All focus turned to a woman who pushed herself down to the front in a wheelchair because of an auto accident, she had no movement or feeling in her lower body, and hadn't walked in about five years. She spoke in a confident but soft demeanor: "After listening to your message on healing, I want to be healed."

The Lord prompted me to pray for her as there was an anointing for her miraculous healing. As I began praying over her, I felt a very strong, heavy and tangible anointing like fire falling and it encompassed her. I had to steady myself, as the power came suddenly and nearly knocked me to the floor. She yelled, "I've got feeling in my legs. I can move my feet! I can move my legs and hips. Oh my God; I'm healed!"

The church stirred with excitement as I proclaimed with bold authority, still under the heavy anointing, "In the name of Jesus, get up and walk!"

Her face beamed with joy and a supernatural radiance as she stood to her feet in amazement, and shouted, "God just healed me!"

To my shock, her husband ran to the front of the church where she stood in awe, quietly praising the Lord. Before she could take her first steps, he shoved her back into the wheelchair, and scowled, "No, my wife! I need the money we have coming from your insurance."

She immediately fell back into the wheelchair. I felt a very deep agony and terrible grief in my spirit. The power of God just lifted right off her. She looked down and muttered, "I can't move anything now." The people in the meeting seemed to hold their breath as she broke the awful silence with weeping and loud sobs. Her husband was cold and nonchalant as he pulled her chair around and wheeled her out the backdoor of the church. What a stinking filthy dog that man is.

In that instance, a spouse stood in the way of healing because of selfishness and greed, and the love of money. Sounds strange, doesn't it, but **it is the truth**. Some people come forward for prayer saying they want to be healed. They talk the faith talk and can quote scriptures, but in their heart of hearts, it is all for show. When the church, friends, or family members see that nothing happens when they pray, they blame God or the preacher.

Another Incredible Personal Testimony from My Australian Ministry

The year was 1988, two years before I came to the United States to live. A pastor from a large church in Brisbane, Australia, who I'd been doing revival meetings for, called me to see if I'd go and check on a lady who had been miraculously healed in one of his meetings about six weeks earlier. He hadn't heard from her or seen her in church for over a month. He said she had been in a road accident and broke her back and was confined to a wheelchair, completely disabled before the lord healed her.

The pastor gave me her address and phone number, and I called her on the phone, and then went to see her the next day. When I got there, her husband met me at the door and let me in the house. To my surprise, she was all crippled up in her wheelchair; her neck was bent over and twisted. Her arms were also slightly twisted as well, and she could barely speak.

I said, "Oh my God, sister, what happened to you? I heard you were completely healed, walking around normal." She said, "That's absolutely true as to what happened to me. The Lord healed me powerfully by His Holy Spirit, and for about a month I was getting around, driving my car, going out with friends for dinner, and shopping—just normal, like everyone else.

"Then my lawyer got in contact with me and said (one insurance company had already given her a lump sum of money), "We have won an appeal in your accident case and the judge has ordered the other insurance company to pay up as well. But that insurance company's doctors wanted to check you out one more time before paying up. If your condition is the same, they would clear you for a final payment of $270,000.00, plus they'll pay all costs, including your legal bills."

Well, it wasn't the same; she was healed. **What you are about to read next, will blow you away. It's very deep, but it's the truth!** This is what she said to me; "I wanted that money more than anything else, so I then renounced my healing because I want that amount of money, too." The next day as she went to get out of bed, she found she could hardly move, let alone get out of bed. Well people, the rest is history, she got her money and became a cripple again, only this time she was worse than she was before. I heard through the grapevine that about 18 months later she died. God is not mocked. What a man (or woman) sows, that will they reap.

> *"...the love of money is the root of all evil..."*
>
> **—1 Timothy 6:10a, KJV**

> *"For if after they have escaped the pollutions of the world through the knowledge of the Lord and Saviour Jesus Christ, they are again entangled therein, and overcome, the latter end is worse with them than the beginning."*
>
> **—2 Peter 2:20, KJV**

Some people realize that if they lose their benefits, they will need to go back to work. For sheer laziness they would rather just cling to their problems for the money. Others enjoy the emotional pay-off from the attention they receive from their condition.

I wonder how the Holy Spirit must feel when people choose money and attention over healing and wholeness. We don't know what is in a person's heart, and can't assume it is faith and good motives when we see somebody who doesn't receive healing.

REASON #20: PRAYER AND FASTING

You don't pray a demon out, you must cast it out, otherwise the person will never be free, or healed.

I've seen people praying for the sick and nothing was happening and I knew the person they prayed for needed deliverance first before healing would come.

> *"Then the spirit cried out, convulsed him greatly, and came out of him. And he became as one dead, so that many said, 'He is dead.' But Jesus took him by the hand and lifted him up, and he arose. And when He had come into the house, His disciples asked Him privately, 'Why could we not cast it out?' So He said to them,* **'This kind can come out by nothing but prayer and fasting.'** *"*
>
> —Mark 9:26-29, NKJV

Over the years I've had to fast for days and pray sometimes for many hours in the Holy Ghost before I got the breakthrough in the Spirit to be able to sense His leading to pray for the sick and dying. **But the demons won't go out through prayer, but rather, you have to cast them out in Jesus' name, then you can go ahead and pray the prayer of faith to heal the sick.**

Jesus would sometimes pray all night before preaching in the villages and praying for the sick. He came in the flesh and as a man, but needed to be empowered by the Holy Spirit and led by the Spirit to minister, just like we do. His habit was to set Himself apart to pray. He was seeking the will of the Father, because He didn't speak or do anything except what He saw His Father in heaven speak or do.

The Authority of the Son According to His Father's Command

> *"So, because Jesus was doing these things on the Sabbath, the Jewish leaders began to persecute him. In his defense Jesus said to them, 'My Father is always at his work to this very day, and I too am working.' For this reason they tried all the more to kill Him; not only was He breaking the Sabbath, but He was even calling God His own Father, making himself equal with God. Jesus gave them this answer: 'Very truly I tell you, the Son can do nothing by himself; he can do only what he sees his Father doing, because whatever the Father does the Son also does. For the Father loves the Son and shows him all he does. Yes, and he will show him even greater works than these, so that you will be amazed. For just as the Father raises the dead and gives them life, even so the Son gives life to whom he is pleased to give it. Moreover, the Father judges no one, but has entrusted all judgment to the Son, that all may honor the Son just as they honor the Father. Whoever does not honor the Son does not honor the Father, who sent him.' "*

—**John 5:16-23, NIV**

> *"Then Jesus said to them, **'When you lift up the Son of Man, then you will know that I am He, and that I do nothing of Myself; but as My Father taught Me, I speak these things.'** "*

—**John 8:28, NKJV**

> *"'For I have not spoken on My own authority; but the Father who sent Me gave Me a command, what I should say and what I should speak. And I know that His command is everlasting life. Therefore, whatever I speak, just as the Father has told Me, so I speak.'"*
>
> —**John 12:49-50, NKJV**

Jesus said that He did nothing of Himself, but only as He saw His Father in Heaven do. We must spend time in prayer sometimes to get a breakthrough in the Spirit and hear from the Lord. Sometimes, the Lord puts it on my spirit to fast. The Lord will empower you to break the bands of oppression and the yokes of bondage and sickness when we seek Him, are led by Him, and do as He directs, which was the secret to Jesus' powerful ministry.

When we had the big tent ministry (the tent was 180' x 60' and seated 2,000 people), in the first year alone, we saw 3,654 people give their lives to Jesus, over 5,300 out-of-church backsliders come back to the Lord, 29 people get out of wheelchairs, plus 57 people on canes, crutches, and walkers healed. Twenty-seven were healed from cancer —confirmed by a doctor's report, plus over 1,700 people were healed from other sicknesses and diseases.

As I said above, we saw hundreds healed and saved everywhere we put up the big tent. But there was a very powerful battle going on in the heavenly realm. I found myself fasting often, but more so, praying many hours every day in the Holy Ghost, and when I felt in my spirit that I had the breakthrough, I'd quit praying, and then we always got the victory. This is **called praying through—something most of this modern church today doesn't understand, nor care to.**

Souls were saved, and people were healed (Look at our website **EagleTabernacleHealingMinistries.com** to see all the before-and-after miracles of people getting out of wheelchairs, etc.). Prayer and fasting will always work, if it's done by the leading of the Holy Spirit and not in the flesh.

> *"With all prayer and petition pray [with specific requests] at all times [on every occasion and in every season]* **in the Spirit***, and with this in view, stay alert with all perseverance and petition [interceding in prayer] for all God's people."*
>
> —**Ephesians 6:18, AMP**

This means that every prayer we pray—no matter what type of prayer it is—should always start in the Spirit and not in the flesh.

> *"Is this not the fast that I have chosen: To loose the bonds of wickedness, To undo the heavy burdens, To let the oppressed go free, And that you break every yoke?"*
>
> —Isaiah 58:6, NKJV

This means, let's have a powerful revival.

REASON #21: THE TRADITIONS OF MEN WILL HINDER

Some say that God doesn't heal anymore, and they also say that the healing power went out with the end of the apostles.

> *"And Jesus answering said unto them, Do ye not therefore err, because ye know not the scriptures, neither the power of God?"*
>
> —**Mark 12:24, KJV**

The traditions of men—which nullify the true meaning of the scriptures—will never ever be supported by the Holy Spirit.

> *"Making the word of God of none effect through your tradition, which ye have delivered: and many such like things do ye."*
>
> —**Mark 7:13, KJV**

> *"That your faith should not stand in the wisdom of men, but in the power of God."*
>
> —**1 Corinthians 2:5, KJV**

> *"Let no man deceive himself. If any man among you seemeth to be wise in this world, let him become a fool, that he may be wise. For the wisdom of this world is foolishness with God. For it is written, He taketh the wise in their own craftiness."*
>
> —**1 Corinthians 3:18-19, KJV**

> *"For laying aside the commandment of God, ye hold the tradition of men, as the washing of pots and cups: and many other such like things ye do. And he said unto them, Full well ye reject the commandment of God, that ye may keep your own tradition. It's the same thing today, people!"*
>
> —**Mark 7:8-9, KJV**

"To the law and to the testimony: if they speak not according to this word, it is because there is no light in them."

—Isaiah 8:20, KJV

"Every Word of God is pure: he is a shield unto them that put their trust in him. Add thou not unto his words, lest he reprove thee, and thou be found a liar."

—Proverbs 30:5-6, KJV

"And if any man shall take away from the words of the book of this prophecy, God shall take away his part out of the book of life, and out of the holy city, and from the things which are written in this book."

—Revelation 22:19, KJV

*"Beloved, when I gave all diligence to write unto you of the common salvation, it was needful for me to write unto you, and exhort you that **ye should earnestly contend for the faith which was once delivered [or given] unto the saints.**"*

—Jude 3:1, KJV

"But we are bound to give thanks always to God for you, brethren beloved by the Lord, because God hath from the beginning chosen you to salvation through sanctification of the Spirit and belief of the truth: Whereunto he called you by our gospel, to the obtaining of the glory of our Lord Jesus Christ. Therefore, brethren, stand fast, and_hold the [true] traditions which ye have been taught,_whether by word, or our epistle."

—2 Thessalonians 2:13-15, KJV

They heard and experienced what the word was really all about. They saw the people getting healed, and the apostles said, "Follow what we are doing;" and that goes for this generation as well.

> *"Be ye followers of me, even as I also am of Christ. Now I praise you, brethren, that ye remember me in all things, and keep the ordinances [paradosis i.e. original traditions], as I delivered them to you."*
>
> **—1 Corinthians 11:1-2, KJV**

> *"Believe Me that I am in the Father and the Father is in Me—or at least believe because of the works themselves. Truly, truly, I tell you, whoever believes in Me will also do the works that I am doing. He will do even greater things than these, because I am going to the Father. And I will do whatever you ask in My name, so that the Father may be glorified in the Son."*
>
> **—John 14:11-13, BSB**

> *"Jesus Christ is the same yesterday, and today, and to [all] the ages."*
>
> **—Hebrews 13:8, BSB**

> *"I, the LORD, [will] never change."*
>
> **—Malachi 3:6a, GW**

> *"Then said the Lord unto me, "Thou hast well seen, for I will hasten My word to perform it."*
>
> —**Jeremiah 1:12, KJV**

Consider My Personal Testimony; How I Came to Christ

G'day Mate, Dan Nolan here. I was born in Australia, the Great Southland of the Holy Spirit, in 1952. I moved to the United States in 1990 and currently reside with my wife, Charlotte, in Arizona.

I was raised in Adelaide, Australia, in a very poor, dysfunctional, and abusive family. After dropping out of school I became a street kid at age 15. By 19, I was a biker gang leader, involved in drugs, rock 'n roll, and the occult. When I was 21, I had a work accident that took me off the job and in need of a major back operation. It was so severe that the doctors wanted to stick two rods up my back and they said that if I didn't, that by my mid-30s I would be confined to a wheelchair for the rest of my life. I was angry, broken, and had no hope...and was not a born-again Christian.

My brother eventually took me to a church that prayed for the sick. The preacher called me out by a word of knowledge, and God did an instant, creative miracle in my back. I was completely healed. Being overwhelmed with God's love, I accepted Christ into my heart. I was filled with the Spirit and I have loved God ever since.

Shortly after, the Lord healed my mind from a learning disability and told me to go back to school to complete my G.E.D. While completing my high school courses, I unexpectedly found myself laying in a hospital with a severely damaged smashed foot, with many broken bones from a sporting accident. The doctor said I would be in a cast up to my hip for three months, with more surgeries to follow. He added that I would probably walk with a limp the rest of my life. After the doctor left the room, I prayed and told God if He would heal my ankle, I would tell everyone what He had done. Suddenly, a pillar of fire came down from the ceiling and stood at the end of my bed. Out of it came the words, "I have called you to carry my healing anointing around the world." I was then healed instantly. I was shocked at what I saw and undone by what I heard Him say I was called to do.

I obtained my GED, and went on to get a Technical Building College associates degree. Afterwards, I entered the Panorama Business College, and received 97% for accounting and 86% for the other studies. By the time I was 34, I was working in middle management for one of Australia's biggest building companies (The Jennings Building Corporation) and enjoying my success when God spoke to me to go into full-time ministry. **I obeyed and have been in full-time ministry 31 years as of writing this book.**

Anytime we teach from the Bible, we take great care to distinguish between the traditions of men and the doctrines of God as revealed in His Word. Jesus Himself condemned those who would teach the traditions of men as biblical truth. He said:

> *"You hypocrites, rightly did Isaiah prophesy of you: 'This people honors me with their lips, but their heart is far away from me. But in vain do they worship me, teaching as doctrines the precepts of men.'"*
>
> —Matthew 15:7-9, NASB

The KJV uses the word "ordinances" where the ASV uses the word "tradition" in 1 Corinthians 11:2. "Now I praise you, brethren, that ye remember me in all things, and keep the ordinances [traditions, ASV], as I delivered them to you." Paul told the Corinthians that what he delivered unto them was what he had received by revelation of the Lord (1 Corinthians 15:3). Further, he said "that which I write unto

you are the commandments of the Lord" (1 Corinthians 14:37), but were "of my fathers." Paul warned the Colossians, "Beware lest any man spoil you [rob or deceive you]) through philosophy and vain deceit, after the tradition of men.

> *"Once God has spoken; twice have I heard this: that power belongs to God,"*
>
> **—Psalm 62:11, NASB**

> *"But if it is by the finger of God that I cast out demons, then the kingdom of God has come upon you."*
>
> **—Luke 11:20, ESV**

> *"But Jesus looked at them and said, 'With man this is impossible, but with God all things are possible.'"*
>
> **—Matthew 19:26, ESV**

Healing comes under the category of all things.

> *"And God is able to make all grace abound to you, so that always having all sufficiency in everything [healing is included in everything], you may have an abundance for every good deed."*
>
> **—2 Corinthians 9:8, ESV**

> "Now to Him who is able to do far more abundantly beyond all that we ask or think, according to the power that works within us."
>
> —Ephesians 3:20, ESV

All is included, that's healing too.

> "and being fully assured that what God had promised, He was able also to perform."
>
> —Romans 4:21, NASB

God has promised us healing.

> "but you will receive power when the Holy Spirit has come upon you; and you shall be My witnesses both in Jerusalem, and in all Judea and Samaria, and even to the remotest part of the earth."
>
> —Acts 1:8, NASB

> "in the power of signs and wonders, in the power of the Spirit; so that from Jerusalem and round about as far as Illyricum I have fully preached the gospel of Christ."
>
> —Romans 15:19, NASB

> "My message and my preaching were not in persuasive words of wisdom, but in demonstration of the Spirit and of power, so that your faith would not rest on the wisdom of men, but on the power of God."
>
> —1 Corinthians 2:4-5, NASB

> *"for our gospel did not come to you in word only, but also in power and in the Holy Spirit and with full conviction; just as you know what kind of men we proved to be among you for your sake."*
>
> —**1 Thessalonians 1:5, NASB**

> *"For the kingdom of God is not a matter of talk but of power."*
>
> —**1 Corinthians 4:20, NIV**

> *"Jesus Christ is the same yesterday and today and forever."*
>
> —**Hebrews 13:8, ESV**

If He healed then, He'll do it now. Just believe. Don't let the spiritually dead, foolish virgins, kill your faith.

> *"For I am the LORD, I do not change;"*
>
> —**Malachi 3:6, NKJV**

REASON #22: NOT SERVING GOD WITH A GLAD HEART

David, "a man after God's own heart" (Act 13:22), loved to worship God. He was glad when asked to go to the house of the Lord (Psalm 122:1).

"The king shall have joy in Your strength, O LORD; And in Your salvation how greatly shall he rejoice!"

—Psalm 21:1b, NKJV

"And now my head shall be lifted up above my enemies all around me; Therefore I will offer sacrifices of joy in His tabernacle; I will sing, yes, I will sing praises to the LORD."

—Psalm 27:6, NKJV

"Be glad in the LORD and rejoice, you righteous; And shout for joy, all you upright in heart!"

—Psalm 32:11, NKJV

"O clap your hands, all ye people; shout unto God with the voice of triumph. For the LORD most high is terrible; he is a great King over all the earth. He shall subdue the people under us, and the nations under our feet. He shall choose our inheritance for us, the excellency of Jacob whom he loved. Selah. God is gone up with a shout, the LORD with the sound of a trumpet. Sing praises to God, sing praises: sing praises unto our King, sing praises. For God is the King of all the earth: sing ye praises with understanding. God reigneth over the heathen: God sitteth upon the throne of his holiness. The princes of the people are gathered together, even the people of the God of Abraham: for the shields of the earth belong unto God: he is greatly exalted."

—Psalm 47:1-9, KJV

Singing is an important element of "serving the Lord with gladness."

> *"Therefore by Him let us continually offer the sacrifice of praise to God, that is, the fruit of our lips, giving thanks to His name. ¹⁶ But do not forget to do good and to share, for with such sacrifices God is well pleased."*
>
> —**Hebrews 13:15-16, NKJV**

> *"'You shall worship the LORD your God, and Him only you shall serve.'"*
>
> —**Luke 4:8b, NKJV**

In Old Testament times who delighted in singing (Psalm 63:3-5), Christians are taught to worship God in a similar way (James 5:13).

We Need to Serve the Lord with Gladness

God desires that we be so convinced of His tender love, so persuaded He is at work bringing us into His best, that we will have continual joy and gladness in our walk with Him! Moses warned Israel, **"Because you did not serve the LORD your God with joy and gladness of heart, for the abundance of all things, therefore you shall serve your enemies,** whom the Lord will send against you, in hunger, in thirst, in nakedness, and in need of all things" (Deuteronomy 28:47-48).

God is saying to us today, "Be glad and rejoice in what I have already done for you! If you go around moping, murmuring, and complaining, you will forever be spiritually starved and naked—a prey to your enemies!" God wants us to so trust in His love for us that we will be testimonies of gladness and good cheer! He wants preachers who are glad at heart, filled with a gladness that is based on truth.

His truth produces a wealth of gladness that flows naturally outward from the heart:

"Serve the LORD with gladness; come before His presence with singing" (Psalm 100:2). "He brought out His people with joy, His chosen ones with gladness" (Psalm 105:43). "Be glad in the LORD and rejoice, you righteous; and shout for joy, all you upright in heart!" (Psalm 32:11). "Let the righteous be glad; let them rejoice before God; yes, let them rejoice exceedingly" (Psalm 68:3).

You may ask, "How long can I expect to maintain joy in my service to the Lord?" Many believe that it lasts only as long as seasons of refreshing come from on high or as long as things go right. No, we are to have joy at all times! That is exactly what the Bible says:

> *"Oh, satisfy us early with Your mercy, that we may rejoice and be glad all our days!"*
>
> **—Psalm 90:14, NKJV**

> *"But be glad and rejoice forever in what I create; for behold, I create Jerusalem as a rejoicing, and her people a joy."*
>
> **—Isaiah 65:18, NKJV**

We are "the Jerusalem from above"—reborn and living for Him with a spirit of gladness and rejoicing! Trust the Father, believe His **Word** about Himself, and see His gladness pour forth from your life.

Jesus taught us to be meek.

> *"Blessed are the meek, for they will inherit the earth."*

—Matthew 5:5, NIV

"Take my yoke upon you and learn from me, for I am gentle (KJV "meek") and humble in heart, and you will find rest for your souls."

—Matthew 11:29, NIV

When people lose their joy in serving the Lord, this is what happens next: They crave things other than God's way, by walking in the flesh and not the spirit of life in Christ Jesus:

The following is an excerpt from the article *Rebellion Against Moses' Leadership (Numbers 11-17)* by Dr. Ralph F. Wilson[18]

> **Demand for other food (Numbers 11), and complaints and fire at Taberah (Numbers 11). Before long, people started complaining again.**
>
> *"Now the people complained about their hardships in the hearing of the LORD, and when he heard them his anger was aroused."*
>
> —**Numbers 11:1a, NIV**

---

[18] Wilson, Dr. Ralph F. "Rebellion against Moses' Leadership (Numbers 11-17)." *Rebellion against Moses' Leadership (Numbers 11-17). Moses Bible Study.*, www.jesuswalk.com/moses/8_rebellion.htm#_ftn1

God punished their complaining with fire at Taberah, but that didn't seem to stop them.

The next complaints were about manna **(John 6:34; Jesus answered, "I am the bread of life, that came down from heaven...")** and began with some of the non-Israelites who had left Egypt with them (Exodus 12:38; Leviticus 24:10-11), referred to here as "rabble."[1]

"The rabble with them began to crave other food **(other than the manna)** and again the Israelites started wailing and said, 'If only we had meat to eat! We remember the fish we ate in Egypt at no cost—also the cucumbers, melons, leeks, onions and garlic. But now we have lost our appetite; **we never see anything but this manna!**'" (Numbers 11:4-6).

This manna symbolizes the walk of the Spirit in Christ Jesus our Lord.

They start salivating when they remember all the tasty variety of foods they had in Egypt. It's interesting that even a few complainers in a group can spread the complaining spirit to others. It is a general dissatisfaction with one's condition, but often the general dissatisfaction latches onto some specific issue—**in this case, manna, boring manna**. The complaints of a few had infected the camp.

"Moses heard the people of every family wailing, each at the entrance to his tent. The LORD became exceedingly angry, and Moses was troubled." (Numbers 11:10)

Hebrews 3:7-19

Warning Against Unbelief = No joy = rebellion = hardness of hearts = hardened by sin's deceitfulness = not getting into the Promised Land and dying in the desert.

> ***"So, as the Holy Spirit says: 'Today, if you hear his voice, do not harden your hearts as you did in the rebellion,*** *during the time of testing in the wilderness, where your ancestors tested and tried me, though for forty years they saw what I did. That is why I was angry with that generation; I said,* ***'Their hearts are always going astray, and they have not known my ways.'*** *So I declared on oath in my anger, 'They shall never enter my rest.'* ***See to it, brothers and sisters, that none of you has a sinful, unbelieving heart that turns away from the living God.*** *But encourage one another daily, as long as it is called 'Today,' so that none of you may be hardened by sin's deceitfulness. We have come to share in Christ, if indeed we hold our original conviction firmly to the very end. As has just been said:* ***'Today, if you hear his voice, do not harden your hearts as you did in the rebellion.'"***
>
> —Hebrews 3:7-9, NIV

God warns us today, that we need to be careful that we do not fall into this same trap of hardness of heart which leads to rebellion, and the sin of unbelief; therefore they didn't enter into his rest.

> *"**Who were they who heard and rebelled?** Were they not all those Moses led out of Egypt? And with whom was he angry for forty years? Was it not with those who sinned, whose bodies perished in the wilderness? And to whom did God swear that they would never enter his rest if not to those who disobeyed? So we see that they were not able to enter, because of their **unbelief.**"*
>
> —Hebrews 3:16-19, NIV

Many of the religiously unlearned will say, "Hey man, that was Old Testament law." **(If you think that, why don't you read Hebrews 3:7-19?)** God is also saying, "This is for this modern New Testament church age as well."

> *"Jesus replied: 'Love the Lord your God with all your heart and with all your soul and with all your mind.'"*
>
> **—Matthew 22:37, NIV**

If we love and serve the Lord with our whole heart, we will never serve our enemies. Sickness is an enemy, and the majority of the Christians today are as sick as the people in the world. This should never be so, but it is. Turn to the Lord and be healed in Jesus' name. God bless you now!

REASON #23: LACK OF GIVING CAN HINDER PHYSICAL HEALING

> *"Whoever shuts his ears to the cry of the poor will also cry himself and not be heard."*
>
> **— Proverbs 21:13, NKJV**

> *"**Blessed are those who have regard for the weak [and give to] the poor];** the LORD delivers them in times of trouble. The LORD protects and preserves them— they are counted among the blessed in the land— he does not give them over to the desire of their foes. **The LORD sustains them on their sickbed and restores them from their bed of illness.**"*
>
> **—Psalm 41:1-3, NIV**

"'Give, and it will be given to you: good measure, pressed down, shaken together, and running over will be put into your bosom. For with the same measure that you use, it will be measured back to you.'"

—**Luke 6:38, NKJV**

"*Is not this the kind of fasting I have chosen: to loose the chains of injustice and untie the cords of the yoke, to set the oppressed free and break every yoke?* **Is it not to share your food with the hungry and to provide the poor wanderer with shelter—when you see the naked, to clothe them,** *and not to turn away from your own flesh and blood? Then your light will break forth like the dawn,* **and your healing will quickly appear;** *then your righteousness] will go before you, and the glory of the LORD will be your rear guard. Then you will call, and the LORD will answer; you will cry for help, and he will say: Here am I. "If you do away with the yoke of oppression, with the pointing finger and malicious talk, and if you spend yourselves in behalf of the hungry and satisfy the needs of the oppressed, then your light will rise in the darkness, and your night will become like the noonday. The LORD will guide you always; he will satisfy your needs in a sun-scorched land and will strengthen your frame.* **[Healing to the body]** *You will be like a well-watered garden, like a spring whose waters never fail. Your people will rebuild the ancient ruins and will raise up the age-old foundations; you will be called Repairer of Broken Walls, Restorer of Streets with Dwellings.*"

—**Isaiah 58:6-12, NIV**

He who is a giving, generous person is blessed.

- He will be delivered in the time of trouble (Psalm 41:1).

- He will be preserved by a particular providence (Psalm 41:2)

- He shall be kept alive amidst infection and danger (Psalm 41:2).

- He shall be blessed on the Earth in his temporal concerns (Psalm 41:2).

- His enemies shall not be able to spoil or destroy him (Psalm 41:2).

- **The LORD sustains them on their sickbed and restores them from their bed of illness** (Psalms 41:3).

CHARITABLE GIVING

You will see more miracles of finances in your ministry through charitable giving and prayer. Our alms and offerings open the heavens! Tabitha's good works and charitable deeds caused God to raise her from the dead **(Acts 9:36-41)**, and God brought salvation to Cornelius' house because of his giving **(Acts 10:1-2)**. Alms are not tithes. They are resources given to the poor beyond the tithe. They are love offerings—special gifts to the poor or for God's children—for the sake of love and mercy, deep from your heart to theirs.

I have been in the ministry for 39 years (8 years part-time & 31 years full-time) and I've learned some things. One of those things is that those who are loving, caring, and giving **(not a tight-fisted person)** will never want for any good thing, **including healing.** I've seen people's lives transformed very quickly when they do the following from their hearts. **So, love God, love people, be a giver, and see the good Lord take care of you always.**

What Does the Bible Have to Say About Giving?

1. Supply the needs of the saints. *Extend hospitality to strangers* (Romans 12:13).

2. Do not neglect to do good and to share what you have, for such sacrifices are pleasing to God (Hebrews 13:16).

3. And the people asked him, saying, What shall we do then? He answereth and saith unto them, He that hath two coats, let him impart to him that hath none; and he that hath meat, let him do likewise (Luke 3:10-11).

4. Anger gives a foothold to the devil. If you are a thief, quit stealing. Instead, *use your hands for good hard work*, and then give generously to others in need (Ephesians 4:27-28).

5. Give to everyone who asks you for something. Don't turn anyone away who wants to borrow something from you (Matthew 5:42).

Be Generous!

1. Whoever has a bountiful eye will be blessed, for he shares his bread with the poor (Proverbs 22:9).

2. The one who is gracious to the poor lends to the Lord, and the Lord will repay him for his good deed (Proverbs 19:17).

3. Give, and it will be given to you. A large quantity, pressed together, shaken down, and running over will be put into your lap, because you'll be evaluated by the same standard with which you evaluate others (Luke 6:38).

4. For the choir director: A psalm of David. Oh, the joys of those who are kind to the poor! The Lord rescues them when they are in trouble. The Lord protects them and keeps them alive. He gives them prosperity in the land and rescues them from their enemies. The Lord nurses them when they are sick and restores them to full health (Psalm 41:1-3).

5. The righteous considereth the cause of the poor: but the wicked regardeth not to know it (Proverbs 29:7).

6. Charge them that are rich in this world, that they be not highminded, nor trust in uncertain riches, but in the living God, who giveth us richly all things to enjoy; That they do good, that they be rich in good works, ready to distribute, willing to communicate (1 Timothy 6:17-18).

Blessed

1. Good comes to those who lend money generously and conduct their business fairly. Such people will not be overcome by evil. Those who are righteous will be long remembered. They do not fear bad news; they confidently trust the Lord to care for them (Psalm 112:5-7).

2. In every way I showed you that by working hard like this we should help the weak and remember the words that the Lord Jesus himself said, **"It is more blessed to give than to receive."** (Acts 20:35.)

3. The godly always give generous loans to others, and their children are a blessing (Psalm 37:26).

4. The liberal soul shall be made fat: and he that watereth shall be watered also himself. He that withholdeth corn, the people shall curse him: but blessing shall be upon the head of him that selleth it. He that diligently seeketh good procureth favour: but he that seeketh mischief, it shall come unto him (Proverbs 11:25-27).

5. They have freely scattered their gifts to the poor, their righteousness endures forever; their horn will be lifted high in honor (Psalm 112:9).

Greedy vs. Godly

1. *Some people are always greedy for more*, but the godly love to give! (Proverbs 21:26.)

2. Whoever gives to the poor will lack nothing, but those who close their eyes to poverty will be cursed (Proverbs 28:27).

Give not with a grudging heart.

1. Each of you must give what you have decided in your heart, not with regret or under compulsion, since God loves a cheerful giver. Besides, God is able to make every blessing of yours overflow for you, so that in every situation you will always have all you need for any good work (2 Corinthians 9:7).

2. Be sure to give to them without any hesitation. When you do this, the Lord your God will bless you in everything you work for and set out to do (Deuteronomy 15:10).

Be kind to one another

1. But the Spirit produces love, joy, peace, patience, kindness, goodness, faithfulness, humility, and self-control. There is no law against such things as these (Galatians 5:22-23).

2. And be kind to one another, compassionate, forgiving one another just as God has forgiven you in the Messiah (Ephesians 4:32).

3. As holy people whom God has chosen and loved, be sympathetic, kind, humble, gentle, patient, and loving towards others (Colossians 3:12).

Giving to your enemies

1. Therefore if thine enemy hunger, *feed him*; if he thirst, give him drink: for in so doing thou shalt heap coals of fire on his head. Be not overcome of evil, but overcome evil with good (Romans 12:20-21).

2. If your enemy is hungry, give him some food to eat, and if he is thirsty, give him some water to drink (Proverbs 25:21).

3. But love ye your enemies, and do good, and *lend, hoping for nothing again*; and your reward shall be great, and ye shall be the children of the Highest: for he is kind unto the unthankful and to the evil (Luke 6:35).

Reminder

1. If there should be a poor man among your relatives in one of the cities of the land that the Lord your God is about to give you, don't

be hard-hearted or tight-fisted toward your poor relative. Instead, be sure to open your hand to him and lend him enough to lessen his need (Deuteronomy 15:7-8).

Examples

2. Jesus said to him, "If you would be perfect, go, sell what you possess and give to the poor, and you will have treasure in heaven; and come, follow me." (Matthew 19:21)

3. And all the believers met together in one place and shared everything they had. They sold their property and possessions and shared the money with those in need. They worshiped together at the Temple each day, met in homes for the Lord's Supper, and shared their meals with great joy and generosity (Acts 2:44-26).

4. All they asked was that we should continue to remember the poor, the very thing I had been eager to do all along (Galatians 2:10).

God wants all of us to be loving, caring, giving people. That's who our Father in heaven is, so let's be like Him.

God has given you the opportunity to *be a blessing to someone*. Scripture makes it clear that when your heart is set on blessing others, God will bless you in the process.

> *"But seek ye first the kingdom of God, and his righteousness; and all these things [that the gentiles eagerly seek after] shall be added unto you [as well]."*
>
> —**Matthew 6:33, KJV**

If you were in need, wouldn't you want someone to help you? Instead of judging, ask yourself that question whenever you see the needy. Always remember that those in need are Jesus in disguise.

REASON #24: LACK OF PRAYING IN TONGUES WILL HINDER HEALING

When I'm holding healing revival meetings, I often spend the whole night in prayer. I sleep by day, and then I get up and go into a very powerful Holy Ghost revival service. The power of the Holy Ghost always comes down like a fire, and heals the people big-time.

> *"Ask, and it will be given to you; seek and you will find; knock and it will be opened to you. For everyone who asks receives, and he who seeks finds, and to him who knocks it will be opened."*
>
> **—Matthew 7:7-8, NASB**

In 1988, when I was pastoring in Brisbane, Queensland, Australia, I was holding a healing revival in a church in another city, when a woman came up to me and said, "Would you please come to the hospital to pray for my very sick husband?" She gave me her phone number, address, and hospital room number.

I said to her, "The first thing I need to do is pray in the Holy Ghost until I've heard from the good Lord on this matter. When I hear from the Lord, I'll give you a call, okay?" So I set myself aside in my church office to fast and pray in the Holy Spirit until I'd broken through into the Spirit realm and heard from the Lord. The Lord finally said, "Go and raise up Lazarus."

This took nearly three days of fasting (no food, just water to drink) and praying in the Holy Ghost (praying in tongues) except for minimal sleep time. I then made a call to her husband's hospital room. She was there, but said, "I think it's too late now, preacher. He's got the death rattles, and our immediate family and our pastor and doctor are all in the hospital room, because—according to the doctors—he's got just a few hours to live." I said, "**Not so**. The Lord told me to go and raise him up."

When I got to the hospital room, there they were, about eight or nine unbelieving fearful Christians, wailing, weeping, bawling, and crying. I said to them, very nicely of course, "Please, you can all leave the room, except the man's wife and his pastor." I then said to the wife, "If you want this man to live, then do as I say, okay?" She got them out of there (Jesus did the same thing in Matthew 9:23-24) and then I worshiped the Lord for a while in the Spirit. Then, when I felt the Holy Ghost, I walked over to the man's bed and I said from the Holy Ghost, "You spirit of death, you spirit of infirmity, you spirit of sickness and disease, leave this man's body now in Jesus' name." I prayed for his healing, then turned to the woman and said, "Here's my business card. Give me a call in three days because that's when he'll be going home from this hospital being made completely whole." (The doctor looked shocked.) Then I walked out, and spoke to no one. Remember, the doctors gave him just a few hours to live.

Three days later, about 10A.M., she called me and said with overwhelming joy, "He's completely healed and going to come home this afternoon about three o'clock." I said, "I told you God will raise him up, didn't I?" About 10 months later, I saw his doctor in a supermarket, and I said, "How is John doing these days." "Oh," he said, "He's perfectly well, no cancer, no sickness at all. He'll presently be on vacation with his family up the north coast, and will be going back to work as a police captain real soon." Then he added, "Although I'm a Christian myself, I've never seen anything like what God did to that man."

This is what praying in the Holy Ghost will do if you know how to pray through, until the veil is broken in the Spirit, and the way opens up for the power of God to flow through.

> *"For he that speaketh in an unknown tongue speaketh not unto men, but unto God: for no man understandeth him; howbeit in the spirit he speaketh mysteries... He that speaketh in an unknown tongue **edifieth himself;** but he that prophesieth edifieth the church. **I would that ye all spake with tongues**, but rather that ye prophesied: for greater is he that prophesieth than he that speaketh with tongues, except he interpret, that the church may receive edifying... **For if I pray in an unknown tongue, my spirit prayeth,** but my understanding is unfruitful... I thank my God, I speak with tongues more than ye all... If any man think himself to be a prophet, or spiritual, let him acknowledge that the things that I write unto you are the commandments of the Lord.** But if any man be ignorant, let him be ignorant. Wherefore, brethren, covet to prophesy, **and forbid not to speak with tongues.***
>
> —**1 Corinthians 14:2, 4-5, 14, 18, 37-39, KJV**

> *"Beloved, building yourselves up on your most holy faith, praying in the Holy Spirit; and keep yourselves in the love of God."*
>
> —**Jude 1:20-21, NASB**

"Pray without ceasing."

—1 Thessalonians 5:17, KJV

Praying in tongues will increase your prayer power a hundredfold big-time!

In 1 Corinthians 14:2, God reveals to us a secret of increasing our prayer power a hundredfold. "For he that speaketh in an unknown tongue **speaketh not unto men**, but unto God: for no man understandeth him; howbeit in the spirit he speaketh mysteries." Ever wanted to pray the prayers that gets God's attention and answers to healing every time? Here this verse opens to us a depth that many Christians rarely understand, appreciate, or even experience. Praying in the Spirit will increase the effect and potency of your prayer power.

When we pray in the Spirit, the Holy Spirit takes over our thoughts, mind, and vocal cords. Man was originally created to a tripartite being of spirit, soul, and body. The inner man, the human spirit, was to rule over the soul and the body. It is impossible to please God when this order is not maintained. Adam functioned this way before his tragic fall (Romans 3:23). Our Lord Jesus exemplified this perfect life of dominion while on planet Earth.

Although God (Jesus did not live as God then as a man; He **had to rely on the Holy Ghost, and be led by him just like we do),** Jesus was and is that perfect pattern son. The moment we are born again, our spirit-man becomes new, infused with God's zōē[19] life.

---

[19] Greek *the absolute fullness of life, both essential and ethical, which belongs to God (Strong's Greek Lexicon).*

1 Corinthians 6:16 says, "But he that is joined unto the Lord is one spirit." **So praying in the Spirit is when our spirit prays by the help of the indwelling Holy Spirit.** The primary way God leads His children is through our spirit…that still, small inner voice. What we call conscience is the voice of our human spirit. **Praying in the Spirit energizes—or charges up—our spirit man.**

> *"That he would grant you, according to the riches of his glory, to be strengthened with might by his Spirit in the inner man;"*
>
> **—Ephesians 3:16, KJV**

The key to living in the glory is to be energized in our spirit being. The human spirit does not think; he just knows. Thinking is the function of our soul and not the spirit. All of God resides in us according to Ephesians 3:19: "And to know the love of Christ, which passeth knowledge, that ye might be filled with all the fullness of God." When we let the spirit-man dominate our soul and body, miracle abundant living is the result. Meditate on this. When this revelation is understood and received, it will change your life forever. Begin this year with a determination that you are going to walk in dominion by allowing **your inward man to dominate your outward man. Then you will be able to pray with great Holy Ghost power the right kind of prayer that will heal the sick.**

> *"In the same way, the Spirit helps us in our weakness. For we do not know how we ought to pray, but the Spirit Himself intercedes for us with groans too deep for words. And he who searches our hearts knows the mind of the Spirit, because the Spirit intercedes for the saints according to the will of God."*
>
> **—Romans 8:26-27, BSB**

The Prayer of Faith Shall Save (Heal) the Sick One

> *"Is any one of you suffering? He should pray. Is anyone cheerful? He should sing praises. Is any one of you sick? He should call the elders of the church to pray over him and anoint him with oil in the name of the Lord. And the prayer offered in faith will restore the one who is sick. The Lord will raise him up. If he has sinned, he will be forgiven."*
>
> **—James 5:13-15, BSB**

Praying in the Spirit gets God's instant attention, simply because this is God's inspired prayer. It's a spirit-birthed prayer. His kinds of prayers through us are always answered. The easiest way to pray God's will is to get it in the Spirit. **1 Corinthians 14:2 says that we pray directly to God when we pray in the Spirit.** That means these prayers bypass human intellect, human error, and demonic barriers. Satan does not understand the prayer language, neither does he have what it takes to hinder or block the answers from coming. It's a heavenly-coded prayer language that all of Hell and his cohorts do not have any answer to. The Holy Spirit understands our needs, our weakness, our strength, and that very missing "puzzle piece" in our life. He is our helper and if we let Him, He will pray through us and for us. There is a big distinct difference in praying with understanding and praying in the Holy Spirit.

Begin to pray in the Spirit, daily. For the next 21 days, make a commitment to pray for at least one or two hours a day. Others, who are able, go for two or five hours every day for the next 21 days. **The more time you spend in praying in the Spirit,** the more spiritual power reserve for your use and the more spiritually sensitized and activated you become. The doors of the miraculous will be open to you, as you have never experienced before. The crooked path will be made straight. You will receive wisdom that will put you over this year. You will become more intuitive and sensitive to the leading of the Lord than you have ever been. Pray in the morning, during the day, and at night. Saturate your next three weeks with Spirit-led, Spirit-guided, and Spirit-inspired intercessory prayers and your life will never be the same again. The Bible gives a number of reasons why every Christian should pray in tongues, and many ways that praying in tongues will tremendously benefit any Christian that will do what God said to do. That is, I would that you all spoke in tongues. (See **1 Corinthians 14:5.**)

More Benefits of Praying in the Spirit

Praying in the Spirit opens the heavens for personal refreshing from God's presence, leading us to that rest of faith. (See **Hebrews 3; Isaiah 28:11-12; 1 Corinthians 14:21.**)

Praying in the Spirit helps us to pray God's perfect will, even when we don't know how to pray or what to pray for. **(Romans 8:26-27)**

3. Praying in the Spirit edifies us. Like a battery, when we pray in the Spirit we are recharged, strengthened, energized, and empowered. We are built up on our most holy faith which helps us to stay in the love of God. **(Jude 20-21; 1Corinthians 14:4.)**

5 Ways Praying in Tongues Will Change Your Life Forever

Based on *The Glory Within* **by Corey Russell**[20] here are five ways that praying in tongues will change your life forever.

---

[20] Russell, Corey. *Glory Within - Corey Russell.* Destiny Image. 2012: 176. Paperback.

1. Praying in tongues gives you supernatural understanding of God's mysteries

> *"For he who speaks in a tongue does not speak to men but to God, for no one understands him; however, in the spirit he speaks mysteries."*
>
> —1 Corinthians 14:2, NKJV

Many describe the Holy Spirit as a very powerful **search engine of heaven.** God is mysterious, yes, but the Spirit who knows everything about the mysterious, expansive, glorious God is the same Spirit who lives inside of you! And furthermore, He wants to reveal mysteries to you about God, His will, your life, and the circumstances you are facing.

How do we access this revelation? Communion with the Holy Spirit on His level—in His language. Remember, Paul defines the Holy Spirit as the One who "searches out everything and shows us God's deep secrets" **(1 Corinthians 2:10, NLT).** As you pray in the Spirit, you will discover things that were previously mysterious and unknown will start coming into greater focus and clarity.

> *"But when he, the Spirit of truth, comes, he will guide you into all the truth. He will not speak on his own; he will speak only what he hears, and he will tell you what is yet to come."*
>
> —John 16:13, NIV

2. Praying in tongues grants you access to other revelatory gifts of the Holy Spirit

> *"For to one is given the word of wisdom through the Spirit, to another the word of knowledge through the same Spirit ... to another prophecy, to another discerning of spirits, to another different kinds of tongues, to another the interpretation of tongues."*
>
> —1 Corinthians 12:8, 10, NKJV

Praying in tongues actually unlocks other revelatory gifts of the Holy Spirit in your life, namely the word of wisdom, word of knowledge, prophecy, and discerning of spirits. Remember, you are not praying on a natural dimension, but rather engaging on a purely spiritual one. Don't be surprised if, while praying in tongues, the Holy Spirit gives you supernatural insight about something, leads you to pray for people, and unlocks clarity over people, situations, and even regions, enabling you to effectively pray for and break off the spiritual strongholds that are influencing them.

3. Praying in tongues opens up the Bible in a new, living way as you read it

> *"However, when He, the Spirit of truth, has come, He will guide you into all truth; for He will not speak on His own authority, but whatever He hears He will speak."*
>
> **—John 16:13, NKJV**

For some modern believers, reading the Bible can feel like a life-draining experience. It's not just history. It is not a mere record of facts. Scripture isn't just stories. The same Holy Spirit who inspired the writing and assembly of the Holy Scriptures lives inside of you. He wants to guide you through the Bible, make the words jump off the page, give you understanding on confusing matters, empower you to apply God's Word to your everyday life, share prophetic promises with you and help you discover your role in God's unfolding story. Many describe praying in tongues as a way the Holy Spirit "shines a flashlight on Scripture."

4. When praying in tongues, you are speaking directly to God

> *"For he who speaks in a tongue does not speak to men but to God."*
>
> **—1 Corinthians 14:2, NKJV**

As you pray in tongues, you have a direct line to the President of the Universe. Sometimes while praying in our native language, we have the tendency to veer off and get distracted. We may start complaining. We may start going through the routine laundry list of prayer requests—and by the time we are finished reading them off to God, we feel more burdened than refreshed because we actively thought of every single one of those circumstances as we listed them off in prayer. Tongues keeps us talking directly to God, praying in agreement with His perfect will **(Romans 8:26-28).**

5. Praying in tongues empowers you to engage spiritual warfare from the position of victory

> *"With all prayer and petition pray [with specific requests] at all times [on every occasion and in every season] in the Spirit, and with this in view, stay alert with all perseverance and petition [interceding in prayer] for all God's people."*
>
> **—Ephesians 6:18, AMP**

Jesus assured us that in this life we will experience tribulation (John 16:33). In the same passage, the same Jesus declared that He has overcome the world. Victory has already been secured at Calvary.

In times of trial and assault, it is easy for us to become weary in the place of prayer, often not knowing what or how to pray. Praise God for the Holy Spirit! Paul reminds us *"For we do not know what we should pray for as we ought, but the Spirit Himself makes intercession for us..."* **(Romans 8:26b NKJV).** When in the heat of spiritual combat, it is easy to start praying prayers that agree with the size of the attack, emphasizing the problem rather than focusing on the size of the blood-bought victory that Jesus purchased at the cross. Praying in tongues empowers you to agree with God's victorious battle plan for your life and your circumstances, no matter what is going on around you. It does not deny reality; it simply positions you to agree with the higher truth of Scripture: Victory has been purchased, and it is yours through Jesus Christ.

Tongues Reveals the Wisdom of God

Again, praying in tongues does not make you a better Christian. It does not instantly elevate you into spiritual superstardom. There are many believers who speak in tongues but live like the devil. However, tongues is a relevant and available gift to true believers today. Keep in mind that you are dealing with the King of the universe who arrived on Planet Earth in a manger surrounded by farm animals. He is the holy God who died the death of a criminal on a Roman cross to make atonement for the sins of the world. Our God is the One who deals in wisdom that is so infinitely superior to what our natural minds can comfortably wrap around that, at first glance, such methods appear downright foolish. Birthing His church with wind, fire, and speaking in tongues would be another such demonstration of God's otherworldly wisdom. But consider the words of the apostle Paul:

> ***"But God has chosen the foolish things of the world to put to shame the wise, and God has chosen the weak things of the world to put to shame the things which are mighty; and the base things of the world and the things which are despised God has chosen, and the things which are not, to bring to nothing the things that are, that no flesh should glory in His presence."***
>
> **—1 Corinthians 1:27-29, NKJV**

Just because our minds cannot understand the whys of God's ways, that does not give us permission to ignore them. Speaking in tongues is surely a mystery, but at the same time it is a powerful gift that will not only enrich your personal prayer life but will bring you into deeper intimacy and communion with the Holy Spirit.

> *"Wherefore, brethren, covet to prophesy, and forbid not to speak with tongues."*
>
> —1 Corinthians 14:39, KJV

The Prayer of Faith

> *"Is anyone among you suffering? Let him pray. Is anyone cheerful? Let him sing praise. Is anyone among you sick? Let him call for the elders of the church, and let them pray over him, anointing him with oil in the name of the Lord. And the prayer of faith will save [**this word means to heal**] the one who is sick, and the Lord will raise him up. And if he has committed sins, he will be forgiven. **Therefore, confess your sins to one another and pray for one another, that you may be healed."***
>
> —James 5:13-15, ESV

The prayer of a righteous person has great power as it is working, **but this power comes only to those who know how to pray in the Holy Ghost until they have broken through in the Spirit. Then you will see the results in praying for the sick.**

REASON #25: TOUCHING GOD'S ANOINTED WILL HINDER HEALING

Over the years, I've encountered a lot of opposition against the ministry of healing (the Devil used them and they didn't even know

it), but when they say healing is of the Devil, or they say healing went out with the apostles, those type always come to great destruction in their lives. Once I had a whole fundamental Christian family oppose me to my face about the healing ministry. About a year later they were divorced. He couldn't take the pressure, backslid, went to jail for a drug problem, and the children ended up in foster homes. Later I heard the wife died from a horrible accident.

Another Form or Type of Touching God's Anointing

Although I have already shared this testimony in the front of the book, I felt in the Lord to reiterate on this theme again, for the purpose of showing how we can touch God's anointing; even in our own ministries.

God said to me in January 1990, "Son, it is time for you to leave Australia and evangelize and help towards bringing a revival to America." The Holy Spirit spoke clearly into my spirit. This was a rekindling and a reminder of a powerful word I'd received from the Lord, about 11 years before, then again four years later, and still again a year earlier in 1989.

I felt like I was nearly knocked out of my chair the moment He spoke. "But Lord," I reasoned, "I like pastoring this nice church. I am enjoying my life, things are good." Plus the Assemblies of God churches in Perth, Western Australia, want me to do a citywide revival there in a few months. The truth was, I really, really, adamantly did not want to go to America to live. Period. "Lord," I said again, "things are good here."

He did give me a choice. I could stay to pastor the church, but the powerful anointing to minister in healings and miracles would be lifted, **and He'd give it to another**. I hesitated. I could continue to pastor the church with all the perks and benefits or leave everything behind to go to

America. **His anointing** and blessings went with the calling to evangelize and bring revival. The choice was mine.

After moments of wrestling with my flesh (which was quite happy and content doing what it was doing in Australia), I decided that I couldn't fathom a halfhearted existence of attempting to minister out of my flesh—**with a gift-only approach**—without His anointing and power. I imagined standing behind the pulpit, preaching nice little sermons and having men's breakfasts, church workdays, and potlucks with the anointing upon me to minister in power....**gone forever.** I could go through the motions of pastoring that church in God's permissive will, or I could follow Him, in His perfect will, with purpose, anointing, covering, and blessing. **His anointing was my life**. It was greater than the comforts of a good job with full benefits. It was my covering, my protection, so I made my decision. I said yes to the good Lord's calling to go to America. Doing God's will is not always easy, but we must do it if we really love Him. Jesus said, "If you love me, obey me..." **(John 14:15a TLB).**

I believe with all my heart that if I had said no and didn't come to America, **I would've been touching God's anointing over the ministry**. I've known a number of preachers who have had similar healing ministries as mine, but they said no and didn't move on with God. Today they are either dead (some died young) or not in the ministry at all. Several others I know who used to have big churches now have shrunken churches with just a few hundred in their congregations. The anointing and power were gone, and everyone knew it. WOW!

Many years ago, I was holding a revival in a very large church in California, and the healings and miracles were bringing in and filling that church to overflowing. Hundreds were being healed, touched, and saved. Even after two weeks, the place was supercharged with the excitement of revival, and increasing. One night, the Lord said to me, "Ask the pastor to take this revival on for two more weeks, because I want to heal and save hundreds more."

So, I went to see the pastor before the revival meeting that night, and I told him what the Lord had said to me. His response: "Well brother, that's not going to happen. Tomorrow night is the last night because then we have the whole church come and watch the Super Bowl on the big screen in this church. Dan," he said, "this is what we do every year, and it's not going to change now. So again, brother Dan, tomorrow night will be the last night for this revival. Okay?"

I walked away and felt an agonizing and a very deep sadness in my spirit. The Holy Ghost said to me, "The blood is not on your head, my son; but theirs." Later, that pastor—who was about 46 years old—his marriage fell apart. Later he died from cancer and his church dissolved down to just a few hundred folks.

How deaf are those who will not hear and how blind are those who will not see.

Listen, God's precious people, I'm not against sports because I'm an ex-boxer and I'm an internationally trained and accomplished deep-sea scuba diver. But when the church puts the things of this world before the things of God, we have a very big problem and God is not amused.

Here's Another Heartbreaking Testimony

I was holding a powerful revival in a 2,500 member big-city Pentecostal church every Sunday night for over a year. In that period of time thousands of people had been healed, including a number of folks in wheelchairs. The deaf received their hearing, and many people with cancer were healed as well. Plus, many hundreds of souls came into the kingdom of God. The Lord spoke to me one night and said, "Tell the pastor I told you to take this revival on for several more months, because the Holy Ghost wants to heal and save many hundreds more souls."

I shared this word with the pastor and he said, "I've been feeling in my spirit the same thing. Yes, we need to take this on for about another three to four months." So, two days later, when I turned up for the Sunday night service, he took me aside and said, "Dan, I shared with my church board about us going on for another three to four months and they adamantly said no, so we need to finish up the revival tonight."

That night as I was driving home, I felt a sadness as if someone close to me had just died. That night, I had a dream where I saw that church split into fragments as if a bomb had hit it. About three years later the pastor was out of the ministry (he was still a young man) working in a secular job, and the church was no longer going. They had to sell the building to another group. How sad!

Still Another Heartbreaking, Gut-wrenching Testimony

I was preaching in a big, **seeker-friendly** church once and the Lord said to me, "There are a lot of people in this church living in sin, and I want you to deal with it." So, I shared and preached on the following text: *"Everyone who makes a practice of sinning also practices lawlessness; sin is lawlessness. You know that he appeared in order to take away sins, and in him there is no sin. No one who abides in him keeps on sinning; no one who keeps on sinning has either seen him or known him. Little children, let no one deceive you. Whoever practices righteousness is righteous, as he is righteous. Whoever makes a practice of sinning is of the devil, for the devil has been sinning from the beginning. The reason the Son of God appeared was to destroy the works of the devil. No one born of God makes a practice of sinning, for God's^j seed abides in him;*

and he cannot keep on sinning, because he has been born of God. By this it is evident who are the children of God, and who are the children of the devil: whoever does not practice righteousness is not of God, nor is the one who does not love his brother" (1 John 3:4-10).

After I preached this message, the Lord said to me, "Call all those who are not saved, and get them to come to the front, especially those who are living in sin, and get them to repent. Twelve people came to the front crying and repenting (the anointing was very strong) and I got them to give their lives to Jesus and start to live a holy life from then on. Then the Lord said to me, "Call out those who are saved, but they are still sleeping around and living a double lifestyle." They came out in numbers (23 in all) and repented, and I instructed them to live holy separated lives unto God from now on. Then the power of God fell in the house of God (holy awe was in the house) and the front of the church was filled with weeping and repenting Christians. God healed hundreds of them, to His glory. Thank You, Jesus, for your love, grace, and mercy.

Now are you ready for the news of the week? The pastor took my wife and me aside after the meeting that morning, and said, "Brother Dan, that was a nice service, but that's the kind of preaching that empties churches out, and we don't need that type of stuff here, okay?" That church didn't want our ministry anymore. People, that's called quenching, stifling, or touching the anointing. That pastor quit the ministry sometime later. They wanted to draw a big crowd by any methods and by any means other than the Word and the power of God. For them, it was let's just keep the crowds coming, and entertain them, and get all their money. They are so caught up in their fleshly, seeker-friendly churches that I think they forget the Day of Judgment is coming. Then we'll see where they stand.

"According to the grace of God given to me, like a skilled master builder I laid a foundation, and someone else is building

upon it. Let each one take care how he builds upon it. For no one can lay a foundation other than that which is laid, which is Jesus Christ. Now if anyone builds on the foundation with gold, silver, precious stones, wood, hay, straw—each one's work will become manifest, for the Day will disclose it, because it will be revealed by fire, and the fire will test what sort of work each one has done. If the work that anyone has built on the foundation survives, he will receive a reward. If anyone's work is burned up, he will suffer loss, though he himself will be saved, but only as through fire. Do you not know that you[j] *are God's temple and that God's Spirit dwells in you? If anyone destroys God's temple, God will destroy him. For God's temple is holy, and you are that temple, so live a holy life."*

—1 Corinthians 3:10-16, NKJV

Blasphemy against the Holy Spirit is when people say that the works of the Holy Ghost are the works of the Devil. According to Jesus, this will not be forgiven them in this life or the life to come. (See Matthew 12:22-32.)

Over the years I've had a number of ministers greatly oppose me about the healing ministry. This is absolutely true: they always ended up in destruction. Three even died young. Galatians 6:7 says, *"Be not deceived; God is not mocked: for whatsoever a man soweth, that shall he also reap."* God will always protect His servants who preach the truth. He does not back up those who preach lies that rob and hurt and all they want to do is entertain God's people.

"Do not touch my anointed ones; do my prophets no harm."

—Psalm 105:15, NIV

Although this scripture was referring to the Old Testament anointed kings and prophets, the anointed ones and prophets are still part of the kingdom of God today.

> *"But unto every one of us is given grace according to the measure of the gift of Christ. Wherefore he saith, When he ascended up on high, he led captivity captive, and gave gifts unto men. (Now that he ascended, what is it but that he also descended first into the lower parts of the earth? He that descended is the same also that ascended up far above all heavens, that he might fill all things.) And he gave some, apostles; and some, **prophets;** and some, evangelists; and some, pastors and teachers; For the perfecting of the saints, for the work of the ministry, for the edifying of the body of Christ."*
>
> **—Ephesians 4:7-12, KJV**

Psalm 105:11-15 says, *"To you I will give the land of Canaan as the allotment of your inheritance."* This was when they were few in number, indeed very few, and strangers in it. When they went from one nation to another, from one kingdom to another people, God permitted no one to do them wrong; yes, He rebuked kings for their sakes, saying, *"Do not touch My anointed ones, and **do My prophets no harm.**"*

Notice in this Scripture that God protected His anointed (Israel) and His prophets from the enemies of Israel to bring physical or spiritual harm.

First of all, this is not saying we are not to speak out against and expose false, so-called anointed teachers. Actually the opposite is true.

Romans 16:17 commands, **"Mark those who are contrary to doctrine and avoid them."** To mark them you have to **identify them,** and to avoid them you have to know who you're avoiding. There are many false teachers today saying, "The Lord doesn't heal today." This is a lie from the pit of hell itself. Stay away from these false teachers, because the Devil wants to use them to rob you of your healing or miracle, whichever God chooses.

The Devil is using their tongue as a lie to hurt the bride of Christ, or the real Christians.

So, this subject is about those who would like to destroy the word of God's true teachings. The Devil is using them! For this case study, we are dealing with the subject of healing and how God is still healing today.

"Jesus Christ is the same yesterday and today and forever."

—Hebrews 13:8, ESV

"For I am the LORD, I change not."

— Malachi 3:6, KJV

"God is not a man, that He should lie, Nor a son of man, that He should repent; Has He said, and will He not do it? Or has He spoken, and will He not make it good."

—Numbers 23:19, NASB

"The counsel of the LORD stands forever, The plans of His heart from generation to generation."

—Psalm 33:11, NASB

> *"Every good thing given and every perfect gift is from above, coming down from the Father of lights, with whom there is no variation or shifting shadow."*
>
> **—James 1:17, NASB**

> *"If you believe, you will receive whatever you ask for in prayer."*
>
> **— Matthew 21:22, NIV**

Healing would come under the category of all things. So, **ask God to heal you, okay?**

> *"Sanctify them by Your truth. Your word is truth."*
>
> **—John 17:17, NKJV**

Unless someone is speaking the word correctly, they are not teaching the truth. It doesn't matter if they call themselves anointed, or how big or successful a ministry they have, they are *wrong when they say God doesn't heal today.*

> **"He who justifies the wicked, and he who condemns the just, both of them alike are an abomination to the LORD."**
>
> **—Proverbs 17:15, NKJV**

For one to find out what is true or false, they must look into the matter and hear both sides before they make a final judgment.

> *"The heart of the prudent acquires knowledge, and the ear of the wise seeks knowledge"*
>
> **—Proverbs 18:15, NKJV**

> *If they speak not according to this word, it is because there is no light in them."*
>
> **—Isaiah 8:20b, KJV**

They are religious, and there's no Holy Spirit in them at all.

Blasphemy Against the Holy Spirit Will Not Be Forgiven

> *"Then they brought him a demon-possessed man who was blind and mute, and Jesus healed him, so that he could both talk and see. All the people were astonished and said, 'Could this be the Son of David?' But when the Pharisees [**the so-called fundamental Christians**] heard this, they said, **'It is only by Beelzebub, the prince of demons, that this fellow drives out demons and heals.'** Jesus knew their thoughts and said to them, 'Every kingdom divided against itself will be ruined, and every city or household divided against itself will not stand. If Satan drives out Satan, he is divided against himself. How then can his kingdom stand? And if I drive out demons by Beelzebub, by whom do your people drive them out? So then, they will be your judges. But if it is by the Spirit of God that I drive out demons, then the kingdom of God has come upon you. Or again, how can anyone enter a strong man's house and carry off his possessions unless he first ties up the strong man? Then he can plunder his house. Whoever is not with me is against me, and whoever does not gather with me scatters. **And so I tell you, every kind of sin and slander can be forgiven, but blasphemy against the Spirit will not be forgiven. Anyone who speaks a word against the Son of Man will be forgiven, but anyone who speaks against***

> *the Holy Spirit will not be forgiven, either in this age or in the age to come.*
>
> —**Matthew 12:22-32, NIV**

According to the above Scripture, those who say that the things of the Holy Spirit are actually the things of the Devil are standing on dangerous ground, and that won't be forgiven him in this age or in the age to come. Jesus said, *"Whoever is not with me is against me, and whoever does not gather with me scatters."* This means that those who oppose the healing ministry—even though it's of God's Spirit and Word—are against Jesus. They are scattering God's people, and causing great pain and harm. Yes, God will judge them big-time.

In conclusion, ask God to heal you. Please keep away from all those who would rob you of God's best for your life. Let the dead bury the dead, and come and follow Jesus.

> *"Every good thing given and every perfect gift is from above, coming down from the Father of lights, with whom there is no variation or shifting shadow."*
>
> —**James 1:17, NASB**

This means only good things come down from God. Healing is a good thing, is it not?

> *"Beloved, I wish above all things that you may prosper, and be in good health, even as your soul has prospered."*
>
> —**3 John 2:1, ESV**

100 Healing Scriptures

"So shall My word be that goes forth from My mouth; It shall not return to Me void, But it shall accomplish what I please, And it shall prosper in the thing for which I sent it."

—**Isaiah 55:11, NKJV**

The following are commonly known as the healing Scriptures. I encourage you to print these Scriptures and meditate upon them. Put them on your refrigerator, bathroom mirror, or by your bed. Get God's Word into your heart and it will produce faith in your heart so you can declare it with expectancy to receive.

All scriptures are quoted from the English Standard Version.

Old Testament

1. I am the Lord that healeth thee (Exodus 15:26).
2. You shall be buried in a good old age (Genesis 15:15).
3. You shall come to your grave in a full age like as a shock of corn cometh in its season (Job 5:26).
4. When I see the blood, I will pass over you and the plague shall not be upon you to destroy you (Exodus 12:13).
5. I will take sickness away from the midst of you and the number of your days I will fulfill (Exodus 23:25-26).

6. I will not put any of the diseases you are afraid of on you, but I will take all sickness away from you (Deuteronomy 7:15).

7. It will be well with you and your days shall be multiplied and prolonged as the days of heaven upon the earth (Deuteronomy 11:9, 21).

8. I turned the curse into a blessing unto you, because I loved you (Deuteronomy 23:5 and Nehemiah 13:2).

9. I have redeemed you from every sickness and every plague (Deuteronomy 28:61 and Galatians 3:13).

10. As your days, so shall your strength be (Deuteronomy 33:25).

11. I have found a ransom for you; your flesh shall be fresher than a child's and you shall return to the days of your youth (Job 33:24-25).

12. I have healed you and brought up your soul from the grave; I have kept you alive from going down into the pit (Psalm 30:1-2).

13. I will give you strength and bless you with peace (Psalm 29:11).

14. I will preserve you and keep you alive (Psalm 41:2).

15. I will strengthen you upon the bed of languishing; I will turn all your bed in your sickness (Psalm 41:3).

16. I am the health of your countenance and your God (Psalm 43:5).

17. No plague shall come near your dwelling (Psalm 91:10).

18. I will satisfy you with long life (Psalm 91:16).

19. I heal all your diseases (Psalm 103:3).

20. I sent My word and healed you and delivered you from your destructions (Psalm 107:20).

21. You shall not die, but live, and declare My works (Psalm 118:17).

22. I heal your broken heart and bind up your wounds (Psalm 147:3).

23. The years of your life shall be many (Proverbs 4:10).

24. Trusting Me brings health to your navel and marrow to your bones (Proverbs 3:8).

25. My words are life to you, and health/medicine to all your flesh (Proverbs 4:22).

26. (My) good report makes your bones fat (Proverbs 15:30).

27. (My) pleasant words are sweet to your soul and health to your bones (Proverbs 16:24).

28. My joy is your strength. A merry heart does good like a medicine (Nehemiah 8:10; Proverbs 17:22).

29. The eyes of the blind shall be opened. The eyes of them that see shall not be dim (Isaiah 32:3; 35:5).

30. The ears of the deaf shall be unstopped. The ears of them that hear shall hearken (Isaiah 32:3; 35:5).

31. The tongue of the dumb shall sing. The tongue of the stammerers shall be ready to speak plainly (Isaiah 35:6; 32:4).

32. The lame man shall leap as a hart (Isaiah 35:6).

33. I will recover you and make you to live. I am ready to save you (Isaiah 38:16, 20).

34. I give power to the faint. I increase strength to them that have no might (Isaiah 40:29).

35. I will renew your strength. I will strengthen and help you (Isaiah 40:31; 41:10).

36. To your old age and gray hairs I will carry you and I will deliver you (Isaiah 46:4).

37. I bore your sickness (Isaiah 53:4).

38. I carried your pains (Isaiah 53:4).

39. I was put to sickness for you (Isaiah 53:10).

40. With My stripes you are healed (Isaiah 53:5).

41. I will heal you (Isaiah 57:19).

42. Your light shall break forth as the morning and your health shall spring forth speedily (Isaiah 58:8).

43. I will restore health unto you, and I will heal you of your wounds saith the Lord (Jeremiah 30:17).

44. Behold I will bring it health and cure, and I will cure you, and will reveal unto you the abundance of peace and truth (Jeremiah 33:6).

45. I will bind up that which was broken and will strengthen that which was sick (Ezekiel 34:16).

46. Behold, I will cause breath to enter into you and you shall live. And I shall put My Spirit in you and you shall live (Ezekiel 37:5, 14).

47. Whithersoever the rivers shall come shall live. They shall be healed and everything shall live where the river comes (Ezekiel 47:9).

48. Seek Me and you shall live (Amos 5:4, 6).

49. I have arisen with healing in My wings [beams] (Malachi 4:2).

New Testament

50. I will, be thou clean (Matthew. 8:3).

51. I took your infirmities (Matthew. 8:17).

52. I bore your sicknesses (Matthew. 8:17).

53. If you're sick you need a physician. (I am the Lord your physician) (Matthew. 9:12; Exodus 15:26).

54. I am moved with compassion toward the sick and I heal them (Matthew. 14:14).

55. I heal all manner of sickness and all manner of disease (Matthew 4:23).

56. According to your faith, be it unto you (Matthew 9:29).

57. I give you power and authority over all unclean spirits to cast them out, and to heal all manner of sickness and all manner of disease (Matthew 10:1; Luke 9:1).

58. I heal them all (Matthew 12:15; Hebrews 13:8).

59. As many as touch Me are made perfectly whole (Matthew 14:36).

60. Healing is the children's bread (Matthew 15:26).

61. I do all things well. I make the deaf to hear and the dumb to speak (Mark. 7:37).

62. If you can believe, all things are possible to him that believeth (Mark 9:23; 11:23-24).

63. When hands are laid on you, you shall recover (Mark 16:18).

64. My anointing heals the brokenhearted, and delivers the captives, recovers sight to the blind, and sets at liberty those that are bruised (Luke 4:18; Isaiah 10:27; 61:1).

65. I heal all those who have need of healing (Luke 9:11).

66. I am not come to destroy men's lives but to save them (Luke 9:56).

67. Behold, I give you authority over all the enemy's power and nothing shall by any means hurt you (Luke 10:19).

68. Sickness is satanic bondage and you ought to be loosed today (Luke 13:16; 2 Corinthians 6:2).

69. In Me is life (John 1:4).

70. I am the bread of life. I give you life (John 6:33, 35).

71. The words I speak unto you are spirit and life (John 6:63).

72. I am come that you might have life, and that you might have it more abundantly (John 10:10).

73. I am the resurrection and the life (John 11:25).

74. If you ask anything in My name, I will do it (John 14:14).

75. Faith in My name makes you strong and gives you perfect soundness (Acts 3:16).

76. I stretch forth My hand to heal (Acts 4:30).

77. I, Jesus Christ, make you whole (Acts 9:34).

78. I do good and heal all that are oppressed of the devil (Acts 10:38).

79. My power causes diseases to depart from you (Acts 19:12).

80. The law of the Spirit of life in Me has made you free from the law of sin and death (Romans 8:2).

81. The same Spirit that raised Me from the dead now lives in you and that Spirit will quicken your mortal body (Romans 8:11).

82. Your body is a member of Me (1 Corinthians 6:15).

83. Your body is the temple of My Spirit and you're to glorify Me in your body (1 Corinthians 6:19-20).

84. If you'll rightly discern My body which was broken for you, and judge yourself, you'll not be judged and you'll not be weak, sickly or die prematurely (1 Corinthians 11:29-31).

85. I have set gifts of healing in My body (1 Corinthians 12:9).

86. My life may be made manifest in your mortal flesh (2 Corinthians 4:10-1111).

87. I have delivered you from death, I do deliver you, and if you trust Me I will yet deliver you (2 Corinthians 1:10).

88. I have given you My name and have put all things under your feet (Ephesians 1:21-22).

89. I want it to be well with you and I want you to live long on the earth. (Ephesians 6:3).

90. I have delivered you from the authority of darkness (Colossians 1:13).

91. I will deliver you from every evil work (2 Timothy 4:18).

92. I tasted death for you. I destroyed the devil who had the power of death. I've delivered you from the fear of death and bondage (Hebrews 2:9, 14, 15).

93. I wash your body with pure water (Hebrews 10:22; Ephesians 5:26).

94. Lift up the weak hands and the feeble knees. Don't let that which is lame be turned aside but rather let Me heal it (Hebrews 12:12, 13).

95. Let the elders anoint you and pray for you in My name and I will raise you up (James 5:14-15).

96. Pray for one another and I will heal you (James 5:16).

97. By My stripes you were healed (1 Peter 2:24).

98. My Divine power has given unto you all things that pertain unto life and godliness through the knowledge of Me (2 Peter 1:3).

99. Beloved, I wish above all things that you may...be in health (3 John 2)

100. Whosoever will, let him come and take of the water of life freely (Revelation 22:17).

About The Author

Healing evangelist Dan Nolan (Th.M.)

G'day, Mate. I was born in Australia, the Great Southland of the Holy Spirit, in 1952. I moved to the United States from Queensland, Australia, in 1990 and currently reside with my wife, Charlotte, in Phoenix, Arizona.

I was raised in Adelaide, South Australia, in a very poor, dysfunctional, and abusive family. After dropping out of school I became a street kid at age 15. By 19, I was a biker gang-leader, involved in drugs, rock 'n roll, and the occult. When I was 20, I had a work accident that took me off the job and in need of a major back operation. Plus, I'd already had several motorcycle bike accidents. My spine was twisted and most of the vertebras were sitting on top of each other with very little disk padding. This terrible back injury was so severe that the doctors wanted to stick two rods up my back. They said that if I didn't that by my mid-30s I would be confined to a wheelchair for the rest of my life. I was angry, broken, and had no hope. I was a very wicked sinner and all I wanted to do was get drunk. I was not a born-again Christian.

Over a period of three years, and with the last set of four x-rays done on my back, the doctors said I would be having spinal surgery in two weeks, and they said I'd be on government disability payments for the rest of my life. The following Sunday, my brother conned me into going to his church, saying I owed him a favor. So I went with him and sat down at the back. My brother said, "This pastor always prays for the sick folks at the end of the meeting."

After the preaching the pastor started calling different people out by the words of knowledge. He then called me out by a very detailed word of knowledge and prayed for me in Jesus' name. I fell under the power **(the catchers laid me on the floor)** and a ball of fire shot into the right side of my body, and moved up and down my spine. The fire of God did an instant, creative irrefutable awesome powerful miracle in my back. I was completely healed. Then the preacher asked me if I'd like to accept Jesus into my life as Lord and Savior. Of course, I said yes. **That was on July 6, 1975, at about 8 p.m.** I was so overwhelmed with God's miracle gift of healing and salvation, and after I accepted Christ into my heart, I was filled with the Holy Spirit, and I have loved God ever since.

Shortly after, the Lord healed my mind from a learning disability and told me to go back to school to complete my G.E.D. While completing my high school courses, I unexpectedly found myself lying in a hospital bed with a smashed foot twisted around behind me. It was so severely damaged, with many broken bones from a sporting accident. The doctor said they were going to do special surgery **with plates and screws, etc.,** and I would be in a cast up to my hip for three months, with more surgeries to follow. He added that I had a 75 percent chance I would walk with a limp the rest of my life.

After the doctor left the room, I prayed and told God if He would heal my ankle, I would tell people all over the world and everyone I could what He had done. Suddenly, a pillar of fire came down from the ceiling and stood at the end of my bed. Out of it came the words, "I have called you to carry my healing power and anointing around the world." I was then healed instantly. I was shocked at what I saw and experienced. My crushed, twisted, and very swollen ankle just shrunk, turned, and was instantly made whole, just like the other one. I was absolutely in awe at this whole ordeal and the mercies and love of our great God, and the Holy Ghost, and His power. I'm still to this day undone by what I heard Him say I was called to do.

I obtained my GED and then went on to get a Technical Building College associates degree from the Marleston Technical building college in South Australia. Later I entered the Panorama Business College, also in South

About the Author

Australia, to study accounting, finances, and marketing. When finished, I received 97% for accounting and 86% for the other studies. By the time I was 34, I was working in middle management for one of Australia's biggest building companies (The Jennings Corporation) and enjoying my success when God spoke to me to go into full-time ministry. I obeyed!

During my four years of full-time ministry in Australia, before I came to the good ol' U.S.A. to live permanently, I pioneered four churches. Our team would go out and have a powerful Holy Ghost revival. People would pour into the meetings because of all the miracles, and many souls would get saved. Our head church and my team would then raise money and start a new church in that area. When we got it up and running, we would hand it over to a new pastor and his wife who came out of the main churches' Bible College. I was ordained by The Full Gospel Church in Australia for those four years before coming to the United States.

I have traveled and ministered extensively throughout America, had several radio programs, preached on TBN 23 times, plus I was the main revivalist for Sunday-night services of a 3,000-member church for two years running. I have now been in full-time ministry for over 31 years. Powerful signs, wonders, and miracles have followed everywhere I minister to the glory of God. Everywhere my wife and I travel, the Lord's Holy Ghost and fire turns up and people are healed and delivered because of the fire of the Holy Ghost.

God is a powerful miracle-working God. We also had a big white, 2,000-seater tent and did tent revivals for four years where we saw thousands healed and saved. Praying in the Holy Ghost big-time is the key to keeping that type of ministry on the road. At one time I also preached in a 2,500-member church every Sunday night for 16 months straight. The big question is, why would a big church like that get an evangelist to preach so long in one church. The reason being signs, wonders, and miracles which draw the people big-time to each service, and they love it.

This ministry has seen the lame walk, the blind see, the deaf hear, and creative miracles happen. The wounded in body, soul, and spirit are touched by the anointing and the healing power of Jesus. The Holy Spirit moves powerfully through this ministry, releasing words of knowledge, prophecy, and a wonderful miracle anointing. There are thousands of amazing testimonies of how God has used this ministry to change lives, heal, deliver, revive, restore, and set free! When we had the tent ministry going, in just one year we saw 29 people get out of wheel chairs and that led to several thousands of souls being saved. That's why God loves to do these types of miracles. He is still doing these miracles today. The fire of the Holy Ghost and the anointing moves powerfully in our meetings. The end results are lots and lots of souls are saved. All to Jesus be the glory!

Conclusion

God's Word—Old and New Testament—declares that Jehovah Rapha is our healer. So, when we come to the Lord for healing, we must first believe that it's His will to heal us, according to His Word. Then we need to say, "Jesus, if there are any hindrances in my way for me to be able to receive my healing, please show me so I can deal with it. Then I can move on into my glorious healing that You paid for through Your stripes, and walk confidently and be absolutely blessed in Your finished work."

By his stripes you were healed (1 Peter 2:24).

> *"May God himself, the God of peace, sanctify you through and through. May your whole spirit, soul and body be kept blameless at the coming of our Lord Jesus Christ."*
>
> **—1 Thessalonians 5:23, NIV**

> *"Dear friend, I pray that you may enjoy good health and that all may go well with you, even as your soul is getting along well.*
>
> **—3 John 2:1, NIV**

> *"My son, pay attention to what I say; turn your ear to my words. Do not let them out of your sight keep them within your heart; for they are life to those who find them and health to one's whole body. Above all else, guard your heart, for everything you do flows from it. Keep your mouth free of perversity; keep corrupt talk far from your lips. Let your eyes look straight ahead; fix your gaze directly before you. Give careful thought to the paths for your feet and be steadfast in all your ways, and God's health and healing blessings will always work for you."*
>
> **—Proverbs 4:20-26, NIV**

For further contact go to our web site:
WWW.EAGLETABERNACLEHEALINGMINISTRIES.COM